Credit And The Two Sources From Which It Springs:

The Propensity to Save
&
The Propensity to Consume

A Treatise On Gold,
Interest And Discount

VOLUME III

BY

PROF. ANTAL FEKETE

Credit and the Two Sources from which it Spring: The Propensity to Save and the Propensity to Consume - A Treatise on Gold, Interest and Discount:

Published by Pintax cvba - May 2019

Pintax cvba
Industrial Estate C 102
Betekomsesteenweg 19
3200 Aarschot
Belgium

Depot Nr. D/2017/14.095/5
ISBN 978-90-820655-58

Published by Pintax cvba Belgium - May 2019

Available in this series :

By Antal E. Fekete

– **Critique of Mainstream Austrian Economics In the spirit of Carl Menger** (2017) ISBN 978-90820655-27 (Hardcover)

– **Credit Volume I : Money and Credit - The Essential** (February 2019) ISBN 978-90820655-34 (Hardcover)

– **Credit Volume II : Money and Credit in an Unhampered Market** (March-April 2019) ISBN 978-90820655-41 (Hardcover)

– **Credit Volume III : Money and Credit in a Mixed Economy** (April-May 2019) ISBN 978-90820655-58 (Hardcover)

– **Credit Volume IV : Money and Credit - Reconstruction** (April-May 2019) ISBN 978-90820655-65 (Hardcover)

By Peter. M. Van Coppenolle

– **The Austrian Business Cycle Revisited** (2012) ISBN 5800094365307

– **De Oorsprog van Geld (Carl Menger) translated to Dutch** (2015) ISBN 978-90820655-10 (Hardcover)

– **In Search of Order - History of (Junk) Ideologies** (target date October - November 2019) (Hardcover)

By Rudy Fritsch

– **Beyond Mises - Based On The Work Of Antal E. Fekete** (2010) ISBN 978 -06153734-09 (Softcover)

By Darryl Schoon

– **Time of The Vulture** (ISBN 978-0615677088)

Online video resources that belong to the Money & Credit Series:

–https://www.youtube.com/channel/UCnz5gMwVp6VVTuxbHjZaB7Q

Advanced Research Topics

– https://purelytheoreticalresearch.com

Discussion fora and applied investment strategies by NASOE members

– https://bullionplay.com

– https://lbnow.co.nz

– https://drschoon.com

– https://monetary-metals.com

– https://goldstandardinstitute.us or .net

– https://survivethecrisis.com

- https://beyondmises.com

► Para libros españoles sobre economía austríaca : Amazon | Juan Ramón Rallo & https://www.juandemariana.org

Prof. Dr. Antal E. Fekete

About The Author

Antal E. Fekete, Professor, Memorial University of Newfoundland, was born in Budapest, Hungary, in 1932. He graduated from the Loránt Eötvös University of Budapest in mathematics in 1955. He left Hungary in the wake of the 1956 anti-Communist uprising that was brutally put down by the occupying Soviet troops. He immigrated to Canada in the following year and was appointed Assistant Professor at the Memorial University of Newfoundland in 1958. In 1993, after 35 years' of service he retired with the rank of Full Professor. During this period he also had tours of duty as visiting professor at Columbia University in the City of New York (1961), Trinity College, Dublin, Ireland (1964), Acadia University, Wolfville, Nova Scotia (1970), Princeton University, Princeton, New Jersey (1974). Since 2005 he has been Professor at Large of Intermountain Institute for Science and Applied Mathematics (IISAM), Missoula, Montana.

Professor Fekete is an autodidactic expert on monetary economics. During his associations with various universities and institutions he has done research and lectured on economics. On one such occasion, in 1974, he gave a talk on gold in the seminar of Paul Volcker, then Senior Fellow at Princeton University, soon to be named as President of the Federal Reserve Bank of New York and, later, as Chairman of the Federal Reserve Board.

In 1984 Professor Fekete was invited by the American Institute for Economic Research in Great Barrington, Massachusetts, to spend a year there as Visiting Fellow. He served as Editor of the Monograph Series of the Committee for Monetary Research and Education, then headquartered in Greenwich, Connecticut, while contributing several monographs to the Series, reproduced on his website. He also acted as Senior Editor for the American Economic Foundation in Cleveland, Ohio, and produced the popular pamphlet series *Ten Pillars of Sound Money*, also reproduced in Volume I of this series. When in 1984 South Africa celebrated the 100th anniversary of discovering gold in the Witwatersrand, at the conference Gold 100 commemorating that event in Johannesburg, Professor Fekete delivered the keynote address entitled Gold in the International Monetary System, also reproduced on his website.

In 1985 Congressman William E. Dannemeyer of Fullerton, California, invited Professor Fekete to join his staff in Washington, D.C., to work on fiscal and monetary reform. While on this assignment, lasting for five years, he gave numerous lectures on Capitol Hill as well as in California. Ultimately the proposals hammered out in Congressional offices under his chairmanship were taken to the White House by a delegation of ten Republican Congressmen led by Congressman Dannemeyer. According to these proposals the runaway government deficit could be reined in by refinancing the entire U.S. government debt through issuing gold bonds. The historic meeting took place in the Oval Office in October, 1989, and was duly reported by The New York Times. Having listened attentively to the presentation of Mr. Dannemeyer, President George Bush, Sr., instructed his Treasury Secretary, also present at the meeting, to let the Congressional and Treasury staff meet and put forward a joint proposal. This initiative came to nought as the Treasury deliberately derailed negotiations through procrastination.

Contents

List of Illustrations

List of Abbreviations

BIS	: Bank for International Settlements
FED	: Federal Reserve Bank (System)
GFC	: Global Financial Crisis
GNP	: Gross National Product
GDP	: Gross Domestic Product
IMF	: International Monetary Fund
NPV	: Net Present Value of a cash flow
OECD	: Organisation for Economic Cooperation and Development
PV	: Present Value
QE	: Quantitative Easing
QTM	: Quantity Theory of Money
RBD	: Real Bills Doctrine
SCC	: Social Circulating Capital
WACC	: Weighted Average Cost of Capital
ZIRP	: Zero Interest Rate Policy

Introduction

Although all four volumes belong together, they can still be read separately. This Volume III of Money and Credit treats the practical consequences of ignoring a gold standard, theorised in Volume II of this 4 Volume series. Antal Fekete stresses the importance of an unadulterated circulating gold coin standard. 'Unadulterated' needs attention at this point, because in Part Seven - Forensic Analysis of Ideological Warfare, the U.S. and U.K. banking people promoted a 'gold standard', ostensibly to promote hard money, but ideologically, the banking people coveted the seigniorage obtained from conversion from silver to gold coinage and simultaneously the illicit interest arbitrage between the short term cheaper bill market and the more expensive longer term bond market. The result is a maturity mismatch and bank run, several in a row, if word hits the street. Moreover, lax credit standards allowed brokerages to sell unsuitable and ill timed products to an exuberant public on little to no margin – under the flag of 'financial innovation' Borrowing short and lending long, or taking money from the Social Circulating Capital to spend in the speculative market comes at a price, when the speculative venture proves a bridge too far for a critical mass of 'investors'. One such crisis hit Vienna in 1873. Carl Menger owned two volumes of *Die Spekulationskrisis von 1873*, by Joseph Neuwirth. Unfortunately, we had as yet no opportunity to read his remarks, if ever he made some, inside this volume. All tis sounds strange as if professional bankers would not know what they are doing. One reason to explain this oddity would be that the friends and representatives in government made sure to extend some legal protection for banks and that banks would be well advised to fogg up their actions and spray lots of mist. And so it happened. Menger's excellent theoretical work was burried before him. Apparently Menger felt the palpable crisis early.

In Britain, Barings Bank brought down The City in 1890 in the first 'sovereign debt crisis'. How was that possible under a gold standard? Unfortunately, the 'gold standard' then in operation, showed signs of adulteration, committed by the very people to whom the gold standard was entrusted, by their abuse of fiduciary media and under cover of academic authority such as Ricardo. It explains partially, the aversion people like Keynes had against the 'conservative' banking people who were just seemingly bumbling from one bank run to another.

'Bumbling' although most of them knew very well not to finance long term projects with short term funds. !B. Eichengreen, the modern dualist spin doctor from Econometrics Laboratory, donned no doubt in a white lab coat, hides the crimes against the gold standard with the euphemisms of 'inelasticity of money supply' or behind 'demand for gold' nonsense that does not apply to gold at all. The spin and pressure from 'above' (academia paid by an oligarchic bureaucracy) and the opportunity for profit and greed overcame good sense, both in the present as in the past. The Northern (U.S.) bankers financed the U.S. civil war for profit and although we cannot read minds, their actions speak aloud. Southern farms and plants were taken over on the cheap... As soon as the opportunity arose, gold was arbitraged against silver and greenbacks profitably - not necessarily for the profit of the country or the banks' clients. Banks are no charities. It explains partially why some academics, without so much as a superficial investigation, call the gold standard deflationary, *n'est-ce pas*, Rev. Eichengreen and consorts? To be sure, prices did come down during the reign of the gold standard both in Britain and the U.S. Not because of the gold standard, but because of its *adulteration* by the relentless removal of specie and real bills and gold as reserves from banking balance sheets, replaced by treasury bonds and Federal Reserve Notes. National banks in the U.S. with the help of government granted monopoly, could issue bank notes and credit, i.e. fiduciary money, and make the lot circulate, still redeemable in name, although in practise its redeemability would be severely tested under a bank run. Only the strong arm of the law, forcing people to accept paper notes, could help. The paper notes could be used as tax credit. Not that banks denounced gold – *au contraire*: they hoarded it *en masse*. The opportunity availed itself at the first World War. Emergency money and coupons did circulate, of course under special circumstances of a war. The privately owned National Banks in the U.S. and elsewhere - in collusion with their friends in high places who provided privilege and monopoly – acted *de facto* as reserve banks where the sovereignty of the consumer could have no hold over; interest rates were manhandled downward, together with some prices, wherever no monopoly position could manipulate prices upward without losing customers. (Haberler-Pigou) Moreover, the paper money notes often would not be accepted on equal terms with metallic coins, and often suffered a discount, much to the dismay and affront of the issuer. That discount translates into a higher price in other products and services, called price inflation by some, but that would be nothing else than recalculating an exchange between goods, taking the discount of paper money into account.

The question of demonetising metal, first silver and later gold remains; it is not a search of how, but of who took it upon himself? It would seem to us the entire operation was at best opportunistic, at worst deliberate predation. I do not need to prove a conspiracy – I just look at the facts: as soon as all profit opportunities from demonetising silver first and later gold were exhausted, the gold standard was suddenly relinquished in favour of a new pet project: fiat paper money. Cui bono ? Who operates on a on a global scale and opened all registers to achieve it? Read the IMF charter! The history of money and credit eads like a crime file – cold case, like science fiction and lunatic conspiracy, yet the pilfering experienced is real, the pauperisation is just as real, the employment situation for the entire world population, bar a handful few, is everything but a path of roses and most people have realised their grand pension plans need revision – downwards. Since most people's jobs hang precariously in the balance, speaking, writing or thinking out loud as we do, would be a serious career limiting move. (Almost) Everybody likes 'whistleblowers' but nobody wants to step up and *be* one. The same goes for politicians and people chosen for their 'leadership qualities' and rewarded accordingly, they all want to go to heaven, but none of them want to die. They all stand accused in they eyes of the voting public. Pleading ignorance will not do for professionals, so the (pseudo) academics in so-called economic science stand accused for being accomplices before and after the facts. We will not be the one's accusing them; rather, a day will come and a large mass of unruly, hungry ex-serfs, tired of being harassed will do the accusation. And perhaps more than just the accusation.

For those sane enough to have understood what the economic (and therefore social) situation has come down to, with this book they are forewarned and confident in their knowledge of what is inevitably coming our way. Game on !

P. VAN COPPENOLLE

Belgium

TO LADY FORTUNE

I SHALL BE MODEST
IN MY WISHES
OH, LADY FORTUNE,
I WON'T ASK FOR GOLD OR SILVER
THAT YOU MAY FAIL TO DELIVER,
I SHALL BE MORE OPPORTUNE –
GIMME PLENTY OF BANKNOTES!
(J. Arany -Hungarian poet-, 1850)

VOLUME III

Money And Credit In A Mixed Economy And In The Absence Of A Gold Standard

PART 5

STRUCTURE OF CAPITAL MARKETS IN A MIXED ECONOMY

Chapter 23

Equilibrium & QTM: The Living Superstitions [1]

In the development of economic thought, the early study of economic relations showed little cohesion. Mercantilism, prior to the physiocrats and the observations of Adam Smith did not consist of a set of uniform views, their attempts to theorise fell back to what is now called 'the quantity theory of money'. Its history can be found in reliable sources of the history of economic theory or method. Conceptually based on the phenomenon of 'rising price levels' associated, mostly as a '*post hoc ergo propter hoc*' fallacy, to a growing stock of money or currency, it remains an appealing concept for its simplicity. Compounding the error of its origin, Ricardo argued how the quantity theory of money smoothly merges with a mechanistic view of the field of economic life.[2] Whilst the history and development of economic thought regarding equilibrium and quantity theory of money may be known to historians, its philosophical underpinnings are hardly studied or known.

Organised Witchcraft

Ever since Francis Bacon, writing amidst waves of superstitions of evil witchcraft rolling over western Europe and America, counteracted such misgivings on the strength of biblical passages that knowledge of nature was God given, organised science, under Bacon's slogan 'knowledge is power' managed to break up the marriage between the state and religion. A scientific priesthood, cut off from Vatican financial support, solicited funding from state sources and successfully projected an image of omniscience, based on materialistic and mechanistic methods that brought them huge recognition. And money. People to this day, still believe simplistically, that scientists search for the truth and nothing else, failing to recognise how huge funding has the same effect on people as honey on flies. Owning a white lab coat pays off handsomely. So does government employment. Just look at B. Eichengreen pontificating from the 'Econometrics Laboratory' at Berkeley California.[3]

Clockwork Orange

The prevailing view of the world (in the West) involved ever since antiquity, bodies, souls and spirits forming an organism – that is until Descartes removed souls, buried the organism and became a principal proponent of a mechanistic, almost clockwork view of nature. [4] Newtonian physics somewhat later firmly grounded itself in mathematical exploration of an intelligently *designed machine*, kickstarted by the First Mover – a deists name for God, until He was removed by French intellectuals dismissing First Movers as fodder for the feeble minded.[5]

Scientistic hubris may be charged with instilling spiritual degeneration. A privileged social order incompatible with spiritual order ensued on the back of ideologies fostered by Saint-Simon, Darwin, or Lamarcke. Human minds are but byproducts of brain activity. The surgical removal of the psyche and its functions was now complete. Nature exists mechanically and tolerated no divine intervention. Selection of the fittest vulgarly degenerated into a widely accepted justification for abuse. After all, humans are just machines, endowed with consciousness – spontaneously 'emerging' from complexity. No doubt in their mind artificial intelligence rules the world - one day soon.[6]

Shift to Method

One specific problem bearing importance regarding the destruction of science in the 19th century ought to be reported as the attempt at making the social sciences in general 'objective' through a rigorous exclusion of all 'value-judgments.' The movement came to the end of its humanistically inspired immanent positivist-materialist logic in the person of Max Weber. The Weberian movement can be characterised as perhaps the final phase of positivism in so far as the perversion of relevance stood out as the very principle by which it lived: by way of stressing the importance of a shift from theory to method. Positivism being dead as a doornail, we nevertheless have still not recovered from this devastation.

Deformation

Human reason, severely restricted by materialist-positivist scientific views, glorified by Auguste Comte, Richard Dawkins[7] and others like Daniel Dennett,[8] cannot give closure to he hierarchy of being without exposing their arguments' shortcomings. Part of the gamut of attempts to fill the void of human reason (stripped of its *ultimate purpose* in the sense of the ancients)[9] would become known in economics as the profit motive. The modern deformation of economics, itself not known as a science to the ancients, becomes obvious by the various expressions of its banality: chrematistics. The latter seems the main preoccupation of today's students of economics. The materialist-rationalist (another word for positivist) world view had inspired economic theorist to disregard the untenability of the quantity theory and nevertheless embrace it as well as its sidekick, the equilibrium paradigm. In the pursuit of government funding in exchange for eternal glory and a statue in the hall of fame, formula's – any formula's – including those smacking of alchemy, were elevated to the level of science.[10]

Fame and Glory

God, not impressed with his banishment from his own garden, never left and reappeared regardless to science in the form of a 'big bang theory' and as the 'discovery' of 'dark energy'.[11] In economics, the religious worship of 'Equilibrium' and the 'QTM' degenerated into a tenacious superstition, thanks to the silent merger between the Lausanne school led by Walras and the British school of Marshall. Walras, after all, enrolled at the French school for Mining Engineers. Engineers, then, as now, solve problems and act hands-on. However, engineering or mining would not be the right mindset to tackle human societal problems. Life, despite objections, is not linear and people are in no way bio-mechanical machines that come with a brain attached.[12] Thinking engineers would do well to adapt their frame of mind to the problems of mechanics, not of human relationships. The fields do not relate to each other. Just like a bridge is not build with a meter made out of elastic-like material, human action in economic affairs defy mechanics, equilibrium, overheating, or any other silly metaphor. When all you have is a hammer, the only things you see are nails... Why is it that economic scientists strive for control over the elusive lever from which emanates full control, equilibrium and general welfare in Erewhon? [13]

Today the obscurantist writings of Keynes are credited for recognising speculative money and the claptrap of a liquidity trap. Keynes never formulated any theory of speculation, for he rejected hoarding as pathological. One would be hard pressed to find the place of speculation and hoarding in his equilibrium formula.

Similarly, Milton Friedman, correctly identifying income as discounted present value streams, generated by existing capital wealth, gets credited for integrating monetary theory and capital 'theory'. If both men professed to be scientists, why did Keynes persuade Roosevelt in 1933 to default on the *domestic* gold obligations and why did Friedman in 1968 tried to persuade Nixon to act likewise on its *international* gold obligations? Government funded 'science' still provides payoffs by way of a hall of fame, judging by the ubiquitous listings of 'famous or influential economists.' In the garden of Eden, though, weeds enjoy no eternal life. They succumb to their own internal inconsistencies sooner or later.

The Sound of Catastrophic Failure

The American Austrian School of Economics build its theory of money and credit on the Quantity Theory of Money (QTM). In his defence Mises did say, though, that his was a 'modern' QTM in so far as it realised that there was a delay between the cause (increase in the money supply) and the effect (rising prices); hence those who could lay their hands on the newly created money first (e.g., people with government and bank connections such as special interest groups and various other pressure groups) would benefit at the expense of those who were last in line (e.g., pensioners). Yet this does not address the main fault of the QTM which is this: newly printed money can be spent not only on goods and services (causing prices and wages to increase)[14] but on bonds as well (causing interest rates to fall).[15] It is even conceivable that none of the newly printed money goes to pay for goods and services, but all of it goes to buy bonds. If that is the case, there will be no increase in the price of goods and services no matter how extreme the printing presses may be called upon. Instead, there will be **deflation galore** as the falling interest rate structure translates into a falling price structure and capital destruction.[16] The contemporary experiment with unlimited 'inflation' [17] is a case in point. We have relatively little by way of price increases, but that sucking sound is the sound of capital destruction: capital in the form of tangible industrial bases move or have already moved out of the country in search of asylum elsewhere. The intangible intellectual capital accrued so far in the highly skilled work force, will, due to its being idled and forced to watch TV instead, die out within a generation.

Invalid Non-Science

In the spirit of Menger NASOE criticises the entire concept of 'inflation', 'deflation' and the QTM that at best is a clever mechanical metaphor, at worst, a thoroughly unsound theory without redeeming features. It treats the world as if it were linear when, in effect, it is unpredictably nonlinear. If we check the indexes of Menger's two most important books, the *Grundsätze* and the *Untersuchungen*, we shall not find one single entry related to the QTM. Careful reading of other writings of Menger reveals that he never said anything of substance on the QTM either pro or contra. One should not jump to the conclusion that Menger had no opinion on the validity of the QTM, and would be happy to let his students struggle with the problem. It is more likely that Menger was disturbed by the idea that the QTM made gold and silver appear more or less valuable according to changing supply. He firmly believed that gold's monetary role was due to its supreme marketability that had nothing to do with temporary changes in supply. (see supra.)

> He was alive to the fact that in terms of the ratio of stocks to annual flows gold is far from being scarce: it is more abundant than any other commodity the marginal utility of which declines faster – thus preventing a large build-up of large hoards.

The value of gold (and silver) is not determined by quantity; it is determined by ***marketability***. The powerful concept of ***marketability is the living denial of the QTM***: quality pitted against quantity. If the characteristics of the purchasing medium reflect the material of the highest quality (read: of the most saleable and the most hoardable good), then its value shall be (nearly) constant, regardless of its 'purchasing power'. We simply don't have any other standard to gage the stability of value. [18]

Menger plausibly wanted to develop his theory of interest in a planned second edition of *Grundsätze* on which he was working during the last decade of his life, and he saved his criticism of the QTM for this work.[19] Unfortunately he died before he could do it, and in this sense his *opus* remains incomplete.

Religious Nominalism

Quantity theorists habitually conjure up the bogey man of gold hoarding in an effort to refute the claim that the value of gold is not more variable than the length of the yard in terms of the same yard is. They argue that gold hoarding makes gold scarce, causing prices to fall. Deflation follows. The truth of the matter however, is that talking about gold hoarding makes sense only if we also consider gold dishoarding in the context of the process of the formation of the rate of interest. Gold hoarding is a protest vote: a warning signal that the government and the banks have gone too far in pushing the rate of interest lower. The marginal bondholder is protesting the violation of his time preference. He sells his overpriced bond, keeping the proceeds in gold coins. Should the government and the banks heed the warning and rein in the credit expansion, the public will dishoard gold.

At any rate, if the government wants to eliminate gold hoarding, there is a very simple way to do it. It should allow the interest rate to return to its natural rate, namely, the level of marginal time preference. The marginal bondholder will react by releasing his hoarded gold. He will buy his bond back at a profit. What he is in fact doing is a profitable arbitrage operation between the bond market and the gold market. This arbitrage is very effective: it keeps the government and the banks on a short leash. The profitability of this arbitrage is the guarantee that the government will pursue the enlightened policy of 'hands off' as far as the rate of interest is concerned. This is how God ordained the world. The rate of interest and its variation can only be manhandled at a price: the same steep price Adam and Eve had to pay for their conceit.

> It is the business of the people who retain their distributed control through increasing or decreasing their outright possession of gold.

Nature's Revenge or the Return of God to Eden

All economists have missed this essential role of gold in the formation of the interest rate with the exception of John Fullarton. (1780–1849) He pointed out the connection between gold hoarding and the suppression in the rate of interest in his book *On the Regulation of Currencies,* first published in 1844. Mainstream and contemporary Austrian economists dismiss the Fullarton effect. Von Mises wrote a contemptuous remark calling it *Deus ex machina* ('God crawling out of the woodwork'). This epitaph turned out to be more apt than von Mises intended. The role that gold is supposed to play in the economy to keep it on an even keel was forcibly overruled by the government. By eliminating gold from the monetary system, conceited men eliminated God from economics as well. But conceitedness in the presence of God will be at your own peril, as God had punished the people of the Old Testament for theirs. The contemporary Tower of Babel is made of debt as manifested by the tower of derivatives. This mindless experiment will end the same way. According to the Bible, God confused the language of the builders of the Tower of Babel that was supposed to reach to heaven. After God confused their language they could no longer communicate with one another. The Tower of Babel collapsed and buried its conceited builders under the rubble. In the contemporary episode God is confusing the currencies of the builders of the debt tower. This tower is also doomed. Lamentably, the effect will not be confined to one city. The collapse of the Debt Tower will bury virtually all the inhabitants of the globe under the rubble – punishment for the conceit of our leaders in trying to one-up on God. This raises the question: how is it that our leaders did not see the disaster into which they were leading the people? The answer is: the Quantity Theory of Money has blurred their vision, suffering as they did from linear assumptions and (ideological) projections in a non-linear world.

Endnotes to Chapter 23

[1] Written by Peter M. Van Coppenolle

[2] Murray Rothbard, *Classical Economics, An Austrian Perspective on the History of Economic Thought,* Vol. II, Elgar Publishing, 1995, p. 196.

[3] See B. Eichengreen *'Fetters of Gold and Paper'* for a classic piece of ideological warfare against gold.

[4] Brooke, J.H., *Science and Religion, Some Historical Perspectives,* Cambridge University Press, 1991.

[5] That leaves French Revolutionary ardour firmly grounded in Gnostic dualism. See note note 25 part 6, page 107 and note 32 part 6 page 109 for characteristics and traits, as diagnosed by Dr. Voegelin.

[6] We're not holding our breath nor are we losing any sleep over such contention.

[7] Richard Dawkins maintains atheism as a normal state of consciousness for humans and maintains adamantly the non-existence of God. But the existence of God remains speculative for all humans and no prove either for or against the existence of God can be made without overstepping the line into speculation. Ultimately, the theist is in the same position as the materialist or physicalist. No one can explain the existence of elementary particles, contingent or otherwise. All explanations come to an end. Dawkins ought to know better then argue in a circle with his atheist reasoning.

[8] Daniel Dennett as a philosopher of consciousness turns out rather poor. His argument that consciousness does not exists, hits bottom for his rationale is explaining consciousness away. Dennett asks us to deny your own experiences because the reality of such phenomena seems incompatible with his own scientific materialism which, for him, sets the limits of reality. If this were true, explain please how our own experiences by sight, touch, smell etc. helped our species survive over millennia ? Both Dawkins and Dennett have lost touch with reality. Both of them look completely estranged and derailed in their reasoning. Both of them are maintaining a thesis at all costs. See also note 21 below for an analysis of ideologues and their issue with who's in control ?

[9] See Thomas Nagel, *Mind and Cosmos, Why the Materialist Neo-Darwinian Conception of Nature is Almost Certainly False,* Oxford University Press, 2012.

[10] See the theories of John Law of Lauriston and the fancy footwork it took for him to bamboozle the French public in accepting a negative value like the King's debt (not circulating unless against a discount often exceeding 60%) as a positive value like a gold coin, such as it was before its seignorage reduced its purchasing power. He had to make promises of redemption that were not up to him to keep or even to make. Seigniorage always has been the Kings privi-

lege. See vol. II for a treatment of John Law.

[11] The elliptical argument of God returning is not meant to prove the existence of God. The argument takes a satirical turn, for what else could a *Deus ex machina* be with a big bang theory ? Or 'dark energy' ?

[12] A brain that deludes itself constantly, if we are to believe the famous D. Dennett... Not that people cannot delude themselves, they can. It is however, over the top (and self defeating) to generalise that all human brain activity is delusional to the core. The self-defeating structure of the argument consists in the conclusion that his own utterances must therefore come forth from delusional brain activity.

[13] For the uninitiated, Erewhon is the name of a fictional country Samuel Butler used in 1872 in his novel *Erewhon : or Over the Range*. The sharp minded will already have discovered that reading erewhon backwards lands you nowhere.

[14] That is, if you adhere to the QTM. In our view, this is a discredited theory by simple observation of reality. The QTM has a relatively small operational field in which it fiends suitable application, such as in accounting or in calculating the issue price of new shares in a venture where the first providers of capital do not wish their share of profits deluded by the newcomers.

[15] And interest rates will fall. This is the essence of the FED or ECB or any major Reserve Bank' s operation: open market purchases of Treasury bonds. Nobody disputes this. It is a simple actuarial or mathematical fact.

[16] I use the terms inflation and deflation, not in the monetary sense, but in the sense described by Knut Wicksell, namely the manipulation of interest rates down as deflation. On the rise of interest rates, the Reserve Banks excert minimal control, for it is not in their hands, but the speculators. (E.g. Greece...) For the explanation of how capital destruction works, see vol II and the inserts with calculated examples. Note that both interest rate rises as well as interest rate decreases cause capital destruction, especially for a prolonged time such as the past 40 years of unrelenting interest rate drops. The last four decades have created an atmosphere of a permanently high interest rate environment. Even a ¼ percent can still be diminished never to go below zero.

[17] Seen as unlimited multiplication of irredeemable currency. It is thought by quantity theorists that such action would bring about the Fisherian non sequitur of 'too much money chasing too little goods.' Price inflation seems to be hard to bring about, especially in the commodity markets. 'Money printing' comes about by open market operations via the FED and Treasury in conjunction. The FED overpays for Treasury bonds, resulting in capital gains to the sellers of these Treasury bonds. These capital gains sit on the books of the speculators. It is re-deployed in more speculative action of bond speculation. It is not distributed by helicopter drops. Price increases in daily goods come about due to the absence of the Haberler-Pigou effect on fiduciary money such

as these capital gains, or because some products are rebranded into white products, or their composition changes (horizontal and vertical arbitrage by the producers...). Price increases in the commodity market seem to be elusive. Some speculators in gold, have been impatiently awaiting a price explosion in the dollar price of gold. They may wait for a long time. The price of gold may become extinct first, meaning no fiat bids accepted...See vol. IV.

[18] t may be hard for students to stop thinking in terms of linear units such as the U.S.$ or in terms of the faulty QTM, promoted to scientific level by Irving Fisher. In all our examples, we tried to avoid wherever possible to use a nominalist symbol such as the U.S. $ or U.K. Pound. Value and US$ or any numbers with a symbol are in no way synonymous. See Vol. II part 1 on marginalism for an explanation.

[19] Of course, this would be speculative on our part. Nevertheless, enough remarks and notes remain in existence to show Menger's intent on some issues and problems. E.g. where he used the title *Volkswirthschaftslehre* in 1871 for his dissertation, he crossed out such a title in his notes and replaced it with a new title of 'Pure Theoretical Economics' or in German *'Reine Theoretische Wirtschafslehre'* See Campagnolo, *ibid.* p. 315.

The word '*Volkswirthschaftslehre* had become tainted even during Menger's lifetime. The tainting occurred due to the general atmosphere of social Darwinism and eugenics, the philosophical scions of deranged Gnostic dualism, which pervaded the entire world including Germany at that time. (Hew Strachan, *To Arms*, p. 54. Voegelin, *ibidem.*)The tragedy of the second world war made that much clear. Such atrocities do not just happen overnight nor without broader social context. The social perversion spilled over into science and it had been a very long process of which Menger must have been aware, if we take his *actions* into account. In the same vain, Menger may look on the surface as being associated with his socialist brother. However, that would be a serious blunder to assume both brothers were on the same page. Analysing Menger's actions speak louder than anything else...

Chapter 24

When Ideological Currency Runs The Lunatic Asylum

The largest 'kid on the bloc' in late mediaeval Northern Europe was France. Its population and organisation outran all others. The word 'nation' only started to become coined during the time the French King Charles VIII invaded the Italian 'nation-states' by request of Ludovico Sforza. Machiavelli some years later in 1513 would write *Il Principe* as one of the most misunderstood essays in history, in which he proclaimed his disgust for the use of force against another Christian nation under God, just because one could.[1]

The French Kings always needed money. In 1557, the merchants operating the Lyons bill market had lent large sums to the King. They learned an expensive lesson not to try to gain from such illicit interest arbitrage for the French King stopped paying his debt and had to be considered insolvent for all intents and purposes. To settle his debt, the King issued *rentes* instead for 25-40% of principal due. The Lyon bill market never recovered. Just forty years later in 1597, the King forcibly, that is by law, reduced the yield on these (and other) rentes to 4%. French cardinal Mazarin as court treasurer tried to keep these rentes under control and succeeded in restoring credit-worthiness to the French King. After Mazarin, the King's spending habits spun out of control again and to entice any *rente* takers, the King had to offer double the interest to above 8% at least.

Scarcely two generations of mayhem later, along came John Law of Lauriston. Although he escaped Britain for Holland after killing Edward Wilson (in a duel over a fair lady), this escaped convict and nurderer nevertheless gained the confidence of the Duke of Orange and the French King and established, besides the Mississippi Company, the *Banque Générale* on promises of getting rid of the French national debt. Awesome, but how? In setting up the *Banque*, the subscription capital consisted of one quarter gold coin and three quarters in the King's ... *rentes*. So some holders of *rentes*, rushed and delivered them to subscribe to the venture. With these *rentes* out of the way for the King, Law issued *banque* bills a.k.a. paper money, redeemable on sight.[2] He talked up his paper money, saying that bankers who did not redeem their notes and keep full reserve, deserve the death penalty. For some strange reason, it convinced the French people and his paper money circulated and even went to a premium. Commerce restored and the notes of the *Banque* (remember it was subscribed by ¾ *rentes*, that is the Kings's debt) could now also be used to pay the French taxes. Perfect bamboozlement, for Law succeeded in turning the King's *debt* into an *asset* with a promise he could not make nor keep: to pay the note at the undiluted gold level at the date of transaction. Since the King used seigniorage rather often to his advantage, the people thought of returning him the compliment. Or so it was thought. The rest is history and Law allegedly escaped Paris, dressed up as a woman. The sordid French tales of fortunes lost to conmen, inspired other conmen later. But they had to wait until the dust of the runaway vehicle had settled.[3] Modern Reserve Banks many generations later repeated John Law's tokenisation of securities, but under cover of darkness and mist as the sequel will demonstrate.

Runaway Vibration

Many of the great achievements of the gold standard have been frittered away since 1971, the year governments of the industrialised world declared irredeemable currency 'money', thereby destabilising the interest-rate structure.

During the inflationary period up to 1981, people hoarded marketable goods in protest against too low rates, waiting for capital gains to offset interest losses. The ceiling rate is expresses as a marginal productivity of speculation, typically bonds. A bond represents wealth handed over in exchange for future income. (See Vol. II) The rate of capitalisation is locked in on the day of the agreement, but obviously will soon appear too low. For other people trying to accumulate wealth, hoarding marketable goods would prove much more profitable. All marketable goods would command a higher price some time later, whereby savers had turned into speculative hoarders.

Starting that year the world has been treated to a spectacle of gyrating rates of interest the like of which has never been seen before. First, an arbitrary increase in the level of interest rates rendered a vast amount of capital and labour submarginal, causing the closure of production facilities, resulting in unemployment, inadequate capital maintenance and, ultimately, capital decumulation and destruction. To combat outrageously high interest rates (for them) central bankers enlisted the help of speculators. [Bankers hold government bonds in portfolio. When interest rates rise, their portfolio's present value plunges. It affects banks capacity to lend, because it affects their solvency.] Let us bypass the fact that this intervention was disingenuous as the government itself was responsible for the destabilisation of interest rates in the first place. Let us focus on the fact that not only has speculation aided and abetted by the government brought down the rate of interest, but it is also responsible for making it plunge to zero. Speculation also makes the volume of activity in the credit markets to grow at an exponential rate as derivatives, such as bond futures and options proliferate at a prodigious rate. By now speculative activity represents a high multiple of the volume of productive activity.

Previously, the former was a low percentage of the latter, as speculation was limited to addressing risks created by nature to the exclusion of risks created by 'Man'.

In 1971 this limit was forcibly removed. Speculation addressing risks created by man, that is, by governments and central banks (e.g., interest and foreign exchange risks) started to overwhelm the economy and, by now, it is increasing at an exponential rate in good times as well as in bad. The artificial creation of risks has caused a chain-reaction of speculative activity with unforeseeable destructive consequences. As we shall see, volatility of the rate of interest is matched by that of the price level. Moreover, the two are linked. This linkage leads to resonance between the gyrating rate of interest and the gyrating price level. Resonance brings about runaway vibration as manifested by exponentially increasing amplitude (the exact opposite of the more common phenomenon of damped vibration). The runaway vibration of the rate of interest and the price level hits the economy with ever greater destructive force. Unless a valid policy of stabilisation is put into effect, and soon, the ever widening swings in the rate of interest and the price level threaten the economy with collapse.

Rising Interest Rendering Capital Submarginal

An increasing rate of interest causes capital invested in production to lose value. The reason for this is the mathematical fact that the present value of future income falls when capitalised at a higher rate of interest. Indeed, the present value of income is calculated by discounting future payments at the going rate of interest. Thus any increase in the latter immediately slashes values that owe their origin to capitalisation of incomes. An unwelcome side-effect is that the value of all production goods falls *pari passu* with the rise of interest rates, regardless of their productivity. In particular, much of the park of capital goods society has, is rendered submarginal and, sooner rather than later, their productive life must come to an end. Production and employment will shrink in consequence of rising interest. But since interest rates have risen capriciously as a result of the government's embracing irredeemable currency, there appears to be no real justification for falling production and growing unemployment. Authors of the Brave New World of fiat money have forgotten to take the murderous effect of rising interest on production into account.

Suppose you are a dealer selling tractors, and the rate of interest **rises**. As if by magic, all tractors on your lot lose value instantaneously. Nobody will pay the old price knowing that the contribution to production expected from the tractor is less than the sticker price.

Cost of capital	4%	5%
Yearly yield of tractor for 5 years	5.000	5.000
PV of yields (or max sticker price)	22.259	21.647

Thus, without any change in the tractor's physical condition, or in the circumstances of its application in the field, the value of the tractor has been slashed. The new price is still determined by the present value of future income that buyers expect to derive from its use. But since that income is now discounted at a higher rate, the new price will be lower. Of course, capital goods already deployed in production also lose value for the very same reason. The entire park of capital goods in the country is decimated. (Remember 1971-1981.) Moreover, this loss of value is irreversible. Submarginal capital withdrawn from production will no longer be maintained.

Even if the rate of interest comes down later, value is gone, never to return. Society has been inflicted a permanent loss of capital values which has no justification nor redeeming features. It is the result of insane monetary policies, in particular, the destruction of the gold standard and its consequence: the destabilisation of the interest-rate structure. (See also below — insert 1)

Falling Interest: Happy now ... ?!

Superficial thinking may suggest that if a rise of interest rates is bad, then their **fall** is good. Not so. A falling rate of interest is even more damaging for the economic process than a rising one. I am aware that my thesis is highly counter-intuitive. I have been challenged by other economists who deny the validity of my contention. They argue that if

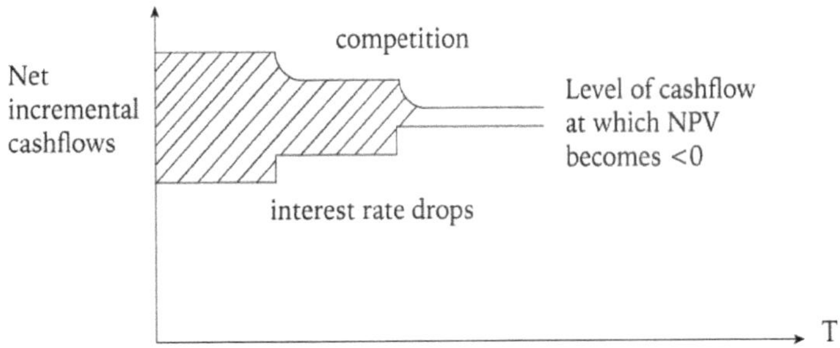

Fig. 1 Capital squeeze : annoy existing enterprises by allowing newcomers better rates. Having spotted spreads that yield a cashflow never fails to attract competition. Every drop in interest rate helps the competition. It finances the competition at lower rates than the existing infrastructure. Would you like to refinance ?
The entrepreneur suffers a triple hit: first the margins get squeezed by new competitors, but secondly authorities consistently work against the entrepreneur in the fiscal and legal field. Thirdly, the entrepreneur needs to come up with more money at the wrong time..

the present value of future income is lower when discounted at a higher rate of interest, then it must be higher when discounted at a lower rate. We may admit that this statement is true. However, it has no relevance to the case under consideration. The firm must be around in order to collect the future income whose present value would be higher as a result of lower interest rates. The point is that many of them won't be, as they succumb to capital squeeze caused by falling rates. Our critics hold that falling interest rates are always beneficial to business and, as such, could not aggravate deflation. (Here deflation means the combination of falling prices and falling interest rates). They are confusing a falling with a low structure of interest rates. While the latter is beneficial, the former is lethal to producers. When interest rates are falling, the low rates of today will look like high rates tomorrow. A prolonged fall in interest rates creates a permanently high interest-rate environment. This paradox explains the reluctance of the mind to admit that a prolonged fall in the rate of interest spells deflation and, possibly, depression.

Worse still, falling interest rates mean that business has been financed at rates far too high. This fact ought to be registered as a loss in the profit & loss statement, and be compensated for by the injection of new capital (much the same as would losses caused by damage to plant and equipment due to war, for example). Instead, businesses choose to ignore the loss, and they merrily go on paying out phantom profits in the form of dividends, further weakening capital structure. When they plunge into bankruptcy, they wonder what has hit them. They don't understand that they have failed to augment their capital in the face of falling interest rates, and their downfall is due to insufficient capital.[4]

Bond Speculation Is No Zero-Sum Game

Once more we see that damage is caused by the destabilisation of the interest rate structure. Under the gold standard interest rates were stable, as were bond prices. Bond speculation was unknown. Arbitrageurs saw to it that bond prices remained stable in the face of temporary setbacks due to natural causes such as floods, earthquakes, and crop failures.

Destabilisation came as the gold standard was destroyed by governments advised by doctrinaire and frankly uninformed economists with vested interest in the church of ideology. They justified inflation (irredeemable currency creation) as 'the lesser of two evils'. (That is: either the curse of inflation *we control* [5] instead of the 'horrible conservative bankers' with their 'deflationary gold' *they control*). Keynes & C° abhorred the thought of 'deflation' - officially; they abhorred even more *they were not in control*. Indeed, it all boiled down to an ideologically perceived *control issue*.[6] They utterly failed to grasp that their policies caused both inflation an deflation simultaneously. (Deflation seen as the destruction of income generating capital. Inflation as the rise of certain prices or shrinking of products due the the absence of the Haberler-Pigou effect on fiduciary money).[7] In fact, they made the Kondratiev long-wave cycle, consisting of alternating inflationary and deflationary spirals, to spin out of control. Criminal negligence of gigantic proportions on their part caused them to never investigate sincerely the more remote consequences of the destruction of the gold standard. Of course, the inflationists realised that their anti-gold policies would destabilise the value of the national currency (for they adhere also to the QTM – when it suits them) and unleash speculators in the foreign exchange markets. Inflationists welcomed this as a salutary development, and pointed to the manipulation of monetary policy as a means to their nationalistic and autarkic ends. They didn't realise that the destruction of the gold standard would also destabilise the interest rate structure, and unleash speculators in the bond market.[8] Fluctuations in interest rates due to the Kondratiev long-wave cycle would be aggravated. Nor did they realise that a prolonged fall in the rate of interest is extremely deflationary [9] and could plunge the economy into a depression. This point is still not widely appreciated, and the world appears to be completely ignorant of the dangers of depression brought about by the destruction of the gold standard albeit with a forty-five-year delay. Economists of the present vintage have been 'trained' (as in 'conditioned') to see in the gold standard the direct cause of depressions. The exact opposite of the truth, as already revealed in Vol. II.[10] Bond speculation does not amount to a zero-sum game. Virtually all speculators choose the long side of the bond market as they want to preempt the central bank in buying the bond.[11] (Note that the central bank makes bond speculation risk free through its open market purchases of bonds) Who is on the short side? Besides the Federal Reserve, raking up losses by overpaying and handing out capital gains to speculators who dump their bonds at the door of the FED: all other holders/managers of fixed capital. That is the entire class of entrepreneurs, of course. They are passive participants with their (own) capital at stake, whether they like it or not. They have literally no choice in the matter. They have been turned into sitting ducks in this unconscionable shoot-out for the benefit of speculators by deliberate government policy. Moreover, the producers are quite unaware of what is going on. In particular, they are completely oblivious to the fact that they are served up as the sacrificial lamb on the altar of government omnipotence.[12] Bond speculation aided and abetted by government is responsible for denuding producers of their capital and for transferring their wealth to the speculators in the form of unprecedented profits on their long positions in bonds. [13]

We may conclude that the best economic climate for all the non-parasitical elements of society is the one with a stable interest-rate structure, such as the one provided by the regime of an unadulterated gold standard. It is charged that in the 19th and the 20th centuries the gold standard failed to stabilise prices. However, in a dynamic economy admitting growth the stabilisation of prices is neither possible nor desirable.

The great merit of the gold standard must be seen in the feat that it has stabilised the interest-rate structure so as to prevent the financial sector from becoming a vampire sucking the life-blood of the producing sector. It must be realised that this is an unstable world, and the best one can do is to stabilise interest rates (as well as foreign exchanges) by adhering to a gold standard. Prices will then take care of themselves.[14]

Exploding the Myth of the Welfare State

Finally, the hexagonal structure of capital markets explodes the myth of the Welfare State.[15] According to this myth the government can finance welfare projects by taxing away some of the profits of the capitalist. However, the activities of the capitalist only arise at the margin, and they represent but the tip of the iceberg. The incomparably greater part of capital society depends on in order to provide annuity income for the aged is furnished by the less visible partnerships of the annuitant and the entrepreneur, as well as those of the annuitand and the inventor. Governmentally dictated social security eliminates, or at least severely curtails, voluntary exchanges of income and wealth, and thereby hampers capital accumulation. The Welfare State confuses charity with entitlement. Its huge commitment to place social security benefits on the basis of universality has no actuarially sound basis in finance nor in economics. The making of these commitments puts the very people out of business whose savings alone can provide the wherewithal of projected benefits.

We cannot help but view the capitalist economy as a highly integrated welfare generating process: individuals voluntarily exchanging goods against goods, goods against services, and income against wealth. In the process they form voluntary partnerships, thus creating wealth by capitalising incomes. The Welfare State cannot invade one part of this machine, taking over its functions, and expect that the other part will go on performing satisfactorily. This invasion means the forcible dissolution of partnerships and the dissipation of their capital. Yet the corresponding liability in the consolidated balance sheet of the nation remains. It will have to be balanced by new assets. The government pretends to do this by printing government bonds payable in irredeemable currency. As long as purveyors continue accepting irredeemable currency in exchange for real goods and services, the game of musical chairs will go on. There have been many precedents in history for such a game, and the music has always stopped at one point or another in all previous episodes. It will also stop in the present one, even though we may be unable to pinpoint the exact timing. Here is the reason why.

The capital of the nation is seriously eroded as it has been deprived of augmentation from capitalising the income of the annuitand in partnership with the inventor. The deficiency of capital eventually shows up as increases in the cost of goods and services. Producers are squeezed and suffer losses. Some will succumb and get out of business; others will raise prices. Either way benefits promised are nullified by the side-effects of the blind policies of the Welfare State: capital destruction and currency depreciation. The alleged benefits must be set against this background: the so-called Welfare State has a hidden scheme to debase the currency and dissipate society's capital.

The Euthanasia of the Bondholder

The cynical phrase 'euthanasia of the bondholder' was first used by John Maynard Keynes. He was well aware what the implementation of his schemes to sabotage the gold standard would mean to bondholders.[16] Keynes treated the bondholder with contempt, as a parasitic element of society. He ridiculed coupon-clipping, calling it the only positive contribution the bondholder is capable of making to the commonweal. In the event, euthanasia turned into a bloodbath, the like of which the world has not seen since the night of St. Barth-

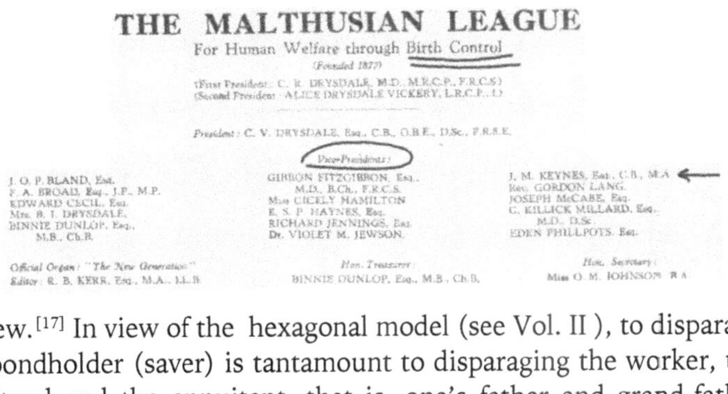

olomew.[17] In view of the hexagonal model (see Vol. II), to disparage the bondholder (saver) is tantamount to disparaging the worker, the annuitand and the annuitant, that is, one's father and grand-father who, after a lifetime of faithful and diligent service expect to have a peaceful and secure retirement. The euthanasia of the bondholder means no less than the euthanasia of dear old grandfather.[18]

It is to the eternal shame of our Western Civilisation that the crime of slaughtering the bondholders was permitted and even glorified, and no case study of the sufferings of the victims was ever allowed to be published. [19]

The euthanasia of the bondholder was the ill star under which 'social security' was born. The latter is a compulsory scheme based on socialistic principles. There is no actuarially sound way to fund the liability incurred by a universal social security program. In fact, it is an unfunded system financed through an open-ended tax escalator. Such a system is easy to introduce, as in the early days a relatively large number of workers support a relatively small number of eligible beneficiaries and the tax rate is nearly negligible. However, as the system reaches maturity a couple of generations later, the number of workers it will take to support one beneficiary declines drastically. This would happen in any case, but birth control, life-prolonging drugs and therapeutic procedures greatly accelerate the process. A reduction in promised benefits is out of the question and is regarded as political dynamite. The only alternative is to escalate taxes that finance the system. Just how long the taxpayers will be willing to carry the open-ended increases of burden is anybody's guess. It will eventually dawn upon young people that they will never benefit as the scheme is bound to collapse before they reach retirement age.

Compulsion can never do what spontaneous association can.[20] We have seen in the previously that the 'social security' scheme introduced in the 1930s dissipates the wealth of the annuitant and induces the annuitand to stop saving. There is also the sinister problem of depriving the inventor of his traditional source of financing, with incalculable consequences as to capital accumulation, in particular the capitalisation of incomes, which society depends upon in order to provide the benefits and comfort to the retired population. Note that none of the problems associated with the compulsory scheme arise under the voluntary cooperation of the annuitand, the annuitant, the entrepreneur, and the inventor discussed previously.

The usual objection goes along the lines that the voluntary system is not universal and it leaves indigent people out in the cold. This is not the place to go into a discussion of the validity of the Biblical admonition that 'the poor will always be with us' and there will always be a need for charity, regardless of the level of affluence that society may reach. We must reconcile ourselves to the objective fact that a compulsory social security scheme promising universal coverage is not viable and cannot be made viable. The idea could be sold politically only because people are prone to fall for Ponzi schemes, to the genus of which 'social security' clearly belongs.

The Rise and Fall of the Yield Curve

Nowadays one hears frequent references to the 'yield curve' or, as the case may be, to the 'inverted yield curve'. It may come as a surprise that there was no yield curve under a gold standard. Multiple interest rates along with multiple foreign exchange rates belong to the paraphernalia of the regime of irredeemable currency, wherein a change in the price of crude oil, for example, could move both rates, and an increase in prices could provoke another increase in prices, as currency debasement looms large. Under the gold standard the rate of interest and of foreign exchange are stable and well-protected from shocks such as that in the price of crude oil, for example.

The yield curve represents the rate of interest as a function of time to maturity. It is considered 'normal behaviour' for the rate of interest to increase as the time to maturity is increased. Moreover, the rate of interest asymptotically approaches a certain value, the theoretical yield of a perpetual bond, as the time to maturity tends to infinity. This means that the normal shape of the yield curve is that of a rising one which nevertheless is bounded from above by the theoretical yield on perpetual bonds. A rising yield curve means that as maturity increases, the yield also increases. This is supported by the Principle of Time Preference (see Vol.II) asserting that, when given the choice between funds available in the remote or nearby future, the economising individual will, other things being the same, choose the latter.

However, under 'abnormal' credit conditions it can and often does happen that, as maturity increases, the yield actually decreases. In this case the yield curve is called 'inverted' as it is falling (apart from a brief sharp spike near zero maturity).

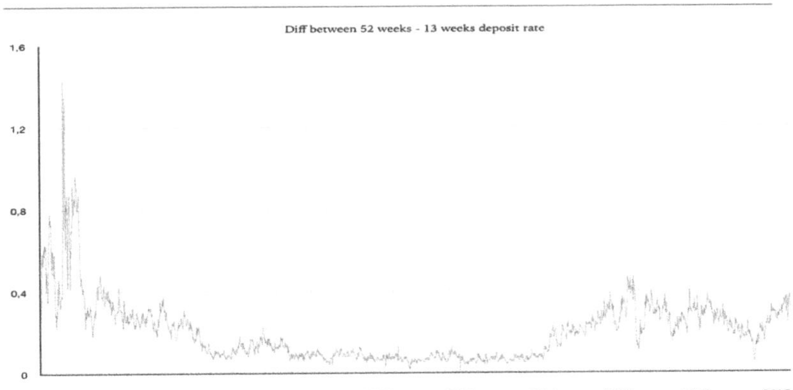

Fig. 2 Flirting with yield inversion.
The difference in % between a 52 week and a 13 week deposit.
Note how graph does not plot a negative rate just yet, unlike 2002-2003. The difference between 52 weeks and 13 weeks does not rise above ¼ % point.

It still approaches the same value asymptotically as the time to maturity tends to infinity, but in this case the yield curve is bounded from below by the theoretical yield on perpetual bonds. Abnormal credit conditions mean that, as a result of loose credit policies pursued by the banks and the government, too many short-term credit instruments approach maturity, which depresses their prices. Cash is scarce and the yield on short-term credit is high. The inverted yield curve may return to its normal state quickly, or it may last for an extended period of time, depending on the depth of the credit crisis which always accompanies it.

None of this may happen under a gold standard where the government and the banks are forced to keep their short-term liabilities safely within the limits of their quick assets. In fact, if all the gold bonds issued have sinking fund protection, as they should, then there is no yield curve. More precisely, the yield is the same constant value for all maturities (graphically: making the yield curve a horizontal straight line). The rate of interest is stable, both in time and across the maturity spectrum. A yield curve, if one existed, would create a temptation for the banks to borrow short in order to lend long. Such an activity would lead to periodic credit crises and the yield curve would get inverted as a result.

The absence of a yield curve under a gold standard does not mean that the rate of interest may not fluctuate. What it means is that all the adjustments are so gradual that they present no temptation for the banks to speculate in the bond market. On the other hand, if certain economic shocks (such as a continental crop failure, or pestilence wiping out a sizeable portion of the working force) calls for a big rise in the rate of interest, then it will be made quickly and expeditiously. Issuers of gold bonds will refund their obligation and sell a new issue with a higher coupon rate. In no case would they allow bondholders to suffer a loss. They take to heart the Biblical admonition that 'tormenting widows and orphans is a sin that cries to high heaven for punishment'.

Arbitrage v. Speculation

I have mentioned repeatedly that there is no bond speculation under a gold standard. Subsequently I got several messages from my readers insisting that speculation actually has a role in stabilising interest rates. However, what my readers referred to as 'stabilising speculation' is no speculation at all. It is arbitrage. The two must be carefully distinguished, something that mainstream economics has failed to do. The distinction becomes clear at once when we consider the objectives of the speculator and the arbitrageur. The former is willing to take big risks in the hope of a big payoff. The latter is not interested in risk-taking at all. The arbitrageur steps in whenever the market shows deviant behaviour. He makes his bet that the deviation will be corrected. Whenever a sufficient number of arbitrageurs do likewise, their market action will be self-fulfilling. Examples are deviations in the foreign exchange rates, or those in the rate of interest, under a gold standard. The arbitrageur takes it for granted that the deeds of the government are as good as its words, and it wouldn't knowingly mislead the market and pocket the illicit gains that originated in deception. Of course, any arbitrageur would quickly come to grief in today's foreign exchange and bond markets where deception is practiced by governments on a regular basis. It is not by accident that mainstream economists have failed to make a distinction between arbitrage and speculation in the bond market. They are lame apologists for the government out to cover up bad faith and chicanery. Arbitrageurs have vacated the field, and speculators have taken over, as a result of the destruction of the gold standard. Contrary to mythology, under the gold standard it wasn't the central bank that kept the rate of interest and foreign exchanges stable. It was the arbitrageurs who believed in the good faith of the government in promising payment on their obligations in gold coin at a fixed rate. Without arbitrage the financial resources of the central bank would have been inadequate to stabilise the foreign exchanges, as well as the rate of interest. This is a problem that mainstream economist are unable to address. It has no mandate from its sponsors to use the language of good and bad faith in market dealings.However, there is no other way to deal with markets under the regime of irredeemable currency but through pointing out the deception regularly practiced by the government and its central bank in order to fool the public. This is why devaluations were always announced during the week-end when markets were closed. Prior to this government and central bank spokesmen had shouted from the rooftop that foreign exchange rates will 'never' be changed. Next week politicians and central bankers had to eat their words. Nowadays this problem is avoided through the mechanism of floating foreign exchange rates. Note that 'floating' is a euphemism for 'sinking', as the international monetary system is merely a cover for competitive currency devaluations. At any rate, the outcome is the same: the fleecing of the producing sector (including the savers) and the enriching of the financial sector (including the treasury).

CHAPTER 24

One Rate or Two?

I have pointed out (Volume II) that the rate of interest is the marginal efficiency of the exchange of wealth and income. It is determined through a market process, similar to that determining the price of wheat. But whereas the formation of the wheat price could possibly be described through a simple diagonal model with the two poles representing supply and demand, the formation of the rate of interest is more complicated as there are at least two types of exchanges involved. Just as the sale of every sack of wheat has an effect on the price of wheat, every exchange of wealth and income has an effect on the rate of interest. My critics point out that if my analysis were correct, then there would have to be two rates of interest, one regulating the exchange of the income of the annuitand for the wealth of the inventor, and another, regulating the exchange of the wealth of the annuitant for the income of the entrepreneur. One rate or two, that is the question.

It is true that for gold bonds, no less than for wheat, the market quotes not one but two prices: a higher asked price and a lower bid price. Transactions take place between these two extremes. The spread between the two has an extraordinary theoretical importance. It is instrumental in setting a limit to the volatility of the rate of interest. In more detail, the higher asked price for the gold bond translates into the floor, and the lower bid price into the ceiling, for the rate of interest.

The reason for the inversion is the fact that the price of the gold bond and the rate of interest move inversely. It is imperative that the reader have a good grasp and perhaps a good visual image of this inverse movement, and the inversion of its extremities. (One way of visualising this inverse movement is a pair of pistons of a reciprocating steam engine as they run up and down in their respective cylinders, always in opposite directions. Another way is the see-saw, a piece of equipment for children to play on, consisting of a long flat piece of wood supported in the middle. A child sits at each end and makes the see-saw move up and down.) We shall make frequent references to the reciprocating movements of the rate of interest and the price of the gold bond, by calling it the 'see-saw'. (See volume II for a full treatment of this inverse relationship of bond and price.

Stable interest rates under a gold standard are explained by the small spread between the asked and bid price of the gold bond. We may verbalise this by saying that the stability of the rate of interest under a gold standard is the flip-side of the narrow bid/asked spread for the gold bond.

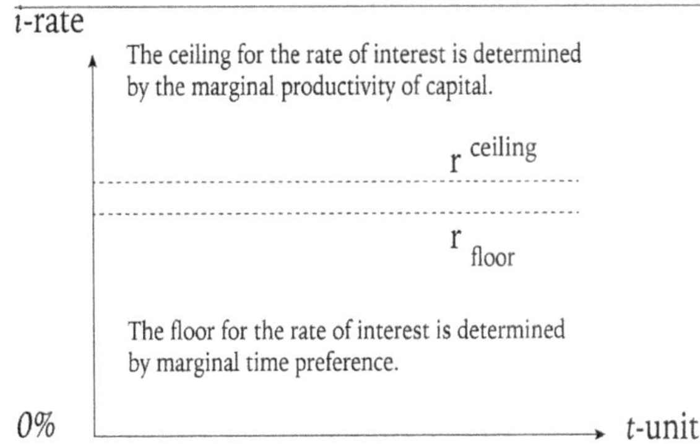

Fig. 3 Stable interest rates can only happen under a circulating gold coin standard, distributing the decision making while keeping all parties in balance to each other. The result is a relative stable rate.

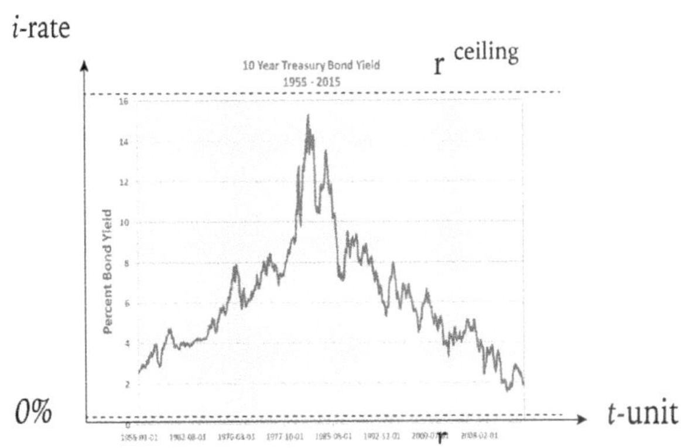

By contrast, wildly gyrating interest rates, as experienced under the regime of irredeemable currency, reflect the yawning gap between the

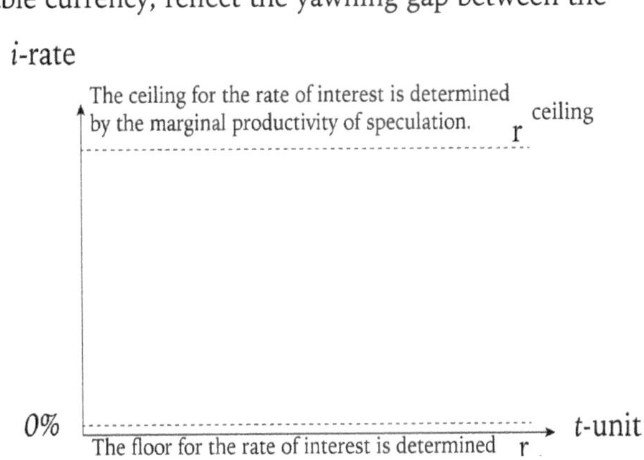

Fig. 4 The result of scientific money management, complements of the central bank and some friendly leveraged hedge funds a.k.a. licensed banks and pension funds. All at your expense, of course.

asked and bid prices of bonds. The gap is the only clue we have to explain unstable credit conditions.

So why is there a unique rate of interest under a gold standard when, on the face of it, there ought to be two, one at which income is exchanged for wealth, and another at which wealth is exchanged for income? Here is the reason why.

> Those who want to exchange wealth for income are the buyers, and those who want to exchange income for wealth are the sellers of the gold bond. To say that the two rates, one involved in exchanging wealth for income and the other income for wealth, are not equal is the same as to say that there is a wide gap between the asked and bid prices of the bond.

The investment banker and the managers of various sinking funds act as market-makers in the bond market. They buy the gold bond at the lower bid price and sell it at the higher asked price. They profit from the existence of a wide spread between the two. As a result of their arbitrage the spread narrows and the two rates get closer. Even though profits from this arbitrage disappear together with the spread, the investment banker and managers of the sinking funds will continue in this business. Their primary task is not to profit from the arbitrage; it is to make a market in bonds. We conclude that under a gold standard the bid/asked spread of gold bonds is negligible, and for all practical purposes the rate of interest is one and the same for all maturities.

Deterioration in the Quality of Credit

If the bid/asked spread for bonds widens, it means that the market-makers in the bond market are hampered in their bid/asked arbitrage. Either the sinking fund protection of bonds is being withdrawn, or the investment banker is intimidated by a torrent of new inferior bond issues. The widening in the bid/asked spread measures the deterioration of credit.

In these terms, the 20th century witnessed an unprecedented deterioration in the quality of credit, one that mainstream economists prefer to ignore. The landmark was the government's default on its gold obligations. This was followed by the dismantling of the sinking fund protection of the bondholders. Finally, the gold clause on bonds were declared 'contrary to public purpose' by the government. As a consequence arbitrageurs have abandoned the field and speculators have taken over. The latter are now in the driver's seat, and bond speculation is increasing by leaps and bounds.

In the 19th century self-respecting governments and companies would not have tolerated that the value of their obligations become a play thing in the hands of speculators. As a matter of fact, there were no bond speculators since there was not enough volatility in the price of the gold bond to make speculation profitable. Things are very different today. Ever since the last link between the dollar and gold was severed in 1971, the volume of bond speculation has been increasing at an exponential rate. Today gold bonds are historical relics. Governments won't put up with any meaningful competition against their obligations denominated in irredeemable currency. They know full-well that their issues would not stand a chance in such an environment.

A gold bond is an obligation that is payable, not in terms of itself, but in value existing outside and independently of the promises of the issuer. A government bond of current vintage is an obligation redeemable in an inferior instrument: a non-obligation, to wit: in non-interest-bearing irredeemable currency. This shatters the logical basis supporting the value of the bond. But this is not all. Ostensibly the value of irredeemable currency is supported by the assets against which they are issued as a liability on the books of the central bank. As these assets are the very same government bonds which promise to pay irredeemable currency to the bondholder at maturity, the logical basis supporting the value of the currency is shattered, too. The relationship between the government bond and the currency is an incestuous one, on which it is not possible to build long-term prosperity. These are fundamental problems that are not being addressed while fair weather lasts. In the meantime forces promoting foul weather are gathering steam. It is doubtful that these fundamental problems can be dealt with after the storm has begun.

Fleecing the Producers

If the logical basis for the value of government bonds has been shattered as it promises to pay its face value in nothing but itself, the question arises what then supports the value of these bonds? The answer is that government bonds are the very chips one needs in order to play in the casino otherwise known as the bond market.

The destruction of the gold standard by the government was thoroughly immoral, but the matter did not end there. It has corrupted the bond market right to its core. Today nobody in his right mind would try to save by holding a bond to its maturity. The bond market is the haunt of speculators. It is a casino for gambling. The bond is the chip used at the gambling tables. Yet there is an important difference between the operation of the bond market under the regime of irredeemable currency, and the gambling casino. In the latter the gain of one gambler is the loss of another. This is also expressed by saying that gambling at the casino is a zero-sum game. Its effect on society at large is nil.

It is quite otherwise with bond speculation. Here we have a casino wherein the players can fleece outsiders.

> Let it suffice here to state the bare fact that the bond market is a casino where speculators risk not their own funds but those of the savers and producers. As a result, the latter are always the losers, even when they haven't the slightest intention to play.

We have an insane arrangement whereby productive activity is penalised and gambling activity is rewarded. As a result, the volume of productive activity constantly shrinks while that of financial activity constantly expands. Moreover, the latter expands at an exponential rate, as the financial markets attract all available funds, gobbling up the capital of the producing sector. Most ominous of all, talent is no longer attracted to production, entrepreneurship, and inventive activity.

> Capable young people choose careers related to the financial sector, the only place where they can hope to earn adequate rewards.[21]

To recapitulate, under a gold standard capital markets function efficiently to channel the funds of savers to finance production for the benefit of the entire society. Their operation is accurately described by the hexagonal model[22] which in particular explains the formation and stability of the rate of interest. Capital markets have been corrupted by the destruction of the gold standard. The rate of interest has been destabilised, inviting bond speculators to turn the capital markets into a gambling casino where the producers and savers can be fleeced. The moral responsibility for this subversion must be borne by the government and the profession of the economists for its failure to inform the public of what is happening.

Insert 1

The capital sum gathered to form the enterprise was calculated to amortise the cash flows a the prevailing rate of 5%, to use our previous example. Using the numbers in the previous table, an enterprise gathered 21.647 as capital to extract income of 5.000 per annum for the next 5 years, the PV of installed capital being discounted at 5% of the total cash flows of 5 x 5.000. When the interest rate drops to 4%, what is the problem? The yearly payouts stay the same and the yield to the advancers of the capital sum is even relatively higher at 5% instead of 4%. Moreover, the principle returned after 5 years is 21.647 instead of 22.259. The enterprise has a windfall no? The problem is indeed not for the entrepreneur, but for the owners of the sums advanced. When repaid after 5 years, the owners of the capital need 22.259 and not 21.647 to reinvest at 4% and **keep income unaffected**. Those who argue that the shortfall needs to come out of provisions from annuities, fail to keep the income unaffected. But, so the argument goes, that is not the problem of the entrepreneur, it is the bondholder's...! Legally, yes, however, economically speaKing, there is no difference between capital from a bond (besides the tax shield) and capital from shares. People provided wealth in exchange for income.
If the capital of the enterprise also belongs to the entrepreneur himself, his capital losses are the capital gains of the enterprise... In that case, why not compensate the capital loss of 621 to the entrepreneur in his private capacity? Economically, the 621 is a loss compensation. But legally, the 621 would be subject to capital gains tax....of all things! Using proper accounting rules, every interest rate drop ought to give rise to extra provisions for capital losses to the owners of the capital. Moreover, rate drops ought to give rise to supplementary amortisation, since profitability of the enterprise becomes more questionable if not precarious after a rate drop. Will the tax authorities smile and go along? All these provisions make extra claims on the spread the enterprise is addressing (in fiscal language: taxable profit the fiscal authorities are about to lose). Interest rate hikes – indirectly but palpably – reduce free cash flow available to the enterprise. In other words they do not show up on the balance sheet, but on your income statement. So, rate drops by your friendly central banker to help you out? The IRS your (not-so-silent) partner? With friends like these, who needs enemies?

Insert 2

Were's My Sinking Fund?

Under a gold standard, bonds were issued by an enterprise under the high protection of the sinking fund manager. When interest rates *hiked*, the sinking fund manager bought the bonds back at the lower market value and kept purchasing them back until ...
... rates went down again and market values were restored back to par. But a rate *drop*? At first glance, it would look beneficial, it does not require a permanent collective higher productivity any longer. But look again.. rate drops have been ongoing for the last 40 years or so! Rates always look too high from that perspective. Consistent rate drops for 40 years (two entire generations) have turned the interest rate structure into a permanent fixture that is experienced as too high. A case in logic can be made that a central bank (e.g. FED, BoE, BoJ, etc.) ought to be the entrepreneur's 'reverse sinking fund'. Every drop in rates, causes a capital gain with the bondholder (mostly banks/pension funds), but an opposite and equal societal loss in the sense that new bidders for the capital will have to bid up prices for no other reason than the rate drop, to ***compensate the loss of income*** for the bondholder (ultimately that would be the retiree's).

Example

To see how a rate drop causes damages, we give the following calculation example of an exchange of wealth for income: We assume that either the income stream and its purchasing power needs preservation at all times. ***A principal of 100.000 is exchanged for an annual income of 4% for the duration of 10 years.*** Coupon payments of 4.000 are made yearly after 1 year of receiving the principal sum. After 10 years, the principal is restituted as well. If the interest rate drops during the 10 year lifetime of the bond to 3 %, the issuer of the bond pays 25% too much on yearly coupons of 4.000, because he could have had coupons at 3% or yearly coupon obligations of 3.000. A 1% drop constitutes a quarter (!) in difference for the issuer. But to the bondholder, who now receives 'too much' (sic) will accrue the agreed income of 4.000 yearly. However, the 100.000 in capital, which will be returned after 10 years poses a problem; in order to preserve his income of 4.000 a year this sum has become totally insufficient under a 3% regime. He now needs 133.333 to invest in a 3% coupon that provides the same income of 4.000 yearly. His capital took a hit of one third (!) in preservation power. Arguments that he can save up from income received defeat the purpose. Either his capital is seriously impaired or his income is seriously impaired by the rate cut. Who will indemnify the holder of the capital ? This income needs to be preserved – it is a pension income ! It cannot be just saved up to fix future capital impairments, without compromise on income.If you cause damage to another person, you are obliged to restitute or compensate the damage, right? Well then... For every rate hike or drop, caused by a central authority, either the FED has to pay compensation or the Treasury has to allow tax shielded compensation provisions to all capital deployed, be it in the form of bonds or equity. This would allow the enterprise to fulfil part of its ethical role in society by providing sinking fund management for all capital handed over to them in exchange for income. Sarbanes-Oxley declarations notwithstanding, the full compensation provided by the Fed or the Treasury in cases of rate changes, indemnifies enterprises who could then put their money where their mouth is through a 'reverse sinking fund' protection. Unpalatable as it is – it may be such an expensive exercise for central authorities that it may deplete tax revenues entirely – it would keep incomes intact and demonstrate the consequences of rate gyrations.

Things Get Worse Instead...

Obtaining compensation from persons that have caused damage may be a normal thing in a lawfully organised society. But the damage is not so simple – in fact completely impossible – to calculate correctly. Using an irredeemable currency causes problems of calculations. Providing 'damage restitution' in more of the irredeemable currency would only work with simpletons. The compensation provided comes in doses of more of the same problem. Providing tax shields then?This non-monetary solution would look attractive, were it not that it would painfully demonstrate the futility of having a Treasury. The so provided tax shield would negate any chance of a positive revenue-income to the Treasury, since more of their revenue will be handed out as restitutions... (Recalling fig. 7 and 23 in Vol. II) the calculation problem of prices in a collectivist-communist society proved its nemesis, but it can be convincingly demonstrated that having irredeemable currency lies at the hart of the problem. (Recall, if you will, its fast declining marginal utility) Which means it affects all those working with an irredeemable currency. Which means all of us.

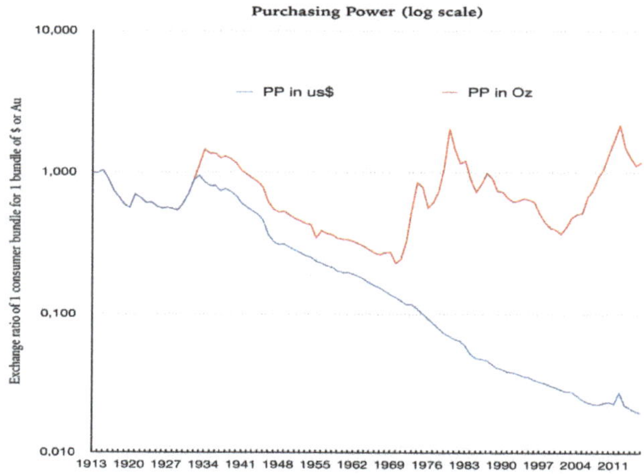

Fig. 5 Cause confusion by suspending the Harberler-Pigou effect on the fiduciary component of money, rake in seigniorage entirely and put yourself above the law with privilege and monopoly.

A Societal Problem

Governments are institutions provided by the people to overcome problems. However, they were not intended to be hijacked. Treasuries and central bankers, if challenged before a judge on charges of check-kiting would face criminal charges. That is not going to happen for a host of mostly legal reasons. It is clear by now, that certain people are more equal than others. If a society would like to maintain itself, it better heed the law of exponential growth: any population, including a parasitical one, will multiply exponentially to the extent that its biotope tolerates it or supports its existence. Certain parasites, however, do kill their hosts, nonetheless. This, however, would not be a problem of economic science, were it not that our economic institutions, churches, schools, and money have become, probably irreversibly, corrupted. So it is a problem, an economic problem also, but a much larger societal problem to be sure.

Insert 3

How a Rate Drop Affects You and Your Bank

A calculation example.
Mortgage banks 'purchase' your cash monthly repayments at the prevailing rate, the mortgage rate. Chances of a rate change over the time span of the mortgage are not difficult to predict. The last 40 years they went nowhere but down. In insert 2 we have seen that in case of a rate drop, only a higher principle amount will repurchase at a lower rate, the same income stream. Refinancing means liquidating the old loan first. Its liquidation value has gone up. To repurchase the same income stream, but at a lower rate, they will need an augmented capital. If after 5 years of mortgage payments of 602.22 per month (at 4 % p.a.), you still owe the bank 81.811,04. If you – refinancing at the lower rate – are offered a lower monthly repayment of 563.38 for the remainder of the 180 months, you win. But you will probably be offered different terms: either a higher amount, say 87.628,50 instead of 81.811,04 or 197 months instead of 180 months – or a combination of both: slightly higher and slightly longer… that is the bank covering her capital loss.
Banks do not only bid for mortgages; they also bid for government bonds. A Treasury bond of 150 million nominal at 2 % will yield a yearly annuity of 3 million. Its PV is 150 million and if 2% is the going market rate, 150 million is its market value. However, in order to force interest rates down accross the board, the Federal Reserve, instead, will (over)bid for the Treasury bonds (held by amongst others banks) and will offer 200 million (instead of its market value of 150 million). The Fed now holds a 150 million bond for which it paid 200 million, receives a yearly coupon for 3 million from the Treasury and so the Fed makes a yield of 1,5 % instead of 2%. Interest rates, when all bonds floating around have been bought, have dropped to 1,5 %. The Fed 'making' a yield is a misnomer. It has lost 50 million per bond repurchased in the open market operation. The gain of the same amount accrues to the bank. This is a capital gain and in many cases this capital gain in the hand of the bank remains tax free. The invitation to speculate in government bonds is a no-brainer.

How a Rate Drop Affects Your Pension Fund

A pension fund is a collection of retiree's who draw on the fund and of employees who contribute and save up for retirement. Whether the capital provider is you, your grandmother or your pension fund (as a representative) makes no difference in financial algebra. A rate drop causes capital losses for the retirees if their annuities or mensualities will remain the same. But what does it do to employees (= current savers)? Their monthly contributions were contracted at the time at say 4%. With a working career of 45 years and yearly contributions of 826.24 their retirement will be funded with 100,000. But if a rate drop occurs, from 4% to 3% (likely during 45 years of FED regime) either their contributions need to increase from 826.24 to 1,078.52 (a 30% increase) or their fund reaches only 76,608.85 instead of 100,000. Even if your pension fund purchases government bonds that provide capital gains, it falls short of the roughly 33% increase needed to guarantee pensions purchasing power. But what is more important: the funds of the employees flow to where the action is: risk-free capital gains in the government bonds. The corporate bond market cannot compete. And what about the enterprise's tools that need renewing and for which purpose theses funds were intended ? See Volume II.

Endnotes to Chapter 24

[1] For the modern misrepresentation and abuse of Machiavelli, see E. Voegelin, 'Machiavelli's Prince: Background and Formation', *The Review of Politics*, Vol. 13, Nr. 2, April 1951, pp. 142-168 available online.

[2] John Law 'tokenised' his securities.

[3] The prestidigitation of turning water into wine or the King's debt into a public asset keeps the imagination of all magicians in monetary matters going, even to this day.

[4] A case can be made that a Central Bank (e.g. the FED) ought to be the entrepreneur's sinking fund. Every drop in rates, causes a capital gain with the bondholder, but a societal loss in the sense that new bidders for the capital will have to bid up prices for no other reason than the rate drop, to compensate the loss of income for the bondholder – as well a a downward shift in marginal productivity of labour! If you cause damage to another person, you are obliged to restitute or compensate the damage, right? Well then... For every rate drop, either the FED has to pay compensation or the treasury has to allow tax shielded compensation provisions to all capital deployed, be it from bonds or shares. It may be such an expensive exercise, it may deplete tax revenues entirely.

[5] Ideologues have a long standing problematic relationship with 'control'. The control problem was already discussed by Eugen von Böhm-Bawerk in his Control or Economic Law. It first appeared in the *Zeitschrift für Volkswirtschaft, Sozialpolitik und Verwaltung*, Vol. XXIII (1914), p. 205-271. The philosophical aspect of this control issue was treated extensively by Eric Voegelin, *Modernity Without Restraint*, Collected Works Volume V. University of Missouri Press, Columbia and London 2000. Any ideologists' problem reduces in essence to an estrangement from reality problem. Ideologues will always *enlist other people* in what amounts to a hare brained scheme to 'improve' this world. To that end, the reality of omnipotence of God and his creation needs to be found wanting and man's skill to help himself seems to be eagerly called for - so the scientists need large funding! All of which is fine, without the hubris of omnipotence and the palace revolution banning God from his own creation. Unfortunately, this amounts to the same idea as Utopia, a toponym made famous by Wells.

Improvements of man's condition during his life time will be eminent but unbalanced if the decision making tends to lay with central organs or bureaucrats, none of which can be counterbalanced by other people's directly opposed interests. Such is the nature of a palace revolution and subsequent murder of the occupant. Most problematic situations only become problematic after a certain level of consciousness and thought has been reached collectively. The so-called 'iniquitous feudal system' nevertheless resolved itself and not only in Europe, China and Japan being prime examples. The typical ideologue will make promises for the future he or she cannot keep and the promises always seems to rest on 'eternal change' (read progress) where eternal bliss always escapes the people, lying just on the other side of the next hill. It reminds one of the proverbial pot of gold at the end of the rainbow. It is a perennial subject of amusement why grown up people and even chrysophobes still chase the 'pot of gold'. Control therefore, is always handed over by grown up people holding out for an irrealis, deluded by estrangement and exploited by con-artists, demagogues and sometimes raw sociopaths playing into the emotions of the masses, like E. Bernays. The essence of the 'Control Issue' comes from a thoroughly dualistic ancient gnosticism: When Plato says that one should love the Creator-Deity and attune oneself carefully to the beauties of his creation, then the Gnostic dualist insist that one should hate the Creator-Deity, who is an usurper and revile the many debased phenomena of creation. When Plato says that it is good to have been born in a beautiful world, then the Gnostic dualist insist that it is intolerable and that 'enlightened' people will seek to be redeemed from the universal miasma or will dedicate themselves to detoxifying existence. When Plato argues for a universal humanity, then the Gnostic dualist insists that humanity is not single, but dual; that there is a vast cohort of the unsalvageable barbarian.

[6] This control problem is only a perceived problem. Under an unadulterated gold standard, the public is in control of rates and consequently productivity and therefore also the degree of employment. However, unadulterated, the gold standard never was. Illicit interest arbitrage had promoted the Acceptance House to the proverbial elephant in the China shop. Bankers like Rothschild, Lazard, Barings etc. all bought political influence with their often ill-gotten gains. Silver could only have been demonetised with the technical know-how and helping hand of these bankers, burdening gold with the load that silver was carrying before. They bought monopolies and high protection from otherwise supposedly public and neutral servants; they financed both or all sides of a shooting war, knowing that they will take 'control' of the winning party's Treasury and tax departments. In that sense, Marx was quite sensitive to these problems of corruption, which were and are still not issues that economic science ought to deal with. The control problem turns violent with Marx and his later followers. Another contemporary epigone such as Graeber, a spin off from the illustrious 'Frankfurt School' of Gnostic dualism and of hard core communist persuasion. He still speaks of 'power games' – a perennial in this school of Marxist ideology – which has nothing to do with economics and certainly not under an unadulterated gold standard. Moreover, we fail to see how fallacious ideology could a) impose itself as a more correct way of doing science or b) provide solutions to societal problems. They are in fact the problem. Nevertheless,

the so-called 'deflation' of gold rest on a complete yet convenient fallacy. See Chapter 11 Vol. II Gold and the Quantity Theory of Money. The 'power' issues that plague this class of people have been described by E. von Böhm-Bawerk in *Control or Economic Law*, and more broadly by Eric Voegelin, *Modernity Without Restraint*, Collected Works Volume V. University of Missouri Press, Columbia and London 2000.

[7] It has been stressed before and we stress it again here : the Haberler-Pigou effect remains without result in an environment of irredeemable money and credit. 'The Haberler-Pigou effect describes how, when monetary authorities keep the current stock of money constant, and falling prices induce a feeling of value increases, people will at some point feel sufficiently wealthier so as to spend more or add to demand. For this to work, we have to assume that the nominal stock of money will remain unchanged...' Keep assuming, it simply cannot happen, for once irredeemable money gets primed and the ball rolling, one always needs to create more irredeemable currency simply to pay the interest on the outstanding principal, especially if taxation will not suffice. This becomes completely impossibly when the differential quotient of newly created GDP to debt dives to or below the ratio of 1. Taxing the entire GDP cannot even redeem the interest on principle then !

[8] Despite Keynes being celebrated as a specialist in interest rates...!

[9] In the sense of marginalising existing capital, by raising the rate of marginal productivity of capital, new AND existing alike. After 40 years of relentlessly falling rates, we now know jobs and capital went Eastward never to return. It even changed location in the East as well.

[10] Inverting truth is a specialist occupation of ideologues like Hegel, Marx, etc...

[11] Note how a Reserve Bank is doing exactly the same as John Law of Lauriston did. Where Law purchased the rentes of the French Crown and de facto receives the cash flow of the Crown's tax money, the Reserve Bank monetises the debt of the Treasury and de facto becomes the recipient of the tax collector. Just like John Law operated under government privilege and monopoly, just like his Mississippi scheme, privatising profits and socialising costs, a Reserve Bank receives monopoly privileges and collects 100% of the seigniorage, partially reduced by the capital gains paid to speculators. As an aside, Chieftains of Reserve banks belong often to the Basel registered BIS or Bank of International Settlements, enjoying complete diplomatic immunity for life, second only to the Vatican (and its bank).

[12] See No Time for T-Bonds by Carl Guttierez, March 28, 2009 Forbes.com

[13] Omnipotence thinking sports as a typical trait of positivism. Could someone please inform these people that economic positivism died after Max Weber? The failure to recognise this could have unpleasant consequences for authorities coming in the form of upheavals or worse. It has happened before.

[14] What would this do to the so-called price-controls, rent controls, etc ?

[15] The Welfare State itself being one of three ideological expressions of socialism: (1) International socialism / communism; (2) National socialism (or NAZISM); and (3) corporate socialism or Welfare socialism (a.k.a. Welfare State)

[16] It was indeed Keynes' ideological obsession. He would at all cost thwart the 'evil conservatives', in his eyes the bourgeois bankers using gold coin, often ill-gained. Keynes was a high profile member of the Eugenics Society, promoting limitations on population growth for those 'unfit' to have offspring, hence his enthusiasm for contraception essentially because the working class was too 'drunken and ignorant' to keep its numbers down. He knew and sympathised with the business of eugenics. In fact, he was Director of the Eugenics Society from 1937 to 1944. Besides promoting contraception for the drunken and ignorant class of labourers, he knew exactly how to prevent those 'unfit' conservatives to live much longer just as well. That they promoted a gold standard was incidental and in any case not interesting for Keynes to study. Both of them had to go. Keynes, in typical fashion of the 19th century positivist attitude, played God by dethroning God and replacing him by Super Man, in charge of His Own Destiny. That is : Keynes in charge of our economic destiny, with Krugman being the second pope in this church of eugenics.

[17] This occurred in the aftermath of the turn of the first millennium, when people in the West generally held the believe in the second coming of Christ. In anticipation of the end of time, an apparent collective madness took over the crowds.

[18] Such moral qualms did not keep awake the Fabianist or Eugenics society members. Bernard Shaw, J.M. Keynes and his ilk, thought that 'the only fundamental and possible socialism is the socialisation of the selective breeding of man' suggesting in a phrase that has inspired Hitler, that defectives be dealt with by means of a 'lethal chamber'. In the same vain, Marie Stopes, a hard-line eugenicist, disinherited her son because he had the audacity to marry a short-sighted woman and in 2008 the Postmaster General of Great Britain honoured her with a postage stamp.... The lunatics that run the asylum all befriend each other, it seems: Shaw and Keynes, Lysenko and J.B.S. Haldane, who warned that the world is in danger of over-producing 'undermen'- a translation of Untermensch ... Such musing show how Keynes never understood in the least the workings of marginalisation: by eliminating via birth control the 'unfit' from society, the remainder of society would -of course!- again be stratified in an elite and the new class of untermenschen. Who did he think would that be ? How moronic does one need to be not to understand it? Simple logic will do, no Auschwitz needed to confront one with reality. In fairness, this strand of social Darwinism did affect all layers of society, not only progressivists. It is the story of how some people became rich in the previous century by cheating and nepotism. Luckily, there still remain entrepreneurs that did not enter into Faustian deals.

[19] Such attitude is visible in the Chinese communities as well. Mao is dead, but not entirely. In order to save face, people simply pretend nothing happened. In the same vain, positivism was eclipsed by Max Weber. Although positivism has been dead ever since, Friedman exhumed its corpse to beat it to life, which is far worse than pretending nothing happened. It is high time to recognise the ideological garbage under the rug as well as in the attic, before it comes crashing down on society in the form of a derivatives collapse. It is time to study the gold standard in earnest and recognise the mistakes of the past; the banning of gold and its clearing house, the real bills clearing practise, was a colossal blunder performed in the name of science but under the influences of a toxic zombie ideology.

[20] Authorities know. In preparation of the coming tax revolt, the G7 meeting in Russia around the 2014 Winter Olympics in Sochi, produced a blueprint for the governmental confiscation of all financial assets known to them, in the aftermath of the financial crises and bail outs of the past few years. To this end, the OECD implemented a cross border financial and fiscal information sharing platform, accessible to tax authorities of OECD member countries. Bank accounts and assets will be at the fingertips of bureaucrats, fully operational from about 2018, ready to 'bail you in' in case another bail out of the Banking sector becomes necessary. Tax authorities like the OECD think they have the situation under control. Compulsion will do the trick. Will it ? Will credit be restored or irretrievably be broken down by such action?

[21] The only sector 'growing' in size is the financial sector. Compare this to the functional distribution sector, where the FMCG sector under a gold sector would provide job security, since FMCG would always be needed and in demand. No more...

[22] See Vol. II part 4 for an explanation of the hexagonal structure of capital markets under a gold standard.

Chapter 25

Essay published on December 2, 2014, by A. Fekete. Invited Address delivered at the International Precious Metal & Commodity Show, at the Event Arena/Olympiapark in München, November 8, 2014[1]

The Counterproductive Monetary Policy of the FED [2]

Introduction

Typically, bond speculators carry on interest arbitrage along the entire yield curve. They sell the short maturity and buy the long, hoping to capture the difference between the higher long rate and the lower short rate of interest (borrowing short and lending long). This arbitrage is not risk-free per se as it has the effect of flattening the yield curve. As a result the normal yield curve could get inverted unexpectedly, that is, turned upside down, making the rising curve into a falling one while turning the speculators' profit into a loss.

However, as a direct result of the policy of open market operations, introduced clandestinely and illegally in 19220 [3] through the conspiracy of the U.S. Treasury and the Federal Reserve (Fed), long before the practice was legalised *ex post facto* in 1935, interest arbitrage was made risk-free. Astute bond speculators could thereafter pre-empt Fed action profitably. **It never fails**: Speculators know that sooner or later the Fed will have go to the bill market to buy in order to boost the money supply.[4] They will buy beforehand. On rare occasions the Fed would be a seller. Then speculators, perhaps acting on inside information, will sell beforehand. This copycat action is an inexhaustible source of risk-free profits. Thanks to the Fed's open market purchases speculators are assured that they will always be able to dump the bonds they bought pre-emptively, at a profit. The more aggressively the Fed persists in its effort to increase the monetary base, the greater the bond speculators' profits will be.

Absolute Bad Faith

Following the disastrous 1921 collapse in the value of U.S. Treasury bonds the ongoing conspiracy between the U.S. Treasury and the Fed was formalised in 1922. The policy of Open Market Operations by the Fed was inaugurated. Ever since federal reserve *credit* has routinely been created on the collateral security of the *debt* of the United States government. Thus the Federal Reserve Act of 1913 was overthrown without fanfare while Congress was looking the other way. As a result the Fed has been subverted. According to the original act, collateral for the note and deposit liabilities of the Federal Reserve banks were to be restricted to real bills, that is, short-term commercial paper originating in the domestic production and distribution of consumer goods. Treasury paper was not listed in the act as an eligible asset. This was not an oversight. No part of Federal Reserve credit outstanding was supposed to be built on government debt. If a Federal Reserve bank was found short of eligible paper in balancing its note and deposit liabilities, it did not matter how great an overflow of Treasury bills it might have in its capital accounts, it was fined according to a stiff and progressive schedule of penalties for deficiency of collateral.

The conspiracy between the U.S. Treasury and the Federal Reserve started in 1914, almost on the same day the twelve Federal Reserve banks opened their doors for business. The decision was made at the highest level by President W. Wilson that the Fed be diverted from its original mission and be put to use in financing the war effort of the *Entente Cordiale*. Naturally, this was kept secret as it violated both the Neutrality Act as well as the Federal Reserve Act of 1913. The latter ruled out any and all purchases of foreign bonds, especially war bonds. The U.S. Treasury was the go-between in providing Federal Reserve credit to the belligerents. [5] The American public opinion that was strongly opposed to the European war was not informed about the *monetary warmongering*.[6]

The conspiracy can be observed plainly in the fact that the Treasury has 'forgotten' to collect the penalty from the Federal Reserve. Indeed, why should it penalise its best customer for its staple product? This was the greatest failing of the Federal Reserve Act of 1913: it put the fox in charge of the chicken coop. By 1920 you could not find a real bill in the portfolios of the Federal Reserve Banks with a magnifying glass. Instead, they were chock-full of Treasury paper. Nor was a serious effort made to return to the norms of the original act after hostilities ended in 1918. Real bills were not allowed to make a comeback by the victorious Entente powers.

We can safely ignore the colourful stories how in 1913 the Fed was conceived on Jekyll Island by a group of malevolent bankers with an agenda to enslave the world as mythological. The Federal Reserve Act of 1913 was not a malevolent document, although it obviously had warts. The conspiracy between the Treasury and the Fed was an unintended consequence, resulting from an unfortunate oversight of lawmakers. This oversight was most skilfully exploited by the sworn enemies of sound money.[7] The dagger went right to the heart of the U.S. monetary system. In 1913 legislators were assured that they were voting for a commercial paper system that could never become an engine of monetising government debt. Should the Federal Reserve banks ever try, they would be confronted with unacceptable losses. Sadly, it did not turn out that way.

When in 1935 the illegal practice was legalised retroactively through an amendment to the Federal Reserve Act of 1913, the introduction of open market operations was presented as an innocent housekeeping change, a technical matter relating to the Banking practice of releasing funds to and draining funds from the Banking system. The fundamental issue, the folly of allowing the Fed to monetise government debt, in itself an unconstitutional act, was hushed up. Congress and the public were never given a chance to scrutinise the matter. They were led astray.

Monetisation of government debt was legalised through the back door, through chicanery and absolute bad faith. It was made the centrepiece of the money-creating process, in complete negation of the intention of the original act (which made the production and distribution of consumer goods in most urgent demand the centrepiece of the money-creating process). Is it any wonder, then, that the new monetary system born in sin has brought disaster to the nation one hundred years later?

Critics focus their demur on the way the Fed creates money 'out of thin air' through sleight of hand. But there is a much larger issue here that has escaped attention. The policy of open market operations has made it possible for the Fed to usurp unlimited power in suppressing the rate of interest on all maturities through the transmission mechanism of risk-free bond speculation, while maintaining the illusion that it had only a very limited power – that of influencing the overnight rate of interest. The impression created is that the world can rest assured: all other rates are true market rates. Nobody took the trouble to dispel this illusion. (The fig-leaf was shed only recently: Quantitative Easing openly embraces direct purchases of T-bonds and agency paper such as those of Fanny Mae and Freddy Mac by the Fed.) (Presumably to hand them capital gains to make up their losses).

Falling Interest Rates as a Destroyer of Capital

Open market operations make for a regime of falling interest rates. My thesis that falling (as distinct from low but stable) interest rates destroy capital across the board is admittedly controversial. I would welcome its examination 'without fear and favour' by a competent and unbiased panel that could also examine the superiority of 'self-liquidating credit' over credit based on government debt (that could be called, tongue-in-cheek, 'self-perpetuating debt').

We shall look at three destructive effects of a rate cut:

(1) the increase in the liquidation value of debt,
(2) labour's deteriorating terms of trade,
(3) the fading of depreciation quotas.

The proposition that the bond price varies inversely with the rate of interest is uncontroversial and universally accepted by friend and foe alike. It describes the effect from the point of view of the creditor. Curiously, people find it hard to comprehend the equivalent proposition describing the very same effect from the point of view of the debtor, namely, that the liquidation value of debt also varies inversely with the rate of interest. In particular, a rate cut increases the cost of liquidating debt before maturity. Liquidation value is what the debtor must pay if he wants to retire his debt ahead of schedule.[8] [Ed. note: a prerequisite for refinancing] As this liquidation value is now higher, falling interest rates make the burden of debt increase. For example, if the rate of interest is cut in half, then according to the rule of thumb the liquidation value of long term debt is doubled (that is, to liquidate the debt will cost twice as much as it did before the cut).

To recapitulate: both the bond price and the burden of debt vary inversely with the rate of interest. Why is it that a fall in the rate of interest increases the market price of the bond? Well, nobody will sell an 'old' bond at face value after interest rates have been cut. The owner will demand, and the investor will pay, a higher price. The reason for this is simple: 'new' bonds that are now being issued produce a lower yield. The higher coupons of the old bond must be worth something. The bottom line is that the cost of the same cash flow has gone up. You must pay more for the same yield. For example, if the rate of interest is cut in half, then you will have to pay twice as much to generate the same cash flow as you have paid before the cut.

Current book-keeping practices ignore the deleterious effect of a rate cut as it increases the burden of debt across the board. Nay, falling interest rates are disingenuously hailed as a blessing designed to help business. It is to the eternal shame of the 'dismal science' that it has let this colossal propaganda lie pass without challenge.

The Present Value of Cash Flow

Having established

(1) the increase in the liquidation value of debt at the occasion of a rate decrease, we now turn to
(2) labour's deteriorating terms of trade as a consequence of suppressing the rate of interest through the policy of open market operations. (See also Chapter 17, Vol. II)

First we dwell a little longer on the problem of the present value of a cash flow (defined as the sum of individual payments discounted at the prevailing rate of interest, each for the period of time between now and when it becomes payable in the future.) Since the rate of interest is being cut, discount at a lower rate is involved. Therefore the present value of the cash flow is increased. For example, if the rate of interest is cut in half, then the present value of a cash flow continuing indefinitely doubles.

What does this mean for the terms of trade of those who need a cash flow for survival, such as all pensioners and all wage earners? Well, the price they have to pay for the cash flow is just its present value. Any cut in the rate of interest by the central bank affects them adversely. (See insert 1 and 2) Their terms of trade deteriorates. For example, if the rate of interest is cut in half, then they have to pay twice as much for the same cash flow as before the cut.

In practical terms this means that wage earners have to work roughly twice as hard to continue earning wages at the same level. As far as pensioners are concerned, their pension fund is devastated. It can no longer support the cash flow they have enjoyed before the cut. (See Chapter 25). Clearly, there is going to be a most serious deterioration in the standard of living for a large segment of society as a result of open market purchases of government bonds.

This reveals the most cruel aspect of open market operations: it hits the weakest members of society hardest. (For a calculation see inserts in the previous chapter.)

'Quantitative Squeezing'

The process undermining the value of money as it is trying to buy a cash flow is not well-understood. It reflects the failure of the public education system. This failure is not an accident. The powers that be under the regime of irredeemable currency have a vested interest in the public being totally ignorant on this matter. If the public realised what was going on, there would be blood in the streets. [9] Take a typical wage earner selling his own labour, namely, exchanging it for a cash flow (that he needs to keep body and soul united). The cash flow represented by his wages is grievously undermined by the policy of Quantitative Easing.[10] One's ability to do profitable work is quasi-wealth. It may well be the only asset the labourer has. The value of this quasi-wealth is rendered inferior every time the rate of interest is cut. For example if it is cut in half, the quasi-wealth of the labourer is halved as well.

> We may visualise the labourer as running on a treadmill the speed of which has just been boosted, say, by 100 percent. Now he has to run twice as fast just to stay abreast. If he wants to retain the value of his labour, he must work that much harder.

Karl Marx called it exploitation. There is no more insidious exploitation of human labour than giving a central bank unlimited power to manipulate the rate of interest downwards through open market purchases of government bonds, mockingly called 'Quantitative Easing'. It would be better called 'Quantitative Squeezing' of labour.

The 'Haircut' of the Rate Cut

Squeezing labour is not an idle theoretical or mental construction. It is very real indeed. The deterioration in labour's terms of trade (exchange labour for income) is clearly shown by the fact that **banks withdraw contract offers on mortgages whenever rates of interest are cut**. Monthly payments as prescribed by the 'old' mortgage contract amortise more slowly under the lower interest-rate regime, so the debt could not be retired on schedule. The 'new' mortgage contract features inferior terms for prospective clients (although this fact is usually obfuscated by the bank).[11] Often a few years are added to the schedule. Maturity is put off or, if this is not an option, then higher monthly payments are inflicted on the new clients. Recall that the mortgage contract is an asset of the bank, the liquidation value of which has just been increased by the rate cut.[12] The bank itself is being squeezed (think of the losses it is suffering on its portfolio of fixed-rate mortgages and other fixed-rate loans). No wonder that the bank is trying to pass on as much of its losses as it can to its clients, often deceitfully, by pressing them to refinance their fixed-rate mortgage at the lower rate to their detriment (by obfuscating some actuarial math calculations.)

We must realise that in the case of a rate cut the best course of

> action is to stay with the original fixed-rate mortgage. [13]

It is definitely not ***always*** beneficial to refinance at the lower rate! The source of confusion is that a rate cut is dressed up as if it were helping the homeowners to cope with the financial burden when the exact opposite is the case! [14]

In reality, the value of the cash flow of wages has been rendered inferior by the rate cut. It has lost so much of its debt-liquidating power. QE pushes labour deeper in debt and ZIRP (Zero Interest Rate Policy) means perpetual bondage for labour. It is modern slavery. 21st century slaves may well 'own' their homes, their cars, their freezers, etc., but their mortgage debt, their auto loans, their credit card debt are just so many evidences of indenture of slavery with absolutely no hope of emancipation under QE and ZIRP.[15]

'We wuz robbed. Dunno by who.' Well, we do. All labourers have been and continue to be pilfered and plundered by the regime of irredeemable currency in allowing the central bank to reduce the rate of interest to zero and beyond through open market purchases of government bonds. Every rate cut is a 'haircut' for labour.

> Shame on Keynes and on the profession of economists for not exposing the culprits, thus becoming an accomplice in the crime of bamboozling the least mathematically gifted section of the population.

They forget the biblical admonition of not doing onto others what you do not wish to be done unto yourself. A self-employed worker putatively uses depreciation quotas on his tools, modest as they may be which, as we shall see in a moment, are subject to fading. Thus self-employed workers are hit twice by the suppression of interest rates through the policy of open market operations. First they are hit on the wage account, secondly, on account of the fading depreciation quotas.

All wage earners are ferociously squeezed by the policy of lowering interest rates through the open market operations of central banks. Worst hit are the marginal wage earners. They are plunged into the hopelessness of permanent unemployment. There is a trade-off between taking on additional debt at the lower rate peddled by the central bank, and firing the marginal worker. Employers find it to their advantage to replace marginal *workers* with additional *machinery* installed and financed under ZIRP. Their collective labour contracts become more burdensome (in the same sense as the bonds they issued at the old rate have become more onerous) in the new lower-rate environment. Worse still for labour, its bargaining power has been grievously undermined through the policy of Quantitative Easing.

> Employers push for renegotiating their collective agreements in order to reduce wage rates to reflect the reduction in the rate of interest.[16] If that fails, they will fire their marginal workers and will apply the cash flow freed up thereby to service additional debt to be used to automate the enterprise or otherwise reorganise it. Either way, the marginal worker is eliminated for good. Unemployment increases across the board as a result.

Much has been made of squeezing labour through the central bank's deliberate inflationary policy. Meanwhile no notice has been taken of the far more insidious central bank policy squeezing labour: QE, ZIRP, and the rest. Union leaders, are you listening?

There is a growing recognition by the establishment of the built-in deterioration of the wage structure, as reflected by a recent essay in the Foreign Affairs magazine (an organ of the Council of Foreign Relations), at least in so far as the need for compensation for the damage caused by central banks is concerned. The amazing title of the essay is: 'Print Less but Transfer More: Why Central Banks Should Give Money Directly to the People.' [17]

Who Will Replace Producer Goods After They Are Scrapped ?

Back to the subject (c) of fading depreciation quotas we may first note their similarity to the fixed coupons of a bond and the fixed wage rates. When the rate of interest is suppressed, there is an upheaval undermining the value of all three.

- ▷ a. The coupons attached to a bond constitute a cash flow the value of which has been undermined by the rate cut.
- ▷ b. Wages of labourers also constitute a cash flow the value of which has been likewise undermined.
- ▷ c. Now we shall see that, no less, depreciation quotas also constitute a quasi-cash flow the value of which has been undermined as well.

Thus we are confronted with a systematic plundering of society through the deliberate suppression of interest rates, that is, through the policy of open market purchases of government bonds by the central bank. It is incredible that while the plunder has been going on unobserved for almost a hundred years, the profession of economists has taken note neither of the wisdom of the framers of the Federal Reserve Act of 1913 in outlawing Federal Reserve credit based on government debt (as the act before the 1935 amendment has done), nor of the untoward consequences of the policy of open market operations: (a), (b) and (c). We shall now see that the fading of depreciation quotas is a consequence of the policy of open market operations.

The depreciation quota of a producer good is an accounting tool revealing how much of its value has been 'used up' over time, due to wear and tear in production, and how much money needs to be put aside to amortise that loss in any particular year. If the rate of interest is pushed down by the central bank, then there is a setback in the amortisation schedule. Just as the fixed coupons of the bond – in the absence of refinancing – are no longer able to amortise the loan in the new lower interest-rate environment (because amortisation has been slowed down by the rate cut, as we have seen it in the case of mortgages), so also the quasi-cash flow of fixed depreciation quotas – in the absence of deploying new capital – are insufficient to guarantee the replacement of the 'used-up' portion of old capital. When looked at in this way it becomes clear that falling interest rates ought to make an upward revision of depreciation quotas mandatory – just like the value of the interest coupons of the bond ought to be adjusted upwards in the wake of falling interest rates, if it is our wish that the market value of the bond (or mortgage) have the same debt-liquidating power in the face of falling interest rates as I suggested in my 2008 paper 'Is Our Accounting System Flawed?' (If this aspect of the policy of open market operations is ignored, then there will be a shortfall in amortisation across the board. Sufficient funds will not have been set aside to pay for the replacement of producer goods when they are ready for the scrapyard.

Capital Destruction

Current bookkeeping practice ignores this effect of falling interest rates. Thereby the renewal of 'worn' capital is rendered impossible. This is capital destruction. The same principle also applies to capital deployed in finance, in particular, in the Banking business. Bank capital that is adequate in a stable interest-rate environment is no longer sufficient in a falling interest-rate environment – as banks in the U.S. and in Europe have found out to their chagrin.

Scandalous as though these omissions in bookkeeping practice are, present accounting standards ignore both effects of the policy of open market operations and the subsequent fall in the interest-rate structure: to wit

(1) increases in the liquidation value of debt,
(2) the fading of depreciation quotas.

Observe the insidious process of concealed capital erosion acting on all businesses simultaneously and indiscriminately. Losses are masked as profits,[18] phantom profits are paid out as dividends and managerial compensation. The process of capital erosion is accelerated by the policy of suppressing interest rates further. Inevitably, the result is deflation, depression or worse, such as breakdown in law and order. Quantitative Easing and any other benign-sounding monetary policy measures aiming at suppressing the rate of interest camouflage the wholesale destruction of capital in the productive and financial apparatus of society. Neither Keynes nor Bernanke [19] understood this process.

We have seen that open market purchases of the Fed are a powerful deflationary force in the economy as they cause interest rates to fall and capital to erode. We shall now see that, with a lag, open market operations are also bound to cause commodity prices to fall. In time, a vicious spiral will be engaged, pulling the economy into an abyss.

Erosion of Capital Causes a Falling Trend of Prices

Erosion of capital affects all producers, some of whom will succumb while others will fight for survival by scrambling to get out of debt. They will aggressively cut prices in the face of weakening demand. Herein we have the classic case of counterproductive central bank action. The central bank wants to snatch the economy from the jaws of deflation by increasing the money supply. Its preferred method is the open market purchases of short-term government securities. But through the transmission of risk-free bond speculation interest rates keep falling for all maturities. As a result capital invested in production everywhere is eroding faster. The burden of debt is increasing. Workers are squeezed. Producers are squeezed. They try to get out of debt by selling more of their product. In desperation, they cut prices but to no avail. Consumers, including workers under squeeze, hold out for more price cuts. They postpone their purchases wherever they can. Demand collapses – as eloquently described by no less of an authority than Keynes himself.

Although the fact is ignored by most economists, speculation plays a major role in the formation of prices. A falling price trend in commodities that started through the erosion of capital is further amplified as speculators redeploy funds from the commodity to the bond market where irresistible risk-free profits are available — not offered to commodity speculators. This is a powerful albeit unrecognised force in the economy triggering a chain reaction as follows:

(1) risk-free bond speculation gives the initial impetus for interest rates to fall,
(2) falling interest rates cause a severe erosion of capital throughout the productive and financial apparatus,
(3) erosion of capital triggers a falling trend in prices,
(4) falling prices further increase the downward pressure on interest rates.

Then the cycle repeats itself. Thus a vicious spiral is engaged: falling interest rates and falling prices chase one another downwards, threatening to push the economy into deflation. Mainstream economics lacks a valid theory of speculation. Hence it has a blind spot and fails to see the destructive nature of open market operations. It completely misses the fact that bond speculators will not stay idle while the show of open market operations put on by the central bank is played out.

Austrian Theory of the Boom-Bust Cycle

The suppression of the rate of interest through monetary policy and the resulting malinvestments made by entrepreneurs is a central theme of the business cycle theory of the post-Mises Austrian school. Our analysis is in the same tradition. But in exposing the actual transmission mechanism that extends the suppression of short-term rates to suppression of the entire spectrum of interest rates we carry the analysis further. The New Austrian School points out that open market purchases of the Fed make bond speculation risk-free with the result that all interest rates will fall. It is not necessary to bring in the malinvestment argument. After all, entrepreneurs could learn from past experience. They might realise that rate cuts are detrimental to their interest and they might fine-tune their investment strategy to take the artificial suppression of the rate of interest by the central bank into account. Could bust be avoided if they did? Our explanation of deflation and depression in terms of destruction of capital automatically brought about by the falling interest rate structure avoids any reference to malinvestments and is, therefore, superior.

Achilles-Heel of Keynesianism

Our destruction-of-capital argument also has the advantage that it exposes the Achilles heel of Keynesianism preaching, as it is, the dangers of 'over-saving' and 'underconsumption'. [20] These concepts are vacuous. They are claptrap. There is no valid reason why society should not be able to accommodate the needs of those of its members who must be net savers (typically the juniors), and those who must be net consumers (typically the seniors).

> The Achilles heel of Keynesianism is found in the treatment of capital, especially in the total negligence of the danger of capital destruction. Keynesianism is oblivious to the fact that if capital consumption occurs for any reason, then the resulting deficiency must be compensated for through the accumulation of fresh capital.

For example, if physical capital is impaired through fire [21] devastating the plant, then the lost value due to fire damage must be written off in the capital accounts of the balance sheet of the firm. In order to escape permanent damage to efficiency, replacement must be made through a periodic reduction in the income statements. The ledger is brought back into balance through entering the present value of the cash flow derived from these reductions.

Loss Under the Rug and Garbage Upstairs

The point is that exactly the same procedure ought to be followed if the loss originated not in a plant fire but as a result of a reduction in the rate of interest. Capital ought to be written off in the capital accounts reflecting the loss caused by the reduction.[22] Replacement ought to be made as follows. Enter the present value of the cash flow derived from a downward adjustment in the income statements into the balance sheet. As observed above, the accounting profession (apparently with the connivance of the tax authorities) fails to do that and the loss of capital due to the reduction in the rate of interest goes unreported. It should be clear that sweeping losses under the rug and kicking the garbage upstairs will not work as a permanent arrangement. The garbage will come crashing down from the attic in due course. Firms live in a fools' paradise. The day of reckoning dawns when the entire capital has been consumed. Such a day, it should be recalled, dawned in 2007 when Lehman Brothers' denuding of capital was discovered. No proper diagnosis was made, losses were papered over and the regime of capital consumption through QE was resumed with a vengeance. Another day of reckoning, possibly even more devastating, is approaching. Society cannot continue living at the same level of comfort and security with capital so seriously impaired as ours is due to QE. If it tries, it makes the crisis of under-capitalisation even more critical. Keynesianism is helpless as it has confused credit and capital, in particular, credit expansion and capital accumulation.

Cause or Effect?

The greatest mistake of Keynesianism is the tenet that the cause of the Great Depression was falling prices due to over-saving.[23] But falling prices were not the cause: they were the effect. The cause was falling interest rates, for which Keynesian fiscal and monetary policies were directly responsible: unbalancing the budget, inordinate increases in overall debt, monetisation of government debt by the central bank. Keynes' idea that open market operations cannot and will not have devastating side effects has become a dogma. This dogma must be discarded forthwith. Open market operations do have consequences, and these consequences are catastrophic. Here is how open market operations of the central bank make bond speculation risk-free, thus causing destruction of capital across the board. Speculators figure out when the central bank is due to make the trip to the open market to purchase its next quota of bonds. They forestall the central bank by purchasing the bonds beforehand, with the idea of dumping them later with a hefty markup. Bond speculators keep pocketing risk-free profits to which they are not entitled as they have not performed any useful service. Rather, they have caused great harm. Bond speculation progressively replaces monetary policy as the driving force behind suppressing interest rates. It may frustrate 'exit strategy' and 'tapering'. The central bank is rendered helpless in facing raging deflation. In the worst-case scenario, risk-free bond speculation will disable the brakes on the runaway car careening downhill and crashing headlong into deflation. These aspects of open market operations are completely missed by economists (Austrian economists not excepted).

Deflation or Hyperinflation?

A frequently asked question remains whether the international monetary system based on irredeemable currency is facing a deflation similar to that of the 1930s, or whether it is on course towards a Zimbabwe-style hyperinflation. Most sound-money observers conclude that the latter is the case. However, a relentlessly increasing money supply is not the only prerequisite for hyperinflation. There is another: lack of suitable outlets for the bloated purchasing power. As risk-free bond speculation made possible by open market operations shows, no matter how much purchasing power is being created by the world's central banks, speculators will always find rising bond values less risky to bet on than betting on rising commodity values.

> In the absence of wars (civil wars) destroying stores of consumer goods as well as the park of capital goods producing them, the logical forecast is deflation, not hyperinflation.[24]

In combating deflation (understood in the Keynesian price decreases) the Fed resorts to counterproductive measures. More government debt is poison for a weak economy. Monetisation of government debt will only *feed bullish bond speculation* and *bearish commodity speculation,* while doing nothing to rebuild the impaired capital base.[25] Bullish bond speculation is responsible for the falling interest-rate structure and destruction of capital, to say nothing of the coming collapse of prices. Increased government spending is the wrong medicine. The right medicine is stable interest rates, more savings, frugality in public spending, and the accumulation of more capital. If it were not so tragic, one could rub in the irony that Keynesianism in trying hard to push the world into the pit of inflation has only succeeded in pushing it into the pit of deflation – the very same pit it was studiously trying to avoid.[26]

Nature Abhors Risk-Free Speculation

According to a Latin proverb, *natura abhorret vacuum* (nature abhors a vacuum). We may add that nature also abhors risk-free speculation in eliminating it just as quickly as it eliminates a vacuum. When on occasion the opportunity for risk-free speculation arises, the very action of speculators quickly removes that opportunity. Only the earliest bird get the worm. However, as we have seen, conditions for the perpetuation of risk-free speculation may be brought about institutionally short-circuiting nature. This is the case with the open market operations of the central bank that frustrates the natural order of things. But nature cannot be abused forever. Sooner or later she will come out on top. According to another adage:

'Whom the gods may want to punish,
First of all will make them go mad'.

That's the fate of the present leadership at the Fed. Men and women in charge of 'monetary policy' exercise their usurped power in a way that is downright counterproductive. They sow inflation and reap deflation.

Endnotes to Chapter 25

[1] Prof. Fekete was introduced as a lifelong student of the phenomenon of interest. His theory eliminates the chasm between the time-preference school and the productivity school of interest. According to him the rate of interest is not monolithic but varies between a floor and a ceiling. The floor is determined by marginal time preference; the ceiling is determined by the marginal productivity of capital. Long before it could push the floor down to zero, the central bank would be frustrated in its rate-cutting fervour by marginal bondholders. He would divest himself of all of his bond holdings and keep the proceeds in gold. He would release his gold only if the central bank desisted and let the rate of interest find its floor once again (known as the Fullarton Effect, after John Fullarton (1870-1849), who correctly questioned and rejected the Quantity Theory of Money, a line of thinking later followed by Carl Menger). Thus there is an inevitable nexus between gold and interest. It is not possible to stabilise the interest-rate structure without allowing a free flow of gold between the Banking system and the general public. This effect works regardless whether a gold standard is formally adopted or not.

With due apologies to Horace we sign off with this thought: *Aurum expellas furca, tamen usque recurret* (You may drive gold out with a pitchfork, yet return it still will; c.f.: Epistles, Book I, x, line 24.)

[2] The German version of this essay can be found in *Das Edelmetall & Rohstoff- magazin*, 2014-2015, GS Management GmbH & C° KG 07806 Neustadt an der Orla, Germany.

[3] A full account is found in Edwin Vieira Jr. *Pieces of Eight: The Monetary Powers and Disabilities of the United States Constitution*, Sheridan Books, 2nd ed. , 2002, 2 volumes. Other authors also discuss the issue. E.g. Charles Rist, *The Triumph of Gold*, 1961, New York

[4] To pay the interest on the outstanding debt....

[5] See also William Boyce Thompson, Director of the Federal Reserve and his role in Bolshewik Russia - Chapter 35 and notes.

[6] The FED replaced J.P. Morgan as the most powerful banker of the U.S. and hence as reserve bank. No sooner was the FED established – with J.P. Morgan as a member of it – or it started financing several opportunities for profit of their members, such as capturing the Russian market at the collapse of Tzar Nicolai Romanov and certain parties in World War I just as the Rothschilds had done in Europe at the occasion of the Napoleonic wars or the establishment of the Kingdom of Belgium. The FED under W. Wilson stepped into the shoes of the 'despised and treacherous high financiers' that financed all parties, so they were always assured of at least one winner, whom they could milk for repayment of war debts. With interest. See Anthony C. Sutton, *Western Technology and Soviet*

Economic Development, Hoover Institute, Stanford University, 1968;

[7] Who then? To answer the question who were or even are the enemies of sound money, just consider that by 1913, the entire world had central bankers, acting as cashiers for the government treasuries. Except the Unites States. More than 750 academics and bankers worldwide had protested against the totalitarian and frankly draconian decision of gold confiscation. Certainly no unanimity understanding existed. However, by this time, governments had the experience of war and war propaganda, thanks to the good services of Freud's nephew, Edward Bernays, a tobacco industry lobbyist and government employee. *Cui bono* ?

[8] If a rate cut occurs and the debtor wants to make use of refinancing at the lower rate, the outstanding debt (that is: the higher liquidation value) needs to be paid up first before refinancing is possible. In case of a bond, one will have to pay the now higher market price. In case of a mortgage or loan, one will have to settle the outstanding debt plus a penalty of ending the contract prematurely, which covers for the lack of market value or lack of bids on the outstanding cash flows, reduced to present value.

[9] 'It is the innate conservation of the people that has kept our money good in spite of the fantastic tricks which the financiers play — and which they cover up with high technical terms. The people are on the side of sound money. They are so unalterably on the side of sound money that it is a serious question how they would regard the system under which they live, if they once knew what the initiated can do with it.' Henri Ford, *My Life and Work*, 1922, p. 179.

[10] Keynes blatantly misrepresents currency debasement as beneficial to society. *A Tract on Monetary Reform*, 1922, p.10 :
'... Besides this, as we shall see below, the benefits of a depreciating currency are not restricted to the Government. Farmers and debtors and all persons liable to pay fixed money dues, share in the advantage....Those secular changes... emancipated them from the dead hand....The tendency of money to depreciate has been in the past a weighty counterpoise against the cumulative results of compound interest...' Where to begin with this nonsense, passed of as scientific promulgations ?

[11] See insert 1 and 2 for a calculated example of how rate drops affect mortgages or how banks refinance mortgages.

[12] Mortgages packed into a bundle represent a cash flow that is amortised over the contractual period. From a financial algebraic or economic point of view, they represent wealth given in exchange for income. Due to an interest rate drop the algebraic equation becomes distorted and the liquidation value is no more 0 (all mortgage debt is paid off) but there will be a remainder. This remainder is the loss of purchasing power to the capital. It now needs to be increased by the amount equal to the loss, to repurchase another contract at the lower rate to keep the income unaffected. In the case of the mortgage, the 'bank' suffers

the loss (better: the unknown owner of the capital given to the bank for investment). It is no different from the owner of capital i.e. bondholder or shareholder who suffers the same loss if not compensated.

[13] Unless you really master financial algebra and discuss the terms of the refinancing in meticulous detail. Often the old loan is replaced by a new loan, the amount of which does not equal the outstanding balance, there are costs added and the length of the schedule is prolonged, or a mixture of all of these.

[14] Mortgages are contractual agreements of exchange of wealth for income. When the wealth has been repaid as contractually agreed, the owner of the capital receives his principal again. During the time he has no possession, he received a certain income (interest) for it. Due to the rate cut, the same capital can only re-purchase a lesser income. The rate cut has added a liquidation value, i.e. a rest value that needs to be added to the principle if it wants to command the same income stream at a lower rate. The refinancing of the mortgage will always need to be done by liquidating the present outstanding debt and then refinance at the lower rate. This refinancing allows the bank (or owner of the capital) to cut the losses and recalculate, often by adding some 'charges' which would cover the loss of purchasing power of the principal and /or by lengthening the repayment periods.

[15] Just like the mortgage, which needs extending in time when amortised at $r'<r$, the same can be said about any cash flow, including the compensation stream for labour provided. A rate hike as well as a drop will affect the purchasing power of this stream of payments.

[16] Completely erroneously. Still they just do.

[17] Mark Blyth & Eric Lonergan, 'Print Less but Transfer More : Why Central Banks Should Give Money Directly to the People,' *Foreign Affairs*, September - October 2014, p. 98-109. Although the authors recognise the central bank intervention as unhelpful in the case they describe, their article ends in a remarkable final paragraph, bringing up ideology and how we should get rid of policy tools invented over a century ago. Unfortunately, the authors seem to be progressivists and they encourage new thinking about the Central Banks. It has not yet occurred to them that Central Banks themselves are indeed the very 'policy tool' (read : problem) that needs ditching. I do not need to draw an image of the snake eating its own tail... I presume.

[18] Losses are marked as profits in that the profits should be less than indicated or that profits are still positive due to not recognising capital impairment. The so called profits may even turn into losses after capital impairment recognition.

[19] Thank heaven for Helicopter Ben: In 2002, in his first major policy speech after joining the Board of Governors of the Federal Reserve, Ben Bernanke spelled out that the only sensible solution to the country's massive debt problem was more debt, lots more. He was going to engineer an unprecedented inflation, quite

oblivious of the deflationary consequences.

[...] 'If the Treasury issued debt to purchase private assets and the Fed then purchased an equal amount of Treasury debt with newly created money, the whole operation would be the economic equivalent of direct open market operations in private assets...essentially equivalent to Milton Friedman's famous „helicopter drop of money'...[...] He did not elaborate how his hare-brained scheme would rain money on people made permanently unemployed by the Fed's open market purchases of government bonds under Quantitative Easing.

Now we shall look at the other side of the same coin, from the point of view of the beneficiaries of the Fed's policy. The text printed in italics below is copyrighted material quoted from *Stansberry's Investment Advisory*, October, 2013, (Permission for reproduction is hereby gratefully acknowledged.) It is tongue-in-cheek, it is clever, it is vitriolic. It is in the form of a prayer addressed to Ben Bernanke the demigod (!), put into the mouth of a super-rich individual as he is boarding his private airplane, noticing that the cost of jet fuel has again been increased.

"Dear Ben, thank you so much for providing us nearly limitless risk-free ways of growing our capital. Please, never for a minute doubt your ability to 'help the economy' by printing more money, thereby making us so, so much wealthier. Never consider whether or not it's fair or proper for the government to impoverish millions so that the very privileged few can gain so generously. And never worry that what you have done will some day lead to a massive inflation and a collapse of the paper money system. While gas prices are making it more expensive to fly this jet, we understand the need to do our part. You can count on us, dear Ben. Amen."

Meanwhile, the people whom Ben fleeced – the workers, the savers, the few Americans left with simple industry and thrift, the kind of folks who would never have believed the government would actively try to hurt them – have been wiped out. They have seen the real value of their wages, savings, standard of living decline by huge amounts...

Bernanke gutted the dollar. He gutted the middle class. He gutted the savings of millions. And he greatly impoverished our country.

And yet, despite it all, Ben Bernanke is still being proclaimed a hero of the Republic. 'When faced with potential global economic meltdown, he has displayed tremendous courage and creativity,' said Barack Obama at a White House news conference. 'He took bold action that was needed to avert another Depression'...

[20] Keynes was aware of the problem of capital destruction (and accumulation) stated by Austrian economists, for he even mentioned it in Chapter 7, par. 2, but then dismisses the issue as 'unclear' to him. Mises' article *The Anti-Capitalistic Mindset* did not get published until after Keynes. But Keynes could have availed himself of Böhm-Bawerk's *Capital and Interest*, a translation in English

was available in 1890. But in Chapter 14, footnote 4, he dismisses the work of Böhm-Bawerk as 'useless'. He had to. It obviously did not fit his world view nor agenda, for the stronger reason that Böhm-Bawerk was also on to all ideologists such as the Historical School, but also Keynes, in his *Control or Economic Law*..

[21] ...fire, terrorist strikes, earthquake or even large scale war...

[22] The bond is floating around in the hands of the public, and the firm has committed itself to the stated rate of return, now higher then the going rate... meaning the Weighted Average Cost of Capital (WACC) may higher than the WACC of some of its competitors. Losses are inevitable and will be reflected in reduced income. (Income Statement) In the balance sheet, other measures ought to be taken, such as a write down, commensurate with the capital loss. Losses will be double, therefore !

[23] Great Depression : 1929-1933, See Charles Rist, *ibidem*, for another cause of the Great Depression.

[24] Deflation in the sense of capital destruction, disappearance of shops, fire-sales, pop-up shops, decreasing velocity of currency, big bank bonuses, bail ins and bail outs, capital gains tax, tax persecution, job cuts, etc… the *déjà vue* of the past 40 years, only worse. The only people at work will be bank jobs and government (subsidised) jobs.

[25] In fact, rebuilding a capital base under irredeemable currency and with the current tax practises will be very hard indeed.

[26] The lecture of Keynes volumes on Money and his General Theory is replete with a pathological Gnostic dualism and hardly disguised contempt for 'savers and capital'. His agenda jumps of the pages: anything he writes is about the 'darn frugal savers who just hoard money and never let it roll'. His typical scapegoat is the conservative, bourgeois, banker or rentier. He barely holds back in writing he wants to bludgeon them all. In a way, he achieves exactly that goal. Too bad for the collateral damage...As the high **Director of the British Eugenics Society**, Keynes and his hardly disguised eugenics theories nicely fit together, but in the light of time, his skeleton rattles loudly in the closet of the left. See Jonathan Freedland, The Guardian, Fr. 17 Feb. 2012. '...Hence the enthusiasm of John Maynard Keynes, director of the **Eugenics Society** from 1937 to 1944, for contraception, essential **because the working class was too 'drunken and ignorant'** to keep its numbers down...' … '...The aim was to do what was best for society, and society would clearly be better off if there were more of the strong to carry fewer of the weak. …'

Keynes (*A treatise on Money II*) : p.175: '...There is nothing worse than a moderate evil ! If wasps and rats were hornets and tigers, we should have exterminated them before now. So with Great Britain's obligations to her rentiers arising out of the war….'.

PART 6

THEORETICAL CONFUSION ON REAL BILLS

Chapter 26

The Wisdom of Adam Smith for Our Own Times [1]

Richard Ebeling in the June 3rd issue of the Daily Bell under the same title contributed a much needed reminder of the relevance of Adam Smith's wisdom to our contemporary world. I am not going to speculate whether the omission of not mentioning Adam Smith's Real Bills Doctrine was accidental or deliberate. However, it is well known that post-Mises Austrian economists have taken a disdainful view of the Real Bills Doctrine and it would have been nice to have Ebeling's coherent articulation of their position. I can do no better than revisiting Adam Smith's great contribution to the theory of money and credit (which, significantly, received the nihil obstat of Carl Menger [2] a hundred years later) for the benefit of the Daily Bell's readership.

Consumption as a Source of Credit

Adam Smith's insight that consumption, next to savings, is another fundamental source of credit was one of the great discoveries of economics, comparable in importance to Carl Menger's subsequent discovery of marginal utility as the source of value.[3] We owe the concept of social circulating capital (SCC) to Adam Smith. By this he meant that part of the flow of consumer goods in most urgent demand that is moving sufficiently fast to the ultimate consumer so that it will be removed from the market in 91 days (the length of the seasons of the year in our temperate zone). For example, items like bread, seasonal garments and firewood in winter will unquestionably be consumed in definite quantities and do thus belong to SCC; items like grain held for speculative gains, unsold garments left over from the previous season and firewood in summer do not. Producers and distributors handling goods that form part of the SCC enjoy special privileges and have special responsibilities due to the special place their product occupies in the constellation of economic goods. They don't have to face uncertainties and don't have to carry risks all other producers and distributors have to face and carry. They do not finance their production under the relatively harsh terms of the interest-rate regime. They can finance it under the relatively more lenient terms of the discount-rate regime.

SCC has been compared to a great river that empties into the infinite ocean of consumption. The salinity of water undergoes important changes downstream as the river gets within earshot of the ocean. A fish habitat prospering in these waters changes. Similarly, important changes occur in the type of credit financing production and distribution of goods downstream as the ultimate consumer is getting ready to remove them from the market in less than 91 days. In particular, the gold coin need not be *saved* in advance of production. Financing is done retroactively with the gold coin *released* by the ultimate consumer.

Drawing a Bill

The wholesale merchant delivers the finished good to the retail merchant (or the higher-order producer delivers the semi-finished good to the lower-order producer).[4] Adam Smith observed that hardly ever does the latter pay with gold coins, and never does the former demand payment in gold coin. Invariably the former, called the drawer, bills the latter, called the acceptor or the drawee of the bill. The face value of the bill is payable in gold coin upon maturity, not more than 91 days later. The signature of the acceptor acknowledges receipt of goods listed on the face of the bill. It also acknowledges his responsibility for payment.[5] The bill so accepted is returned to the drawer. Only in the rarest of instances would the drawer keep the bill and present it to the drawee for final payment upon maturity – as observed by Adam Smith. More commonly he would offer it to his own suppliers in payment when replenishing his inventory. They would be glad to take it because they know that they themselves could likewise use it when it is their turn to replenish their depleted inventory. In other words, the bill goes into spontaneous monetary circulation. Paying the supplier with a maturing bill drawn on a third party is called discounting it since the face value is subject to discount by the number of days remaining to maturity. Discounting is accompanied by the endorsement of the bill on the back, signifying the last endorser's transfer of the title to bearer. When the bill matures, face value is typically paid by the drawer's bank, often the first endorser of the bill.

To suggest that the drawer extends a loan to the drawee, and that the discount represents interest taken out of the loan up front, is a travesty – as Adam Smith and Carl Menger would readily confirm. If anything it is the drawee who is in the stronger position, by virtue of being closer to the ultimate consumer on whose gold coin the whole transaction turns. After all, it is this gold coin that will liquidate a whole string of claims upon maturity. As the bill is passed along from one endorser to the next, the underlying semi-finished good assumes ever greater marketability. The drawee is handling goods more marketable than that handled by the drawer. Put in this light, it is preposterous to suggest that the drawee is a debtor and the drawer is a creditor. The transaction under consideration is definitely not one of borrowing. It is one of clearing: the process of canceling claims and counterclaims at maturity among various parties to the same deal. Their relationship is one of cooperation between collaborators; not one of confrontation between creditors and debtors.

Nor is savings the source of commercial credit. The true source is consumption. The intensity of the demand for consumer goods is the driving force, fully capable of creating its own source of credit quite independently of savings.[6] It is conceivable for commercial credit to exist even in the hypothetical absence of savings. The error in confusing interest and discount, although quite common, could be fatal as I shall show below. The rate of interest is a measure of the propensity to save while the rate of discount is a measure of the propensity to consume. Although in either case the rate varies inversely with the propensity, the two rates spring from entirely different sources, and are shaped by entirely different forces.

How Does Discount Arise?

Discount arises in the first place as an option of the retail merchant to prepay his bills. When due to overwhelming consumer demand he finds himself in the position that his till spills over with gold coins, he will offer to discount his bills, that is, to *prepay* face value discounted by the number of days left to maturity. Implicit in discounting is the discount rate at which the discount is calculated.[7] The fact that the retail merchant insists on a concession in the form of a discount is **not due to time preference**.

> Rather, such discount is due solely to the fact that the alternative of purchasing a bill with the same maturity drawn on a fellow retail merchant at a lower price *is* available to him.

Adam Smith's theory of commercial credit independent of savings was pejoratively named the Real Bills Doctrine by its detractors.[8] They flatly denied the spontaneity of bill circulation. They vehemently insisted that the discount was due to time preference and nothing else. They condemned the whole scheme as a conspiracy, a backhanded way to inflate the money supply. This criticism is plainly wrong: a real bill arises simultaneously with the emergence of new merchandise and it expires together with the removal of that merchandise from the market by the ultimate gold-paying consumer. Inflation of the money supply does not enter into it. This fact makes the real bill the next best thing to the gold coin itself. In one sense it is even better: it earns a return in gold.

Existence of commercial banks is not a prerequisite to bill circulation. But if banks are given, then they cannot have better earning assets than real bills to cover sight liabilities. The demand for real bills is virtually unlimited, so the banks can get ready cash by selling bills from portfolio if they run into unusual drain of gold. Indeed, demand for real bills comes not only from other commercial banks experiencing unusual increase in their gold reserves. Demand also comes from anyone with gold obligations to be met at a future date. For example, issuers of bonds to mature during the next quarter do not accumulate gold itself in anticipation of their obligation. Rather, they accumulate real bills with the same maturity.

SCC is not a fixed quantity. It waxes and wanes together with changes in the propensity to consume. (See Vol. II) The appearance of marginalism a hundred years after *The Wealth of Nations* presented an opportunity to refine Adam Smith's theory of commercial credit by introducing concepts such as the marginal item in SCC, the marginal retail merchant and the marginal productivity of SCC. In particular, the marginal retail merchant is seen as doing arbitrage between SCC and the bill market. At the first sign of falling consumer demand he withdraws his standing order for marginal goods on his shelf and redeploys his capital in the bill market instead. Conversely, when consumer demand picks up again, he will liquidate part of his bill portfolio and orders new marginal merchandise displaying it on the shelves.

Clearly, this arbitrage is the engine behind the variation of the discount rate. Note that the discount rate is much more nimble than the sluggish rate of interest. The discount rate depends directly on the caprice of the consumer. This observation challenges the traditional supply/demand equilibrium theory of price: changes in demand act ***not on the price but on the discount rate.*** The extension of Adam Smith's thought to incorporate marginalism culminates in the theorem stating that the discount rate is equal to the marginal productivity of SCC. (See Vol. II)

An increase in marginal productivity means that the marginal item drops out from SCC so that the productivity of the new marginal item is relatively higher than that of the old. Conversely, a falling discount rate sends a telegraphic message to all producers and distributors to increase their offering: 'consumer confidence' is on the rise once again.

Incidentally, this is the reason why the price of fuel is normally not higher in winter than it is in summer – predictions of the supply/demand equilibrium theory of price notwithstanding.

Relevance of Adam Smith's Real Bills Doctrine

The first casualties of the 'Guns of August', slightly more than one hundred years ago in 1914 were the real bills, financing as they did, world trade in consumer goods. This was not in itself surprising. What was surprising, however, was the failure of real bills to reclaim their former paramount place in financing world trade after the cessation of hostilities in 1918. In retrospect it is abundantly clear that there was an unannounced political decision made clandestinely behind closed doors to block the international trade in real bills. Without such a decision real bills would have started circulating spontaneously right after 'the farewell to arms'. Real bill financing of trade is synonymous with multilateral trade. The victorious Entente powers wanted none of that. They wanted bilateral trade instead.[9] They were scared stiff of German competition. They thought in that way they could control German exports and imports. According to the terms of the peace treaty they had to lift their blockade on Germany but, at the same time, they could block the international bill market to the same effect – and they did. This is the reason why real bills did not start circulating after the cessation of hostilities. They were simply not allowed by the victors. For the same reason they could not make a comeback during the entire span of the intervening one hundred years.

Scarcely did the victorious Entente powers realise that in blocking the bill market they shot themselves in the foot. Their action destroyed the Wage Fund, causing horrendous unemployment and the Great Depression of the 1930s. In the meantime a formidable official propaganda machinery was launched to discredit Adam Smith's real bills doctrine. Economists of the Age of Keynes, Austrians included, failed miserably to discharge their duty to search for and disseminate truth. It never occurred to them that there was a reason why 'structural unemployment' prior to World War I was unknown and non-existent.

Economists should have clarified how the Great Depression was caused by the destruction of the wage fund – a direct consequence of the unannounced and secret decision to block international trade in real bills.[10] Workers producing the great mass of consumer goods cannot wait three months for their wages to be paid when their product is sold for cash. The fact that there was no structural unemployment before World War I was entirely due to the existence of the Wage Fund consisting of real bills in circulation. The unannounced secret decision [11] to block the London bill market sealed the fate of the workers. The wage fund having thus been destroyed left no one around to advance wages of workers before the finished goods could be sold to the ultimate consumer for cash, if need be, three months, thirteen weeks or ninety-one days later. Unprecedented unemployment ensued – following the unprecedented blocking of the bill market. The causal relation between the two events could not be more clear. Structural unemployment had been artificially created that was to plague the world for the next one hundred years, and ever after. A very high price was exacted for ignoring the wisdom of Adam Smith. The great damage caused by the forcible elimination of the bill market has gone unrecognised for a century. It all boils down to a fatal confusion between interest and discount, and to the contest between bilateral and multilateral trade.

The way towards building a better world in the twenty-first century after the catastrophic credit collapse leads through the full and unconditional rehabilitation of Adam Smith's real bills doctrine. Starting with the most marketable staple goods: Food, Fuel and Fodder (the three Capital F's), real bill financing of world trade must be reintroduced forthwith. Since real bills must mature in gold coins (it would be preposterous if they were made to mature in an instrument of lesser marketability – and irredeemable currency notoriously has badly impaired marketability), gold coin circulation must also be restored – a *sine qua non* of the rehabilitation of credit.

Only then will future generations be able to look back on our insane experiment with global irredeemable currency in the twentieth century as a brief reactionary episode, trying to expunge the wisdom of Adam Smith from the memory of mankind.

The error of confusing interest and discount could be fatal to the welfare of society in the future as well through depriving it from acceptable means of exchange as the pool of circulating gold coins could not in itself, unaided by real bills, finance the highly intricate process of transforming semifinished (a.k.a. higher order) goods into finished (a.k.a. first order) goods without creating severe deflationary distress. In order to avoid deflation the gold coin circulation must be augmented by the circulation of real bills that mature into gold coins. Not recognising this fact is among the most embarrassing *faux pas* in the history of science next to the invention of the phlogiston in the 18th century.

Endnotes to Chapter 26

[1] Essay published at the occasion of the 291st birthday of the great Scottish Economist on June 18, 2014, by A. Fekete.

[2] Carl Menger was not the only economist who subscribed to Adam Smith's wage fund theory. See note 1 of the Introduction to Credit. It was the German economist Friedrich Benedikt Wilhelm von Hermann who pointed out the exact location of this wage fund : it is found in the income of consumers who purchased products made by labourers. This version by Hermann together with the additions of Brentano (Lujo) in 1894, was almost universally accepted by German economists, including Carl Menger. The Keynesian and Friedmanite economists of later date disingenuously object however that this would lead to some form of circle reasoning concerning the general wages; more specifically, by the wage-fund theory consumer's income determines wages. These modernist economists would of course say that income equals to a large extent wages and they are troubled to find the causes determining the supply of finished consumer goods and the cause that determines the height of the wages. For the solution ... read on. Spoiler alert: the discount rate determines the direction of the flow of the wage fund and its size. What determines the height of wages then? Marginal productivity of labour. In short: Keynes and Friedman tried to systematise a complex non-linear process with assumptions and inadmissible reductions. That led to this apparent circle reasoning.

[3] Mainstream economists, just as Austrian economists, display a rather condescending attitude towards Adam Smith for being 'bourgeois.' Just one famous example: P.A. Samuelson. It becomes uncanny for the sincere student how mainstream economists' mistreatment of economists like Say, Menger and Adam Smith corresponds exactly to the idolatry of all those that deserve it less or not at all, like Ricardo, Keynes or Marx.

[4] The concept of higher and lower order of production emerges with this well known cornerstone of Austrian economics and contemporary of Carl Menger: Eugen von Böhm-Bawerk, professor of Political Economy in the University of Innsbruck, in his ground typical Mengerian book: *Capital and Interest* (1890) London and New York, Macmillan. For a good understanding of Austrian Economics and of this too, you need to read this work.

[5] In fact the drawee upon his signature is legally committed to payment. The bill leads a 'life' separate from the contractual relationship between the supplier or purchaser (in legal theory). To maximise circulation, once a bill is accepted, the commitment to pay is set in concrete. Even if the goods are deficient the drawee still needs to pay his bill. He has nevertheless a legal recourse on the

supplier in case of faulty goods, on the basis of the contract, but not on the basis of the bill. *Caveat acceptor* !

[6] Fernand Braudel, *The Wheels of Commerce*, London, Collins. St. James Place, (1982), p 183, last paragraph.

[7] This kind of commercial credit is still offered in certain cases !

[8] The 19th Century debate between the Currency School and the Banking School reveals its detractors. Neither the arguments of David Ricardo or Thornton convince us nor did they convince Carl Menger. In general Menger has a lot of remarks to make on Ricardo.

[9] See Röpke, supra, p. 165. '[...]...Countries remaining faithful to the world-economy as a rule themselves, like Switzerland, forced to apply the control-by-planning methods of bilateralism and of clearing-agreements, when dealing with collectivist countries, and it is not always easy to avoid reactions on the domestic economy or on the remaining free commercial relations. In short, every country is sooner or later faced with the serious question whether, in face of the growing uncertainty and unsteadiness of international transactions it must not thoroughly review its relationship to the world-economy.' [Ed. text bolding is mine]

[10] See amongst others, the documents from Lord Robert Cecil, 1st Viscount of Chelwood, serving as Minister of Blockade in the U.K. from 1916. In particular Black List and Blockade, interview with The Rt. Hon. Lord Cecil, M.P. in reply to the Swedish Prime Minister, London, Eyre and Spottiswoode Ltd, 1916. There exist also reports of the American Military Government of Occupied Germany around the time of 1918-1920 touching on the subject of financial instruments and bank blockades.

[11] E.g. The Paris Economic Conference of 1916, during which the Allied Powers tried to isolate the Axis Powers, in such a way that the Wilson Administration in the U.S. became seriously concerned. This concern is still reflected in the United States Code in Title 19, Section 1332(c). During war time such conferences did not receive publicity and the power games behind closed doors due to war could certainly count on discretion and secrecy.

Chapter 27

Essay written by Sean Corrigan in response to A. Fekete, edited by A. Fekete

Unreal Bills Doctrine

To give the reader an opportunity to peruse arguments of the detractors of the Real Bills Doctrine,[1] we shall comment on an unfriendly essay criticising the position taken by this treatise on commercial credit. The reader is invited to search the article online and read it in the original before reading our rejoinder. We reproduce the abstract verbatim:

> " *Despite two centuries of learned refutation, that particular breed of inflationism known as the 'Real Bills Doctrine' has re-emerged once more to confound the unsuspecting layman. However, in its latest champion's eagerness to rebut his critics, he has unwittingly served only to emphasise the crucial importance of savings and capital accumulation to the greater division of labour and to the material advance of mankind which it brings.'*

The essay starts with quoting Ludwig von Mises:

> " *Is the attempt to guide the people on the right road not hopeless, especially when we recognise that men like John Maynard Keynes, Bertrand Russell, Harold Laski and Albert Einstein could not comprehend economic problems?'*

The author continues by referring to the great 18th century debate between the Banking School and the Currency School of credit. It was a high-quality debate that continues to the present day. This treatise is an attempt to continue the argument on the side of the former. Protagonists on the other side include Ludwig von Mises and the American Austrians grouped around the Institute in Auburn, Alabama named after him. It is fair to say that the Currency School discredited itself by taking the wrong position on the nature of money as it only recognised bank credit in the form of the bank's note liabilities to the exclusion of its deposit liabilities. We might rest our case here saying *'historia locuta, causa finita'*. We won't, however, because we wish to bring out some of the finer arguments of the Banking School. Corrigan quotes Mises several times.

" *The Banking School failed entirely in dealing with with these problems [the problem that the demand for paper also depends on the willingness of the banks to suppress the rate of interest]. It was confused by the spurious idea that according to which the requirements of business rigidly limit the demand of the public for credit is a magnitude dependent on the banks' readiness to lend, and that banks which do not bother about their solvency are in a position to expand circulation credit by lowering the rate of interest below the market rate. It is not true that the maximum amount which a bank can lend, if it limits its lending to discounting short-term bills of exchange resulting from the sale and purchase of raw materials and half-manufactured goods, is a quantity uniquely determined by the state of business and independent of the bank's policies. This quantity expands or shrinks with the lowering or raising the rate of discount [Ed. note: here Mises uses the word 'discount rate' indiscriminately: he simply means short-term interest rate.] Lowering the rate of interest is tantamount to increase the quantity of what is mistakenly considered as the fair and normal requirements of business.'*

" *The assertion that lies at the heart of the position of the Banking School, namely, that it is impossible to set and permanently maintain in circulation more notes [bills] than will meet the public demand, is untenable; for, the demand for credit is not a fixed quantity; it expands as the rate of interest falls and contracts as the rate of interest rises. But since the rate of interest is charged for loans made in fiduciary media created expressly for that purpose can be reduced by the banks in the first instance down to the limit set by the marginal utility of the capital used in the Banking business, that is, practically to zero, the whole edifice built up [by the Banking School] collapses.... The quantity of fiduciary media flowing from the the banks into circulation is admittedly limited by the number and extent of the requests for discounting that the banks receive. But the number and extent of these requests are not independent of the credit policy of the banks; by reducing the rate of interest charged on loans, it is possible for the banks to increase the public demand for credit. And since the banks - as even the most orthodox disciples of [the Banking School] cannot deny - can meet all these demands for credit, they can [expand] their issue of fiduciary media arbitrarily.'*

Mises misses the point of the debate. What is at issue is not whether self liquidating credit does or does not exist given the existence of commercial banks. The more penetrating question is whether self liquidating credit exists in the absence of commercial banks. The point maintained by the Banking School (and also by this treatise) is precisely that the answer to this question is in the affirmative. Real Bills are drawn and will circulate spontaneously even in the complete absence of commercial banks, because the wholesale merchant (and the producer of higher-order merchandise) can pay his suppliers when replenishing his depleted inventory of semifinished goods. Mises himself admits that much when he recognises that real bills circulated in Lancashire among spinners and weavers before the Bank of England opened its branch in Manchester.

Fig 6. Example of a bill, accepted in Antwerp in March 1934 by Minerva Motors for 2.786 francs, though the unit of account was the belga since 1926. But there is something wrong with it. Do you know what is wrong with this bill ?

Endnotes to Chapter 28

[1] Several detractors float around. Antal Fekete focusses on one, within the American Austrian School. But Mainstream also knows its fair share of detractors. One such mainstream example was written by Thomas M. Humphrey of the Federal Reseve bank of Richmond, entitled *The Real Bills Doctrine* , Economic Review, September/October 1982. The author sees tokenisation of securities equal to real bills, 'secured by property...' There are a lot of issues with this document, but they are beyond the scope of a note. It suffices here to state that tokenisation of securities was and still is indeed the magic trick performed by John Law, now performed by the reserve banks. But no mention is made of gold, nor of the pesky attribute of gold coin as having the slowest declining marginal utility of all goods in existence. ... 'property' will simply not suffice as vague 'security' !

Chapter 28

Essay published on November 2, 2010 by Antal Fekete.

Real Bills and Gold

The Daily Bell published an interview with Dr. Lawrence H. White, Professor of Economics, George Mason University, on October 24, 2010. One of the questions the interviewer asked was this: 'Please comment on real bills and how they work.'

In his answer Professor White gave the following example. Joe the Baker buys flour from Bob the Miller and gives him a bill promising to pay $1,000 in 90 days.

1. There are several problems with this description. In actual fact it is not Joe who issues the bill but Bob. The bill is *drawn by Bob on Joe* who must accept it before it can have any value. In common parlance Bob bills Joe. Professor White puts the cart before the horse in confusing the concept of a *bill* with that of a [promessory] *note*. A bill originates with the payee, the note originates with the payer. This is no hair-splitting. The difference is important. A [promessory] note is evidence of *debt*. A bill is evidence of *value* added. There is no loan, no lending and no borrowing involved in Joe's purchase and Bob's sale of the flour. None whatever. The transaction cannot be understood except in the context of merchandise maturing into the gold coin that only the ultimate consumer can release – a process that makes the relationship between Joe and Bob one of *coordination* rather than one of *subordination*. If anything, Bob could be considered the subordinate. Joe is one step closer to the boss, the consumer, and he is the one to get the gold coin first. He dispenses bread that is in general demand. Everybody eats bread. Flour that Bob dispenses is only in special demand. It is not as 'liquid' as bread, if liquidity of (finished or semifinished) products is defined by how far removed from the consumer's gold coin they are.

It is preposterous to suggest that Bob is the lender and Joe is the borrower. The two men are partners in a joint enterprise, made ad hoc, in order to provide the consumer with bread. Their role is like that of the two blades of a pair of scissors: neither can do the job by itself. This is not to deny that Bob extends credit to Joe. But extending credit is not the same as lending.[1] To suggest that Joe is in debt to Bob as a result of borrowing is entirely fallacious. Joe is in a very strong position: the bill he has accepted can circulate as money for 90 days. The note of a mere borrower cannot.

2. Professor White goes on to say that Bob the Miller can either wait 90 days for his money, or he can go to a bank and sell his bill. The banker will pay Bob something less than $1,000 because he takes interest due for 90 days out of the proceeds.

Again, there are several problems with this description. The main one is the suggestion that banks are necessary for real bills to be effective and useful. This representation makes facts stand on their head. The question whether bills came first or banks is not a 'chicken or egg' problem. We have the facts certified by Ludwig von Mises, no friend of the real bills doctrine, that bills did.[2] Moreover, we have it on the authority of Adam Smith that real bills do circulate as money on their own wings and under their own steam. By contrast, legal tender bank notes circulate by virtue of the strong arm of the government.

It would have been more correct for Professor White to say that Bob, if he wanted cash (read: gold coins) immediately, then he would go to the bill market and discount his bill (read: exchange it for gold coins at a price discounted by the number of days remaining to maturity, at the prevailing discount rate). But the beauty of real bills is seen in the fact that if all Bob wants to do is to pay for the shipment of grain that is being unloaded at his mill, then he does not have to go to the bill market to get gold. He can simply endorse the bill drawn on Joe, and Dick the Grain Merchant will be glad to take it in payment.

I repeat: the $1,000 face value of the bill does not represent *debt* and the discount does not represent *interest* on debt. Rather, it represents *value* added to the underlying merchandise and it is incumbent upon Joe the Baker to accomplish this feat. Time preference has nothing to do with it. The height of the discount rate is governed by considerations entirely different from those governing the height of the rate of interest, as we shall presently see. Confusing the two rates is the worst mistake economists have ever made, and are still making.

3. Professor White condescendingly admits that bills, while they were still tolerated, used to command a low interest rate because of their 'low default-risk'. This remark confuses the issue further. Risk of default has nothing to do with the level of the discount rate which is not determined on a case-by-case basis but, rather, ***across the board***. In fact the risk of default is so low that it can be taken to be zero. I ask you: how many bakers go bankrupt for each banker that does?

To understand what determines the level of the discount rate, as opposed to that of the rate of interest, we have to go not to the saver but to the consumer. The level of the discount rate is determined, not by the propensity to save, but by the propensity to consume. In more details, the discount rate varies inversely with the propensity to consume (whereas the rate of interest varies inversely with the propensity to save).

A higher propensity to consume means that Joe the Baker experiences increased cash-flow (really, an increased flow of gold coins). It prompts him to get rid of the gold coins by prepaying his bill outstanding. Rather than buying back the bill he has accepted, which may have been endorsed and passed on a dozen times and would be next to impossible to track down, he simply goes into the bill market and buys any bill with three good signatures. The demand for bills has thus increased, making the bill price rise. This means that the discount rate is lower as a direct result of an increase in the propensity to consume. Conversely, a decline in the propensity to consume decreases demand in the bill market as retail merchants have a reduced cash flow and fewer gold coins to get rid of in prepaying their bills outstanding. Decreased demand shows up as a lower bill price or, what is the same, a higher discount rate.

Our argument clearly shows that the credit represented by real bills has absolutely nothing to do with the propensity to save. The source of commercial credit is not savings, it is consumption.

The reason why real bills have been and are badly misunderstood by most students of credit is a poor understanding of gold itself, and the 'next best thing' to gold. Undoubtedly, the next best thing to gold is the bill of exchange representing merchandise in most urgent demand that is moving apace to the ultimate gold-paying consumer, and will be purchased by him before the season of the year changes (causing fundamental changes in the character of consumer demand) that is, in not more than 90 days. The process of supplying the consumer is a maturation process of merchandise that we figuratively describe as the maturing of the real bill into gold coins.

The consumer is fickle, and changes in his taste are unpredictable (to say nothing of hers). The army of merchants and producers must stand on their toes to serve consumer demand efficiently and instantaneously. It is the gold coin that makes the consumer King. If you removed gold coins from circulation, as European governments started doing exactly 100 years ago,[3] then merchants and producers would start serving another sovereign. From then on, they would rather serve the issuer of 'legal tender' bank notes. This change in the person of the sovereign corrupted the economy and caused an upheaval in The Wealth of Nations.

4. Professor White says that 'real bills were an important source

of business credit in the 19th century, and a major category of assets in a typical bank portfolio.' This sounds as if our grandfathers lived in backwater unmindful that there are other, more appropriate sources of commercial credit. The fact is that it was not progress or enlightened thinking but, rather, lust for power, desire to conquer, chicanery, malice, and vindictiveness on the part of certain governments that eliminated real bill circulation.
Two dates stand out:

(1) In 1909 first the French government and then, hard on its heels, the imperial German government introduced legislation making the note issue of their central banks legal tender. This paved the way towards financing the coming war with credit. [4]
(2) In 1918 the victorious Entente powers decided to block a spontaneous return of real bill circulation for they were afraid of multilateral trade. They would have liked to continue the wartime blockade of Germany.

As there is no such a thing as peacetime blockade, they had to settle for something less: replacing blockade with blocKing (real bills circulation, that is). This meant replacing multilateral with bilateral trade. Or, to call a spade a spade, replacing indirect with direct exchange alias barter – a relapse to conditions prevailing during the Stone Age. Through bilateral trade they hoped to monitor and, if need be, control German imports and exports. Under multilateral trade monitoring would be more difficult if not impossible.

The collapse of the international gold standard was the direct consequence of this malicious and vindictive decision. The gold standard could not survive the destruction of its clearing house: the bill market – its most vital organ. The world is still suffering the consequences. 'Structural unemployment' was perfectly unknown while real bills were financing multilateral trade. The elimination of real bill circulation has destroyed the wage fund out of which the wages of workers producing consumer goods can be prepaid. Prepaid, to be sure, because the ultimate consumer's gold coin may not be available to pay wages for up to 90 days. However, the pay envelope must come weekly, rather than quarterly so that the Lord can 'give us our daily bread'. Thus, in a real sense, the Lord's prayer is also a prayer for a speedy return of real bills circulation.

Structural unemployment, plus periodic outbursts of a horrendous tide of unemployment was the result of the destruction of the wage fund. The 1930 episode was blamed on the gold standard. This argument has been exploded by events during the present Global Financial Crisis (GFC) which, in the fullness of times, will be far worse as far as unemployment is concerned than the earlier episode. Real bill circulation has been eliminated along with the gold standard, yet unemployment is still with us. And, curiously, *no one* is inquiring how it can be that the removal of these two arch-enemies of government omnipotence has not deflected the threat of deflation, depression, and unemployment – as promised by Keynes and other false prophets.

Endnotes to Chapter 28

[1] There is a crucial distinction between credit and lending money, which may not be identified. Do you give credit to your toddler for using the potty or do you lend him money for it ?

[2] Unlike his followers, Mises was not a dogmatic person and could admit to facts like the above. There may be many justified reasons and circumstances preventing Mises from reaching the conclusions that were up for grabs, but some of his successors do not elaborate nor expand either Mises or Menger and turned rather dogmatic, which would probably have abhorred both Menger and Mises.

[3] That is just before or during World War I. The German *Bürgerliches Gesetzbuch art. 793 (1909) et seq.* stipulates several changes and additions regarding German fiduciary money. The twenty and fifty mark notes were made legal tender and cheque payments were introduced. See e.g. Benjamin Anderson. *Economics and the Public Welfare. A Financial and Economic History of the United States, 1914-1946,* Liberty Fund, 1979. The French legislator used social law to forbid payment in kind and payment in specie or its alternative, at the option of the employer. See note 14 on p.86.

[4] Benjamin Anderson, *ibid,* p. 25-26. ...There had been accumulation of gold by Germany, Russia and France. The first manifestation came as early as 1912, as German bankers began to take steps to increase their gold supply. In order to take gold out of the hands of the people and carry it to the reserves of the Reichsbank, fifty and twenty-mark banknotes were issued to take the place of the gold in circulation. German agents regularly appeared as bidders for gold in the London auction rooms. Gold was shipped from the United States to Germany, and the famous Spandau Treasure was transferred to the vaults of the Reichsbank. ... France and Russia made strong efforts to increase their gold reserves during the spring and summer of 1914. ...[...]. Also, saying the same, Hew Strachan, *The First World War,* Vol. I.: To Arms, Oxford University Press, 2001, p. 836.

Chapter 29

Essay published on November 3, 2010 by Antal Fekete.

More Fallacies

The first article of my two-part series on the Real Bills Doctrine (RBD), in commenting on the Daily Bell's interview with Professor Lawrence H. White on October 10, 2010, I made the central point that the source of commercial credit is not saving but consumption. The following example will dramatise this point. Assume for the sake of argument that all banks in the whole wide world succumb to the sudden death syndrome simultaneously. What does this mean in terms of the production and distribution of consumer goods? Would we have to go back and start from scratch to save in order to replenish society's circulating capital? Saving is a time-consuming process and people have to get fed, clad, shod, and sheltered in the meantime. We could not restore circulating capital through saving for the simple reason that before we could we would die of starvation.

Luckily, there is no need to go through such a regimen to satisfy the dogma that the only source of capital is saving. Consumption *per se* is a ready and instantaneous source of commercial credit. Real bills drawn on merchandise in most urgent demand will supply all the credit society needs so that consumption can continue without interruption – and the banks be damned. It does not matter if very little gold is available to pay the bills upon maturity. My detractors' 100 percent reserve Banking would be confronted with sky-high prices on account of the scarcity of gold. Under the RBD prices need not be high: the burden of adjustment will not fall on prices, as the quantity theory of money falsely teaches; it will fall upon the discount rate. There is only one interdiction, namely, real bills must not mature in mere promises to pay gold - the proviso of Ludwig von Mises notwithstanding that 'claims to gold are a complete substitute for gold in markets where their security and maturity of those claims is recognised.' [1]

Claims to gold are useless. Bills at maturity must be paid in gold coins, not in claims thereto. Claims to gold coin are inferior to bills that must mature into something superior. The only thing superior to a real bill drawn on consumer goods in most urgent demand is the gold coin. A bill maturing in a mere claim on gold will not circulate.

In commenting on the first part of this paper several of my correspondents asked why the discount rate is getting lower when the bill price is getting higher. Here is the relevant arithmetic. Suppose a bill of 1,000 maturing in 91 days (or 0.25 years) circulates at 990. This corresponds to a discount rate of 4 percent per annum, because 1,000(1 - 4(0.25)/100)=10(99) = 990. If on the next day the bill market quotes the same bill at a higher price, say at 995, then there is a corresponding decrease in the discount to 5, half of the earlier discount of 10. Thus the discount rate has fallen from 4 to 2 percent.

[2]Let us return to the Daily Bell's interview with Professor White. Observing that the RBD has been important in the history of monetary theory, he goes on to say: It is a mistaken idea that if the Banking system lends only by discounting real bills, then it cannot over-expand. It is also a dangerous idea ... because rather than letting interest rates rise to reach their new equilibrium level whenever the business demand for credit rises, the banks will actually make money over-expand.

This is tantamount to blaming the loot, rather than the thief, for the thievery. Why did it allow itself to be stolen? There are uses and abuses of credit. Over-extension of credit is an abuse. For example, drawing two or more bills on the same merchandise is an abuse, and so is rolling over a bill at maturity rather than paying it, regardless whether or not the underlying merchandise has been sold. Such abuses should be dealt with by the Criminal Code in the same breath as dealing with the forgery of bank notes.

Professor White's remark assumes that the discount rate is the same as the short term rate of interest. I shall not pause here to repeat the arguments of my previous article refuting this misconception. Instead, I shall describe what has actually happened when banks first put in an appearance to take a piece of the action in the already flourishing bill market. Banks have arisen because they had a legitimate and useful role to play:

(1) Their credit has a high name-recognition;
(2) Bank credit in the form of bank notes come in standard denomination that is easy to count and make payments with.

The banks in discounting real bills paid with bank notes of their own issue. Thus they substituted their own credit, enjoying high name-recognition, for the sometimes obscure credit of traders in the periphery. Also, they offered standard-denomination bank notes to replace bills with odd amounts as face value that circulated more easily. Because of this, bank notes were welcome: you did not have to scrutinise the credit standing of the drawer and the drawee of the bill. People were glad to pay for this service in the form of foregone discount that accrued to

the bank for facilitating the circulation of real bills further.
The good banks strictly followed the market rate of discount. Upon the expiry of the underlying bill they punctiliously withdrew a corresponding amount of bank notes from circulation. There is no sense in which the reserves of these banks could be called 'fractional.' Bank liabilities were backed 100 percent by reserves, either in the form of gold, or the next best thing to gold: real bills maturing into gold in 91 days or less. Such banks were not exposed to the nemesis of poorly managed banks: the bank run. Every business day on average as much 1 ⅔ percent of their portfolio of real bills matured into gold coins. That was sufficient to meet normal demand for gold coins. If the demand for the gold coin was *abnormally* high, then the banks had to go to the bill market and *sell unexpired bills* from portfolio for gold, in order to meet the extra demand. There was no problem involved in selling real bills for gold. Some other banks experiencing an overflow of gold coins would be scrambling to get earning assets and would buy the extra supply of real bills eagerly. To call these 'fractional reserve banks' is to bark up on the wrong tree.

However, inevitably, there were bad banks as well that did not bother withdrawing their bank notes from circulation when the underlying bills expired but made fresh loans with them on which they collected interest. This was very profitable business for them. Nevertheless, their profits were illegitimate and their loans were fraudulent. In effect, the bad banks were borrowing short in order to lend long. I call such a transaction illegitimate arbitrage between the bill market and the loan market, to take advantage of the spread between the higher interest rate and the lower discount rate. Illegitimate arbitrage is unsound because the short leg of the arbitrage has to be moved forward every quarter and it may not be possible to do at the old rate. The new discount rate may well be higher, and if it is higher than the interest rate on the long leg, then the bank ends up with a loss rather than a profit. In addition, the bank is guilty of false pretences. It pretends that its bank notes are covered by real bills drawn on fast moving merchandise demanded most urgently by the consumers – which could circulate on their own in the bill market. In reality, however, its notes were covered by anticipation bills and accommodation bills or notes of debtors – that could not so circulate. Illiquid and dubious paper: expired real bills on unsold or unsalable merchandise; accommodation bills drawn on the dreams of lunatics, notes of speculators was being aided and abetted by the fraudulent bank that gave shelter to them in its portfolio that was not open for public inspection. Note the difference: bills circulating in the bill market are completely transparent making fraud and conspiracy easy to detect. The common earmark of bad banks is that their assets cannot be readily sold except maybe at a loss.

I have mentioned the notes of speculators that are ineligible to figure among the assets of banks. This is no condemnation of speculation per se. Speculators in agricultural commodities render a great service to society. Trouble starts when they speculate with other people's money without their knowledge and concurrence. The best example of this is the conspiracy committed by Dick the Grain Merchant and Bob the Miller who anticipate an increase in grain prices from which they want to benefit. (See Vol. I) Lacking money of their own to buy grain, they decide to put Dick-on-Bob bills into circulation drawn on grain the movement of which has been arrested.

Such conspiracy would be criminal. The bill market must not be used for the purpose of financing speculation. The market for real bills must be recognised as a social institution that has evolved spontaneously for the benefit of everybody to facilitate the most expeditious movement of consumer goods in greatest demand. Sabotaging the bill market, whether by speculators or the banks, or by the government itself, is a crime against society.[3]

The low discount rate is there to benefit the consumer, and the consumer only. Luckily, by virtue of its openness, the bill market exposes such conspiracies. Trouble starts when the bank is participating in the conspiracy and gives shelter to fraudulent Dick-on-Bob bills.

> It *is* possible to brand the bad banks 'fractional reserve banks' to reflect the fact that a portion of their credit outstanding is not covered by gold coins or real bills maturing into gold coins. The existence of such delinquent banks, however, does not justify disparaging the entire Banking system calling it 'fractional reserve Banking system.' The suggestion that there are no 'good' banks and that, in discounting real bills all banks create money out of thin air, is fanciful and untrue.

The Daily Bell concludes the interview by commending Professor White for 'simplifying the real bills debate.' It adds that 'the real bills debate has raged for some time and Professor White's perspective has clarified matters.' With all due respect to Professor White's perspectives, I demur. Far more careful analysis of real bills and clarification of the difference between the discount rate and the rate of interest is needed than Professor White is willing to offer. Just as my detractors, Professor White has declined to debate the issues on the premise that the merit or demerit of real bills must be decided in the context of complete absence of banks, since real bills can and do circulate on their own wings and under their own steam. Such refusal is especially regrettable at the present juncture, in view of the unprecedented world Banking crisis. There is a real danger that all the banks may simultaneously succumb to the sudden death syndrome.[4] I imagine that Professor White would not dismiss this assumption of mine as outlandish.

Professor White is one of the important and respected protagonists of the hard money movement. In the interest of success, and also to save the world from unnecessary ordeal and much suffering, we should admit that further study of the RBD is needed, including an impartial inquiry about the circumstances under which governments forcibly blocked real bill circulation at the end of hostilities of World War I, and enforced the ban until the gold standard, such as it was, collapsed. It had to collapse because it could not survive the destruction of its clearing house, the bill market: its most vital organ.

It is a fallacy to assume that real bills, thankfully, faded away into oblivion for reasons of being obsolete. It is wrong to conclude that the RDB is a stale, mistaken and even dangerous idea.

The RBD, in making a comeback, may protect lives. It may also save our Western civilisation.

Endnotes to Chapter 29

[1] Mises, *Theory of Money and Credit*, Ch. 15.

[2] All of this arithmetic would be treated in a standard course financial algebra or a course actuarial science. However, not all of my readers would necessarily have followed such a course. It is nevertheless a recommendation to enrol for or engage in a study of financial algebra.

[3] And this is not a victimless crime, for all the members of society are exposed to grave existential losses in their savings, if held in bills kept by the 'acceptance banker'.

[4] A sudden bankruptcy of the entire banking system worldwide is not impossible, but why should we care? Well, it would still inflict such an enormous pain on the world population, that civil unrest and possibly a world war is almost assured. While the present banking system under the fiat dispensation and monetary abuse arrangement could be missed as a bad tooth-ache, worldwide civil strife of a pauperised population turning on each other is no alternative.

Chapter 30

Essay published on March 8, 2009 by A. Fekete.

That Accursed Propensity to Save

'Thank Heaven for little Keynesian Nobel laureates... without them what would little Keynesian Treasury secretaries do...?'

At long last we got the official explanation how we got into this mess. In his March 2, 2009, column in The New York Times under the banner title *Revenge of the Glut*, Paul Krugman tells us, quoting the authority of the Chairman of the Federal Reserve Ben Bernanke, that it is all the fault of the Asians. They save damn too much. They test the endurance of unhappy Americans who bankrupt themselves in trying to work off all that darned excess saving fast enough before it can do more damage. Even though they do their level best, they could not keep up with the prodigious output of the Asians and 'global savings glut' is the result. It was the cause of the U.S. current account deficits in the first place; now it is causing more mischief by creating turmoil in the financial markets and in the Banking system. In this scenario, the good guys are the Americans. They are heroically trying to stave off disaster through their unselfish consumption. The bad guys are the Asians, tormenting their American victims in force-feeding them with overdoses of consumer goods all the way to the bankruptcy court.

Although Krugman does not say it, the implication is all too clear: there is one especially pernicious form of saving, namely, saving in the form of gold. Keynesians, through half a century of hard work, ably assisted by their Friedmanite monetarists comrades, have developed a highly efficient system to embezzle, unobserved, superfluous savings in an antiseptic way. Their sophisticated contra-saving devices through currency debasement anaesthetise those bastard savers so that they can be pilfered and plundered without touching a raw nerve. It is a clean job, causing a minimum of commotion.

Unfortunately, these methods do not work on those who do their vicious anti-social saving in the form of gold. These guys will have to be taken care of by other means, such as threats of central bank gold sales, bubble-bursting and price-busting techniques in the paper gold markets, and other similar tactics. If everything else fails, the guillotine could be reactivated as an instrument of monetary policy, last used in this way during the French Revolution. At that time, if you were found in possession of undocumented gold, your head would be chopped off in summary justice.[1]

It is very doubtful that in the long and checkered history of science there is another episode comparable to this deliberate misuse and abuse of knowledge for the exploitation of those who do not have the full complement of it.[2] What makes it particularly odious is that Keynesian obscurantism and anti-scientific propaganda is put in the service of a hidden agenda: to cover up the mismanagement of the economy through Keynesian precepts, the sabotaging of human cooperation under the system of division of labour, and the destruction of capital through the corruption of the monetary system.[3]

The monetary dispensation was developed to serve and protect society as a whole: savers as well as consumers. After all, at some point during our lives we are (or ought to be) savers, so that later, in our harvest years, we can be consumers. If it does not work in the opposite order, Mother Nature is to be blamed. Saving always and everywhere had to precede consumption. Saving has always been primary and consumption secondary, like it or not.

But Keynesians have overthrown Mother Nature. They say that it is possible to have consumption without prior saving.[4] Having corrupted our monetary system and having destroyed society's capital, Keynesians have rendered people unable to fend for themselves. They treat them as they would treat livestock in the feedlot. In exchange for fattening them (in preparation for the slaughterhouse) livestock is being relieved from the need to gather feed in the summer for winter consumption. Keynesians, self-styled directors of the national economy, reserve the job of the feedlot operator to themselves. They declare savings and capital obsolete. Synthetic credit manufactured at the central bank in the service of collectivism is used as a substitute.

It would be well if Keynesians took to heart the astute observation of Glenn Prickett, Senior V.P. at Conservation International, that 'Mother Nature doesn't do bailouts.'

Apparently it has never occurred to Krugman that the present disaster is not due to his imaginary savings glut but, rather, to the imperfections of the present monetary system.[5] Why can't we have a monetary system that allows people to save to their hearts' content? **Why do we have to have one that sets up the Treasury and the Federal Reserve as partners in the crime of check-kiting**? Maybe the idea of delegating unlimited power to these agencies was not such a good idea after all. Maybe the U.S. Constitution imposed a wise limitation on the power of government in refusing to sanction irredeemable currency. Maybe no one should have the privilege to issue liabilities without assuming countervailing responsibilities. Maybe our corrupt monetary system carries the seeds of self-destruction in allowing structures like the quadrillion-dollar strong derivatives tower to get conceived and grow beyond all limits until it topples on the people of Babel. Why is questioning the efficacy of our monetary system taboo anyway?[6] All these questions are side-stepped by Krugman as he trots out that old Keynesian warhorse, the theory of over-saving.

There is one more disturbing element in Krugman's centrally planned economy.[7] It is the golden thorn in the Keynesian flesh. It is gold, the barbarous relic. Man's greedy little palm is itching to touch the stuff. Visual contact in museums, churches and art galleries will not suffice. Keynesians have a job here that has been cut out for them: they have to 'educate' people that wanting gold is like wanting the moon. They can't have that; at any rate, green cheese is just as good, and the government has an efficient green cheese factory, the central bank, that can manufacture it in unlimited quantities. Those who like gold had better learn to like green cheese.

By the way, this is vintage Keynes. It is in the Keynesian Bible: the moon, the green cheese factory and all, entitled *The General Theory*, written by the Prophet in 1936. Go look it up, and see it for yourself. It shows Keynes' cynicism and his infinite contempt for the intelligence of others.[8]

We are anxiously waiting to see how the Pupils of the Prophet will deal with this piece of unfinished business: to cure man of *auri sacra fames*, 'the accursed hunger for gold.'[9]

Krugman ends his piece on an alarmist note. The savings glut is still out there, ready to gobble us all up. In fact, it is bigger than ever, now that suddenly impoverished consumers have rediscovered the virtues of thrift; now that the worldwide boom that provided an outlet for all those excess savings has turned into a worldwide bust.

One way to look at the international situation right now, Krugman says, is that we're suffering from the 'global paradox of thrift'.[10] Around the world savings exceed the amount that businesses are willing to invest. And the result is a global slump that leaves everyone worse off. The implication seems to be that we need a saviour.[11] We need someone to save us from ourselves and our own destructive saving habits. The Government is our Saviour.[12] It can tax savings up to 100 percent.[13]

It is hard to imagine a worse way of standing facts upon their head.[14] **The exact opposite of what Krugman has the audacity to suggest is true.** The falling interest-rate regimen inspired by Keynes has **destroyed capital across the board.** The only way to replace or to replenish it is through saving. **Krugman adds insult to injury when he suggests that there is too much saving in the world, where in fact there is too little, and that this glut is the reason why businessmen have stopped investing.** So it falls upon the government to take up the slack and start spending ourselves into prosperity. Krugman's is a recipe for the ruination of what is left of the world economy. The trouble is that he and his cohorts at the Treasury and the Federal Reserve have all the means of coercion at their disposal to finish off the job. **They control the monetary system, they control taxation, they control the White House.** They also control the guillotine that is being dusted off just in case it may be needed again as an instrument of monetary policy.[15]

There you have it: Krugman's theory of the savings glut, and my theory of wholesale capital destruction in the world as a result of serial halving of the rate of interest by Keynesian monetary policy. I am ready to submit my thesis to a public debate that it was Keynesian measures that started capital destruction I warned about already eight years ago. If they had any decency, Keynesians should admit that they were wrong and let others come in with the new Obama administration and repair the damage. After all, Keynesians have amassed unprecedented power in Washington with their savings glut fable once before. There is absolutely no reason why they should be given a second chance to try their half-baked theory of over-saving on innocent people. But the idea of giving up power has never crossed their mind. They just won't, even if blood is flowing on the streets of Detroit and Los Angeles.

> That's the nature of the so-called Keynesian revolution. It is not a branch of economic science; it is a branch of Leninism, a blend of collectivist ideology reinforced with unmatched expertise on conspiracy, street fighting and barricades.

In a nutshell, here is my theory of wholesale destruction of capital as a result of Keynesian monetary policy of serial halving of the rate of interest. The regime of falling interest rates is lethal to businesses, whether financial or producing. It makes businessmen lethargic: they understand that the falling interest-rate environment makes their investments go sour. It clandestinely wipes out capital through increasing the liquidation value of debt on past borrowings. Lower rates are not helping business as Keynesian propaganda suggests, because the issue is not the cost of future borrowing. The issue is the historic cost of past borrowings that has rendered existing investments unprofitable. Chartered accountants and bank examiners ignore the erosion of capital due to falling interest rates, most likely with the connivance of governments if not on direct order from them. So there is no advance warning, and the destruction of capital presents a surprise *fait accompli.* When it hits, it is already too late to do anything about it. The wholesale destruction of capital is a social disaster of the first magnitude, in many ways worse than the destruction of physical capital due to war, precisely because wartime damage is expected and preparations are made to cushion it. Capital accumulation is the result of decades or even centuries of arduous saving by hundreds of millions of individuals that, nevertheless, can be frittered away in a matter of a few years. To rebuild the capital base of society will take a concentrated effort to save for decades to come. This great task of reconstruction is certainly not being helped, rather, it is being sabotaged by the vicious Keynesian agitation about a mythical savings glut.

Gold offers the only ray of hope in an otherwise thoroughly gloomy picture. Gold represents that hard core of capital that cannot be destroyed by the credit collapse. Gold is the only asset that survives any consolidation of balance sheets. Other bank assets tend to be canceled out upon the nationalisation of banks. At any rate, they are subject to counter-party performance that becomes questionable in a credit collapse. Gold has no counter-party liability. If our civilisation is to survive, it will have to make a head start in rebuilding capital, the sooner the better. It cannot start capital accumulation from scratch. It must enlist gold in the reconstruction effort. One ounce of gold will go farther than all the make-believe credits created out of the thin air by all the defunct central banks of the world. This is the triumph of gold: it can be bad-mouthed all the Keynesians want. But gold and those who control it will have the last laugh.

Endnotes to Chapter 30

[1] Today's reader may find this rather crude. Please note that historical sources are available. Furthermore, one may recognise the methods of intolerant dogmatism and religious dogmatism. Today's method employed by the secular authorities finds its outlet in the publications of the OECD. This supranational organisation with the innocuous name of Organisation for Economic Development is in fact a boiler room for the fiscal delegates of its member countries, devising and coordinating systems, based on information technology. See e.g. its 'Common General Reporting Standard' after the Cyprus Debacle during which some investors in Cyprus paid for the bailout of the Euro system. This was called a bail-in and the OECD as well as the IMF set up everything that is necessary for future events to repeat this bail-in with a 'Common General Reporting Standard' ... just in case.

[2] Others have diagnosed the 19th century as the period of total scientific ruination with the onslaught of positivism in the person of e.g. A. Comte. Rabelais in the 15th century already satirised the physicists' preoccupation with measuring flea-hops; J. Swift aptly ridiculed the mad scientists of Balnibarbi in *Gulliver's Travels*. Nothing short of an exorcism will do in the case of standard economics.

[3] In *History of (Junk) Ideologies*, [forthcoming] P. Van Coppenolle dedicates a section on the history of political ideas, ideologies and their roots. The Age of Enlightenment seems only an Orwellian 'NewSpeak' term for its opposite. The 19th century obtains the odious distinction for being the century of complete scientific bankruptcy. However, we still have to live with its consequences. *Quousque tandem...* ?

[4] The structure of reality cannot be changed. However, there will always be those who accept the challenge and fail miserably. Eric Voegelin in *The New Science of Politics* diagnoses with a rarely seen clarity these people and calls them 'Gnostics'. See: Eric Voegelin, *Modernity Without Restraint*, Collected Works Volume V. University of Missouri Press, Columbia and London 2000. and Eric Voegelin *From Enlightenment to Revolution*, Duke University Press, Durham, North Carolina, 1975. In *History of (Junk) Ideologies* P. Van Coppenolle extends the analysis of political environments to economics, in which the denial of the structure of reality finds specific applications, especially with modernist economists. The political or sociological derangements and their characteristics can be classified in such groups as the millenarians, the chiliast, the alchemist, the utopians etc...which prof. Voegelin all classified as 'gnostics'. In this work, the author refines and elucidates these classes of 'deniers of reality' and brings up to date

all the classes that may be relevant to economics and that were mentioned by Voegelin in his work of 1952, *The New Science of Politics*. Also Ludwig von Mises in *The Ultimate Foundation of Economic Science, – An Essay on Method,* Indianapolis, Liberty Fund, 2006, treats the subject of reality equally well. See his chapter 5 on *Some Popular Errors*.

[5] See in particular: Charles Rist, *The Triumph of Gold,* Transl. Philip Courtney, Philosophical Library Inc, New York, 1961.

[6] A typical characteristic of an anti-philosophical stance would be the prohibition of questioning, which is at the core of philosophy. There are thousands of examples of this ant-philosophical stances out there. Clear examples are Auguste Comte and Karl Marx, amongst many others. The roots of this anti-philosophical stance are at the core religious, yet grown secular over time. Neither Plato nor Aristotle were 'systematisers' unlike A. Comte, a self-styled judge of humanity, who in his *Catechism of Positive Religion* suggested that the non-positivists or any other recalcitrant creature would be ***'appropriately dealt with in the hell of social oblivion'***; Marx, likewise, insisted to ***'be a good socialist and not ask questions'*** in his earlier works established around 1840.

[7] A centrally planned economy is a typical secular manifestation of denying the structure of reality. There are six characteristics betraying a **gnostic attitude** :

1. Dissatisfaction with present situation.

2. The reason for the dissatisfaction is to be found in the 'wickedness of the world' as given by God or nature.

3. Salvation from the evil/shortcomings of the world is possible.

4. The change to a better world must be a historical process and the road is arduous.

5. Man's own effort makes this change possible.

6. The Gnostic will come out with a 'formula' or 'system' for self- and world salvation. However, do not ask questions, because that would expose the assumptions and lay bare its Gnostic character of denial of reality.

7. There seems to be a 7th characteristic which is the *libido dominandi* or the will to subject all others and which tolerates no contradiction.

[8] Keynes's hubristic cynicism reminds one of A. Comte's condemnations in the same vein. Keynes is no less a late positivist with his scientistic fulminations against 'capital' and 'savings'. But that is not all: he was also the director of the Malthusian League, planning the birth control of *other people,* because these 'other people were too drunk or stupid to keep their numbers down...' See Part 5, Chapter 24 and notes.

[9] Virgil, *Aeneid,* III. 57.

[10] Paradox? Only when reality gets deliberately inverted, to use a Hegelian and Marxian expression by D^3 wizards like Krugman become contradictory situations apparent. (D^3 stands for: Derailed, Deluded and Dangerous) The idiocy

of his conclusion needs covering up in a mantle of scientistic hubris, a.k.a. 'paradox'. Does any of the readers actually experience an undesirable excess in their savings account? Even so, in the charitable case that no single person ever meets his desire for savings to the limit, why would the excess become a glut? Where does glut begin? Where is the proof of the glut and the proof of the undesirable effect? Why would not such excess funds, due to 'too much thrift' be cured by a bit less thrift and so-called labour time sharing as pushed by so many unions these days? Splitting one job over more than one person did not help the unemployment, despite the 'excess thrift', did it now? If we are to take Krugman on his word, we live in a workers paradise, where we all work too hard and have too much money. So why not all work half days, retire mid-career and make room for the youngsters? I hear they experience an unemployment problem.... This so-called 'thrift-paradox' only deserves ridicule if not contempt.

[11] The 'Saviour' symbol is quite typical for ideologies based on guilt, an easy mass manipulation tool. Note also the latests ploy of this type: the Global Warming guilt ploy... in which the Hight Priest exacts a penance in the form of taxation for the redemption of your guilt. Not that one ought not to disrespect the environment, though, which is different. Other ploys may exists, such as the revelation of a problem that urgently need intervention by government: perhaps some terrorism groups?

[12] The religious undertones are unmistakeable. The phenomenon of ideologies have deep religious roots. See e.g. *The Theological Origins of Modernity* by Allen Michael Gillespie, 2009, University of Chicago Press, Chicago and London.

[13] And the OECD is ready for it. All non-cooperative countries are black-listed for international loans and/or 'exposed' by 'leaks' such as the 'Panama Papers', if not humiliated in elaborate public scandals, whipped up by a docile press. We witness taboo's (a.k.a. gag orders) as a favourite tool of suppression ...

[14] Gnostic dualists have a long history of turning things on their heads, even after this mass movement became secular. It has been diagnosed not as a disease of the mind, a psychopathology, but as a disease of the spirit, which is a 'pneuma-pathology.' The affected person suffers from a dream-like state, and now lives in a 2nd reality of his own making, coupled to concupiscence or *libido dominandi*, subordinating all subjects (of the Crown or the legal realm) around them to their vision and direction. The same rhetoric always recurs somehow : obliteration of what is real, together with silencing those who instead point out reality. Often expressions are used involving 'transformation of the fabric of society' or 'radically reordering society's view of reality...' etc. The rhetoric all pertains to reconstructing a 'second or dream reality'. More on this subject can be found in Eric Voegelin, New Science of Politics: ' In the Gnostic dream world . . . nonrecognition of reality is the first principle. As a consequence,

types of action which in the real world would be considered as morally insane because of the real effects which they have will be considered moral in the dream world because they intended an entirely different effect. The gap between intended and real effect will be imputed not to the Gnostic immorality of ignoring the structure of reality but to the immorality of some other person or society that does not behave as it should behave according to the dream conception of cause and effect. The interpretation of moral insanity as morality, and of the virtues of *sophia* and *prudentia* as immorality, is a confusion difficult to unravel.' p.169-170.

[15] Hence, the so-called witch-hunt for perceived 'tax evaders' and 'capitalists' (apparently now a dirty word) has been declared open, worldwide. The Social Justice Warriors have a field day with sponsored web sites, TV appearances and journalists turning miraculously almost overnight into scholarly taxation specialists. Even the best book publishing houses can only dream of such an oiled marketing machine. Of course, this method of mass vilification is a form of public trial without due process and has been used many times in the past. If public prosecutors cannot make their case solid under positivist law, the atomic weapon of public vilification is used such as the public smear campaigns of tax evasion. Remember that All Capone, the maffiosi of the 1930s was not tried for his actual crimes of murder, but for tax evasion. Nevertheless, such witch-hunts have proved popular and are definitely orchestrated events.

Chapter 31

Essay published on June 7, 2010, by A. Fekete.

What You Always Wanted to Know About Gold

The following is a transcript of an interview requested by a gold-friendly hedge fund.

Q.: Professor Fekete, you are known as a staunch advocate of a return to the gold standard. But mainstream economists are saying a gold standard is not practicable and they are fighting the idea with everything they have. How do you answer their criticism?

A.: To say that the gold standard is not practicable is the same as to say that honesty is not practicable, and Constitutions are made to be blithely ignored when convenient. The American Constitution, for example, mandates a metallic monetary standard for the United States in the clearest possible language. Opponents of the gold standard have never been able to muster up the moral fortitude to amend the Constitution so as to formalise the abolishing of the gold standard. Yet in 1933 president Roosevelt confiscated the gold of all citizens, gave them irredeemable paper in exchange, and proceeded to write up the value of gold in terms of the paper by 75 percent. Might makes right: if you cannot do it fairly and legally, then you can use the strong arm of the government to do it through chicanery, backed by the constabulary and the jail cell.

More recently, in our own century, Switzerland changed her Constitution in which the gold standard was also enshrined, through a referendum. Citizens were given *a weekend* to debate and decide the merits or demerits of the proposed constitutional changes. The indecent haste with which they were railroaded through the constitutional process betrayed the bad conscience of the authors.

One of the key principles supporting a gold standard is that jurisprudence cannot tolerate a double standard of justice. The government, its departments and agencies ought to be subject to the same contract law as are citizens. There are no valid grounds to allow the Treasury and the Central Bank to issue obligations which they have neither the means nor the intention to honour – while everybody else doing it will be dealt with according to the Criminal Code. To say that the gold standard is not practicable is the same as saying that the government should be exempted from the provisions of the Criminal Code in its dealings with its subjects.

Q.: What would be the basic steps involved in reintroducing a gold standard? How to proceed?

A.: Three indispensable steps are involved.

First, the government should open the Mint to gold. This means that everybody who wants to convert his gold of the right quantity and quality into gold coins of the realm should be able to do so at the Mint, free of seigniorage charges, and with no limit imposed on the amount. In other words, they would get gold back, ounce for ounce, in coined form, and the cost of minting would be absorbed by the government, the same way as it absorbs the cost of maintaining highways in good repair. Conversely, owners of the gold coins of the realm must have the right to hoard, melt down, or export them as they see fit. This is designed to vest the right to regulate the money supply in the people, rather than in unelected bureaucrats.

Second, 'legal tender protection' of paper money must for once and all be declared unconstitutional. This is designed to remove coercion whereby labour can be forced to accept irredeemable currency for services rendered.

Such coercion was first legalised in France and Germany in the year 1909, just five years before the outbreak of World War I.[1] These countries wanted to make sure that civil servants and military personnel could be paid in chits, thus putting the entire labour force at the disposal of the government – regardless of the state of budget and collection of taxes – in case of war. The motivation behind the second provision is that governments should not be able to wage undeclared and unpopular wars, as could Kings of old, but must raise taxes. World War I would have come to an early end but for the legal tender laws. As soon as treasuries had run out of gold, the belligerents would have been forced to make peace, unless the electorate agreed to pay for the continuing bloodshed and destruction of property. And the world would have been the better for it.

Third, the principle known as the 'Real Bills Doctrine' of Adam Smith should be observed. Bills of exchange drawn on fast-moving merchandise in most urgent demand by the consumers, which mature into gold coins within 91 days (the length of the seasons of the year), must be allowed to enter into spontaneous monetary circulation. This would guarantee the flexibility of the monetary system not through government coercion, but through the voluntary cooperation of producers and consumers in satisfying human wants.

It can be seen that the market for real bills is the clearing house of the gold standard.[2] In 1918, at the end of World War I, the victorious allies decided not to allow the world to go back to multilateral international trade. To be sure, they wanted to go back on the gold standard, witness Great Britain's decision to make the pound sterling once more convertible into gold at the pre-war exchange rate in 1925, but with only bilateral trade allowed. This meant nothing less than the castration of the gold standard: once its clearing house was amputated, it could not perform.

The allied powers did this out of spite and vengeance: they wanted to cripple Germany over and above the provisions of the Versailles peace treaty. Forcing bilateral trade upon Germany was equivalent to peacetime blockade whereby the allied powers could monitor and control Germany's imports and exports. The measure backfired. The Great Depression and the 1931-1936 collapse of the international gold standard was due to the forcible elimination of the multilateral financing of world trade with real bills.

The gold standard did not collapse because of its 'contractionist nature' – as alleged by Keynes. It collapsed because of its clearing system, the bill market was blocked. Falling prices in 1930 were not the ***cause*** of the Great Depression: they were the ***effect***. The cause was falling interest rates. Incidentally, falling interest rates were in turn caused by the illegal introduction of 'open market operations' by the Federal Reserve of the United States in 1921, whereby the central bank pays bribe money, in the form of risk-free profits, to bond speculators for bidding bond prices sky-high.

Q.: To what extent should money be 'covered' by gold?

A.: The Real Bills Doctrine provides the answer to that question. There are on average 75 business days in a quarter. Therefore on each business day, on average, one-seventy-fifth, that is, 1 1/3 percent of the outstanding real bills mature into gold. Sufficient gold must be available at all times to pay the bills at maturity; more if the discount rate is rising, less if it is falling. In normal times the commercial banks should have that much gold flowing to them in the ordinary course of business, with which they can pay the maturing bills. If times are abnormal, banks go to the bill market and sell at a discount a sufficient amount of bills from portfolio to raise the gold. This should be no problem: a maturing real bill is the best earning asset a commercial bank can have. At any given time there are commercial banks somewhere in the world overflowing with gold. They scramble to acquire earning assets. The value of real bills increases every single day through maturity. They represent 'self-liquidating credit'. Sale of the underlying merchandise to the ultimate consumer provides the wherewithal for their liquidation.

Q.: What happens if a country has no gold in its coffers?[3]

A.: Such a country will experience a rise in the discount rate. The appearance of a positive spread between the discount rates prevailing in two countries improves the terms of trade in favour of the one with the higher rate. It can offer lower cash prices on its exports, while paying lower prices (91 days net) for its imports. This means that the country gets the gold for its exports 91 days before its bills payable in gold for its imports fall due. In addition, the higher discount rate will induce an inflow of short term capital that will help finance both exports and imports. We have to remember that imports are financed by exports, not by gold. Gold is there to tie the country over through temporary imbalances.

Should this help not be sufficient to meet the shortage of gold, then consumers, if they want to eat, to keep themselves clad, shod and, in winter, warm, will have to dig into their pockets and come up with the gold coin to pay the bills for their imports upon maturity.

The point is that a shortage of gold need not cause privation: thanks to the discount-rate mechanism it is a self-correcting condition.

Q.: You have announced that in August you will start a school, and call it the New Austrian School of Economics, in Budapest, Hungary. Why new? Why Austrian? Why in Hungary?

A.: The Austrian School of Economics was started by Carl Menger (1840-1921) of Austria-Hungary who deserves the epitaph, along with Isaac Newton, humanis generis decus (pride of the human race). The first members of the school, like Merger himself, were all great monetary scientists who abhorred the idea of irredeemable currency. Keynes introduced the notion that the gold standard is a 'barbarous relic' and should be discarded.[4] Through bribe and blackmail academia was enlisted to rally to the new doctrine, while the Austrian School withered.

When the intellectual bankruptcy of Keynesianism – which turned things upside down in castigating the virtue of thrift and lionising the vice of prodigality – has become obvious, the Austrian School has gone through a renaissance, especially in the United States, calling for sanity and return to the gold standard. However, the 'American Austrians' are vehemently against the Real Bills Doctrine of Adam Smith for doctrinaire reasons, as it contradicts their holy of holies, the Quantity Theory of Money. They do not understand that real bill circulation is spontaneous and its suppression is nothing less than unwarranted interfering in the operation of the free market. They do not see the difference between the discount rate (yield on real bills) and the rate of interest (yield in the gold bond).

This prompted me to start my school in Hungary where I live. It would be a disaster if the American Austrians succeeded in making their '100 percent gold standard' a reality. It would not survive the first Christmas shopping season. Markets would seize up, and the gold standard would be given a bad name for the second time.

Austria and Hungary used to be a dual monarchy during the days of Carl Menger, sharing not only the monarch, but also their scientific and cultural heritage.

Q.: Why a gold standard? Why not pick a basket of precious metals, or of some other marketable commodities to serve as the standard unit of value?

A.: American money doctors are in the habit of ridiculing gold in comparing it to frozen pork bellies that, *horribile dictu*, have been trading in the same pit since gold was expelled from the Monetary Paradise. This reflects a mindset suggesting that gold, at best, is just one of several marketable commodities, and a basket of wider selection could provide a *better* monetary reserve than gold.

This position is ***false***. Gold is no frozen pork bellies – wishful thinking by the American money doctors notwithstanding. The reason is that the marginal utility of the former declines more slowly than that of the latter. In fact, the marginal utility of gold declines more slowly than that of any commodity (or a basket of any commodities) known to man. That's what makes gold what it is: the monetary metal par excellence. That's what makes gold the only monetary asset that has no counterpart as a liability in the balance sheet of someone else. (See fig. 2 Volume II. *ed.*)

Incidentally, there are only two monetary metals: gold and silver. Other precious metals such as platinum and palladium are not monetary metals. What sets monetary metals apart from other precious metals is their stocks-to-flows ratio. They are a high multiple for the monetary metals, but a small fraction for other precious metals.

Q.: Critics say that historically, under the gold standard, the world economy languished, trade was sluggish, technological and therapeutic innovation was unexciting, in a word: the gold standard has never worked well. How do you answer that?

A.: This allegation is just the opposite of the truth. The heyday of the gold standard was during the 100-year period between 1815 (the end of the Napoleonic wars) and 1914 (the start of World War I). This was the age of transcontinental railways, intercontinental shipping, when all the key inventions were made that ushered in the age of electricity, of the internal combustion engine, of aviation, of wireless telecommunication, of the X-ray, etc. Financing these discoveries and their applications in transportation, telecommunication, and therapeutics would have not been possible without the gold standard and the accumulation of capital that it facilitated.

Q.: Introducing a gold standard hardly seems possible today, in view of the gigantic injections of new currency into the economy worldwide. How could the gold standard handle that?

A.: It wouldn't. The new gold standard would let the regime of irredeemable currency run itself aground and boil in its own juices of excess fiat money. When it can no longer handle the task of delivering food and other necessities to the people, when it can no longer provide employment to the majority of the population, the gold standard will spring back to life spontaneously. People have to eat, and they also have other necessities. They must have work to be able to earn a living. It will dawn on the world, maybe unexpectedly for the majority, that gold has a place underneath the Sun. Gold is that hard core of capital that can be destroyed neither by inflation nor by deflation, that will survive any consolidation of balance sheets. Gold is at the heart of the healing process of the world economy that makes survival possible.

Q.: Is a gold standard the ultima ratio to cure the human weakness, the belief that you can multiply wealth by printing money without limits? Is it not true that no central bank could ever stand up to do-gooder politicians?

A.: Friedrich Hayek, the Nobel-laureate Austrian economist thought so. He said that there would be no need for a gold standard but for the propensity of governments to spend beyond their means.

I disagree. I see gold everywhere, independently of government spending propensities. Even without a gold standard, gold has a role to play in forming prices, wages, rents, the rate of interest. It helps to find the balance between short and long-term satisfaction; it determines the marginal productivity of capital and labour. It is like air, we don't see it yet it's there and without it, there is no life.

You need a yardstick to measure value. Gold is the raw material of which that yardstick is made.

Q.: In the past states also went bankrupt, some repeatedly, e.g., ancient Athens, Rome, or France in the 17th and 18th centuries. This shows not only that such occurrences are possible under a gold standard, but also that the powers-that-be could always circumvent limitations put on coining money and restrictions on Banking whenever the idea of scarcity of gold takes hold. What makes you think that a future gold standard may be more successful, and could endure for a long period of time?

A.: There is no hard-and-fast limit on the amount of self-liquidating credit that can be safely built on the unit weight of gold. Improvements in clearing techniques, such as those in telecommunication, freight-forwarding and warehousing will increase the amount of credit outstanding while there is no corresponding increase in gold bearing that credit. It is this property that makes gold the ultimate extinguisher of debt. It is simply not true that restrictions put on an economic process by an unadulterated gold standard are 'contractionist', and that the 'powers-that-be' are justified in breaking those fetters. Gold is not scarce: in terms of its stocks-to-flows ratio gold is the most abundant substance on earth. But for the gold standard to endure, man has to have confidence in the promises of government to pay gold. If this confidence is impaired, gold tends to go into hiding and then the process may break down. The answer to the problem is that the government must keep faith in its subjects without fail.

Q.: What is your opinion of the government's handling of the great financial crisis, the Greek crisis, the crisis of the Euro, and the other currency crises brewing? How long can they contain the 'debt-firestorms'? Will they be able to extinguish it with a shower of new debts?

A.: The governments of the industrialised countries bear full responsibility for bringing the world to the brink of this crisis – the greatest financial and economic crisis ever. They should have resigned in admission of their guilt, and let new governments armed with a better economic theory take over and work out the remedy. Instead, they doggedly cling to power. Their analyses of the causes of the malady are faulty; the remedial measures they have recommended are the old nostrums, incredibly inept, nay, counterproductive.

Take the example of the runaway growth of the debt tower. The great financial crisis, the Greek crisis, and all the currency crises still at the brewing stage, are part of the same problem, namely, the debt problem. It goes back to the year 1971. On August 15 of that fateful year the U.S. government defaulted on its international gold obligations. By now the debt tower threatens with toppling, and burying the world economy under the debris.

The reason for the exponential growth of debt in the world is that the international monetary system has been lacking an ultimate extinguisher since 1971. Total debt in the world can only grow, **never contract**. We should do well to remember that, since time immemorial, gold has successfully acted as the ultimate extinguisher of debt – until it was forcibly removed from the international monetary system in 1971. Paying debt in gold extinguished the debt, period. Since 1971 governments have *pretended* that paying debt in U.S. dollars extinguished it, too. But in fact it did not.[5] Debt was merely transferred from the debtor to the U.S. government and kept accumulating. *Transferring* debt is not the same as *extinguishing* it. Debt accumulation has a natural limit. This limit will soon manifest itself, if it has not already been reached.

Your description of the debt-tower as a firestorm is apt. Governments of the leading industrialised countries will not be able to contain the firestorm they have started. They are just pouring oil on the fire.

Q.: How will the current situation unfold? Do you think resolution will come in the form of hyper-inflation or deflation?

A.: One has to be careful with these terms. Both inflation and deflation mean destruction of wealth through destroying the value of obligations;[6] the former through depreciation, the latter through default. It is also possible to have a mixture of both simultaneously.

But if you insist on my answering your question, chalk me up in the deflation column. Signs of deflation are all around us. Rivers of new money are unable to turn receding prices and interest rates around. Confidence in promises to pay is evaporating. Banks do not trust one another with overnight money. Paper gold is being pushed down the throat of those wanting physical gold. Worse still, vanishing confidence has reached the stage of contagion. Paper wealth is disintegrating before our very eyes. The domino-effect is spreading: the collapse of one firm brings down two others. Most frightening is the shrinking of employment. It is leading to a break-down in law and order. Governments are completely unprepared and think that it is just a matter of printing more money, for which they are superbly equipped, to prevent further contraction.

Q.: Your answer to my next question would certainly interest our readers very much. Are you invested in gold, silver, and other precious metals? Would you still buy them at these elevated prices?

A.: I take exception to your use of the word 'investing'. To my way of thinking holding monetary metals is not investing but more like taking out an insurance policy. I don't think the other precious metals (or stones, for that matter) make for good investments. As far as the monetary metals, gold and silver, are concerned, you would be well-advised to buy some more every month routinely, regardless of the price. You should look at your holdings as you look at your fire insurance policy. If you never need to collect, well, so much the better.

At the optimum, you would track the value of your assets not at their dollar price but at their gold equivalent. In other words, you would carry your balance sheet, both on the asset and the liability side, not in dollar or euro units, *but in gold units* (ounces or grams). It takes self-discipline to do that, but this is the only way to avoid the pitfall of always looking at your own face in a curved mirror. The torsion of the image may easily translate into torsion of the mind.

Q.: I come to my final question, if I may. What do you think the gold price will be in terms of U.S. dollars or euros in three to five years' time?

A.: I am sorry, but I am not a practitioner of clairvoyance. I think I would compromise my reputation as a scientist if I ventured to answer this question. Besides, I don't think I am very much interested in knowing. Guesses at the future price of gold are a dime a dozen. A more appropriate – and interesting – question may be whether *the dollar and the euro will still be around in three to five years.* I am not sure about the euro, but I think the dollar will definitely be around three years from now. Five years – maybe not, but I wouldn't be surprised if the staying power of the dollar extended beyond five years. It is dangerous to underestimate the strength of the poison you have to live and work with.

Endnotes to Chapter 31

1 See note 14, p. 85 above.

2 See e.g. Ernest Sykes, *Banking and Currency*, London, Butterworth & Co. 4th ed. 1920, Chapter XII. 'Clearing Houses.' p. 106.

3 The question has a few unclear connotations: 'country' and 'coffers' are meant to point to the Treasury or does the question point to the inhabitants and their savings ? If a country is on a gold standard, the stock of circulating gold coin is not theirs (that is: any institution's; it circulates at various velocities to extinguish debt. Yet ownership of gold remains private.

4 More clues on recognising the shift from religious to secular movement are treated in Burdach, Karl. *Reformation. Renaissance. Humanismus. Zwei Abhandlungen über die Grundlage moderner Bildung und Sprachkunst.* (1926)

5 See the argumenat about living in a 2nd reality, being estranged from reality.

6 Please consult the glossary in Volume I for the meaning in current language and the meaning that in this work will be attached. '...the value of obligations' means here the entire nation's savings.

Chapter 32

Sad Ending To The Second Greatest Story Ever Told

' Banking was conceived in iniquity and born in sin. The Bankers own the earth. Take it away from them, but leave them the power to create deposits, and with the flick of the pen they will create enough deposits to buy it back again. However, take away that power, and all the great fortunes like mine will disappear — as they ought to in order to make this a happier and better world to live in. But, if you wish to remain the slaves of Bankers and pay the cost of your own slavery, then let them continue to create deposits.'

Sir Josiah Stamp (1880-1941), one time governor of the Bank of England, in his Commencement Address at the University of Texas in 1927. Reportedly he was the second wealthiest individual in Britain.

Make no mistake about it: in this credit collapse we are witnessing the death throes of irredeemable currency. In vain have governments and their client banks tried, for hundreds of years, to graft this repulsive and degenerate bastard on the living organism of society. The result was always the same: the healthy organism rejected the unnatural implant in its own good time. The present episode is no different from earlier ones except, perhaps, in the degree of the conceitedness of the perpetrators, and in their contempt for the native intelligence of man.

When on August 15, 1971, Richard Nixon defaulted on the gold obligations of the United States and declared the irredeemable dollar the 'ultimate' means of payments and liquidator of debt, he was relying on the expert advice of Chicago economist Milton Friedman. Five years later the world's oldest central bank, the Swedish Riksbank would bestow upon Friedman the prize it established in memory of Alfred Nobel. The reward would be in recognition of the brilliance of Friedman's idea that if a central bank robs the people piecemeal (read: it dilutes the currency at a fixed rate of, say, 3 percent per annum) then the victims would not cry 'we wuz robbed!' They would never notice the robbery. In all previous episodes shame and disgrace were part and parcel of the government's default on its promises to pay. Not so in 1971. In this latest experiment with irredeemable currency there was a new feature: far from being a disgrace, the default was presented as a scientific breakthrough; conquering 'monetary superstition' epitomised by gold; a triumph of progress. Sycophant governments and central banks overseas that were victimised by it and had to swallow unprecedented losses due to the devaluation of the dollar were not even allowed to say 'ouch!' They were forced to celebrate their own undoing and hail the advent of the New Age of synthetic credit, irredeemable currencies and irredeemable debts.

The regime of the irredeemable dollar was put to the test soon enough. In 1979 the genie escaped from the bottle. The price of oil, silver, and gold were quoted at twenty times that prior to 1971; in the case of sugar the rate of increase was more like forty times, so much so that the Coca Cola Company found it too expensive to put into coke and started using corn syrup instead. Interest rates were quoted in double digits well past the teens. There was panic across the land and around the globe. Hoarding of goods became a way of life. Everybody was expecting the worst.

It was at this time that the notion of 'targeting inflation' was invented. Previously the claims of central bank power were rather modest. Central banks were supposed to target short-term interest rates. Later they graduated to targeting the money supply. Now they were claiming supernatural powers of micromanaging price increases. It was apparently working, and the genie was put back in the bottle.

In the intervening three decades policymakers and mainstream economists became ever more confident that in inflation-targeting they have found the holy grail of irredeemable currency. Professor Frederic Mishkin of Columbia University, a former governor of the Federal Reserve, published the gospel of inflation targeting with the title Monetary Policy Strategy in 2007. In his book he calls inflation targeting 'an information-inclusive strategy for the conduct of monetary policy.' Martin Wolf, the chief economic columnist of the Financial Times of London explains: inflation targeting makes allowance for all relevant variables — exchange rates, stock prices, housing prices and long-term bond prices — via their impact on activity and prospective inflation. This, then, is the new modified holy grail. Cast your net wide enough to catch all that you want to control. If you do it boldly, you will make people believe that the government can control everything it wants to control. It is amazing how much can be accomplished by piling prestidigitation upon prestidigitation.

Ironically, disaster struck just at the time when the prophets of inflation-targeting became cocky beyond any measure of modesty. They actually had a whole debate going on in American journals, but also English ones. Ben Bernanke, who in the meantime was made the chairman of the Federal Reserve, contributed the keynote address and the title to the debate: 'The Great Moderation'. Their description, up to and including the beginning of 2007 of what was happening in the macro economy, was a reduction in the volatility in the trade cycle: more consistent growth, less bouts of inflation, more stability. The London Times published a jubilant piece as recently as early 2007 with the title 'The Great Moderation' which began with the line: 'History will marvel at the stability of our era.' It was not meant to be a joke. It was meant to be believed. Complacency about the almighty nature of monetary policy reached its peak. They celebrated the success of inflation targeting just when it started to unravel. Policymakers, central bankers, and their lackeys in academia and journalism, felt inordinately proud of themselves. They thought they held the whole world in their hands.

The celebration and self-congratulation was premature. Bernanke & C° did not know that they were about to be humbled by the markets. Blinded by the glare of their own glory, none of them foresaw the coming disaster.

Martin Wolf talks about 'this unforeseen crisis' as an unmitigated disaster for monetary policy. It leaves fiat money with just one last chance to put its act together and save its hide. He says: 'The holy grail turned out to be a mirage. If fiat money is not made to work better than it has, who knows what our children might decide to do in desperation. They might even decide to bring back and embrace gold'. Oh horror of horrors! Wolf still considers the gold standard an absurdity.

It's kind of strange. It is not the regime of irredeemable currency, whereby governments are supposed to create wealth by sprinkling some ink on little scraps of paper, that is considered an absurdity. Of course, Mr. Wolf has the right of wanting to be pilfered and plundered. But he has no right to advocate that the rest of us be cheated through this crudest form of plunder forever and ever.

He is also mistaken when he assumes that Bernanke & C° still has one more chance. The chance they just blew was the last. We are witnessing the closing of the regime of irredeemable currency and irredeemable debt. We may not know how long its death throes will take, but there will be no other chance. Financial journalists and mainstream economists, in their blind stupor acting as cheerleaders for the disastrous monetary policy of the government and the insane credit policy of the banks, have exhausted and destroyed heir own credibility for once and all.

Martin Wolf, like most of his colleagues, is a victim of brainwashing inspired by Keynes that has been going on to discredit the gold standard for some 75 years, but which got a new lift after Friedman inspired Nixon to default. Here are the facts about the gold dollar that should be made available to the world through the opening of the Mint to gold, as demanded by the U.S. Constitution.

The gold standard is an indispensable prerequisite of freedom. Without it individuals are helpless in facing the constant and ongoing encroachment of their property rights by the government and the banks. The right to demand gold in exchange for bank notes and bank deposits far transcends the mere technicality of exchange of one form of money for another. It is the only way to check the unlimited power of the government manifested by the unlimited creation of bank deposits. The combination of governmental power and the power of the banks to create deposits is especially dangerous for the freedom of the individual, because of the double standard involved. The government exempts banks from the effects of contract law in exchange for the banks' special treatment accorded to government debt.

Gold hoarding is not a blemish on the gold standard; it is its main excellence. When a sufficient number of individuals are disturbed by the encroachment of this combination of powers, or disapprove the monetary policy of the government and the credit policy of the banks, they are not helpless under a gold standard. They can withdraw bank reserves, namely gold, from the system, thereby putting the government and the banks on notice that unless they mend their ways, and stop their adventures in debt creation, they will find themselves insolvent and out of power. The gold standard gives people the upper hand. It is no accident that all dictatorships set out by limiting the people's access to gold. It makes no difference whether they march under the banner of national or international socialism. All totalitarian regimes inflict irredeemable currency on the people as an instrument of servitude and bondage. Martin Wolf should know this. The ideal of limited government is meaningless unless reinforced by a gold standard denying to the government the power of issuing unlimited amounts of currency. There is no other way of doing this than making the promises of the government redeemable in something other than more promises of the same shabby kind.

Once the government makes the currency irredeemable, it puts itself in the position to curtail the rights and freedoms of the people as it sees fit. Constitutional government is effectively overthrown. Once the government usurps the public purse, its power becomes uncontrollable. Budget debate in Parliament or in Congress becomes an annual farce. Nothing stands in the way of unscrupulous politicians to undermine constitutional government. The purchasing power of the currency is constantly undermined year in, year out. The banks are freed from constraints on them exercised by the people under the gold standard. Pandora's box of corruption is opened and its contents contaminate the nation's economic, political, and social system.

Governments which employ irredeemable currency grab unconditional control over foreign trade, exchange rates, foreign investments and travel, even the amount of currency an individual can take in or out of the country. The more powerful governments will buy the allegiance of the less powerful. Out of this feudalistic web of allegiances financed by irredeemable currency come various adventures in fomenting and waging wars in far-away lands, spilling the blood of the young people of the nation for causes alien to them.

Under a gold standard prolonged budget deficits and prolonged unfavourable balance of payments cannot occur. There are forces limiting persistent losses of gold which tend to correct the underlying distortion. By contrast, under the regime of irredeemable currency economic distortions can persist indefinitely. They ultimately become destructive. This is so because government bureaucrats cannot possibly provide the same level of wisdom that a people free to act in their own interest can.

As problems in foreign trade mount, governments will find ever more excuses for ever more controls. There is no end to the expansion of government power over the individual until the nation regains the benefits of a gold standard, requiring that the government retire to its proper role of umpire and relinquish its role as dominant partner and dictator.

A government can take total control of the people either by the use of military force, or by the use of irredeemable currency. The former is readily understood, while the latter is a subtle national drug that is not generally recognised as such. Rather, it is readily embraced by its victims. For these and similar reasons irredeemable currency is the favourite device of modern governments that want to bring people under total control. Indeed, it enables the government to succeed in controlling the masses while, at the same time, earning their approval and even their enthusiastic support. Irredeemable currency must be seen as the habit-forming drug that the government uses to intoxicate people. Under this intoxication people will want more and more national spending, more and more government control, and more and more debt.

This intoxication obscures the sad end that arrives when the merry-go-round is coming to a jerky halt, when credit is exhausted or withdrawn, and the kitty is found empty. The nation is facing a most serious economic disaster followed by prolonged economic pain. Unfortunately, government economists, university professors, and financial journalists have taken their share of the fun and they failed miserably in their duty to forewarn people of the coming disaster.

It is useless to expect a mass movement on behalf of a sound currency. The daily experiences of people provide them with a warped outlook. They confirm in their minds the alleged virtues and benefits of an infinitely inflatable currency. People lack sufficient understanding of monetary science to see that no currency can be made infinitely inflatable without inviting disaster. Like a drug addict, people exposed to irredeemable currency do not regard it as a dangerous and undermining narcotic agent. Even the loss of purchasing power does not disturb them to any great extent. Their response is to demand more money, and they take pride in the fact that the government listens sympathetically to their demand. They welcome the soaring stock indexes and real estate prices, and put great stores on them. Heavy taxes and burgeoning debt are not regarded with anxiety. A frequent and common agitation is for ever more government spending.

If we are to be saved from the ultimate evil consequences of the regime of irredeemable currency, needed action must come from the leadership of the opposition party when it is its turn to take over government. The new President and his Secretary of the Treasury, or the new Prime Minister and his Secretary of the Exchequer must be statesmen. They must act as informed and tough monetary surgeons, men who can and will persuade Congress or Parliament to reinstate redeemable currency.

Once that step is taken, the people should experience a breath of fresh air. Government would once more be subordinated to the Constitution, bringing greater freedom to the people. Optimism should be wide-spread, because the currency of the people would once more had integrity. Business should prosper, domestic and foreign trade expand. Imbalances in foreign trade should rectify themselves. Gold should start to circulate and flow in from abroad. The control of the public purse would be returned to the people where it belongs if human freedom is to be preserved and responsible government is to be obtained.

But as the last presidential election in the United States has shown, the needed leadership is lacking. The party of the opposition is just as much in thrall to the same toxic ideology as the governing party.

The last change of guards took place in the middle of a financial and economic crisis involving the destruction of quantities of wealth unprecedented in all history, with more destruction coming. Yet when the new president appointed officials at the Treasury, confirmed others at the Federal Reserve, and named economic advisors, they turned out to be the same men who were responsible for the credit collapse in the first place. Not only do these officials continue the dangerous course of the previous administration, they increase the stakes by several orders of magnitude in announcing more bailouts, more stimulus packages, hence more government spending, more government debt, and more fiat money creation.

The situation is no better in the United Kingdom, another important country expecting a change of guards, which could take the initiative to put a peaceful end to the regime of irredeemable currency now in its death throes. Rather than initiating a national debate on the utter failure of the present financial system which was supposed to end bank runs, deflations and depressions, serial bankruptcies and unemployment for once and all, and on the return to sound money and sound book-keeping, Her Majesty's Loyal Opposition is plotting a course how to cure the collapse of bad debt with the injection of more bad debt.

What this means is that there is no hope for change through peaceful means. When change finally does come, it will be through violence. When the economic pain inflicted on the people reaches unbearable heights, law and order will break down, anarchy and chaos will ensue. Looking at the ruins of our civilisation will be a bitter reminder of what the great monetary tradition of the English-speaking countries, in ruling out irredeemable currency and mandating a metallic monetary standard, was designed to prevent. [1]

Endnotes to Chapter 32

[1] The author has drawn heavily on Walter E. Spahr's article in the quarterly *Modern Age*, Summer, 1960, under the title 'The Significance of the Gold Standard'

PART 7

FORENSIC ANALYSIS OF AN IDEOLOGICAL WARFARE

Chapter 33

Act I : The Incredible Disappearance of Silver

The silver standard did not die a natural death. It was killed deliberately. A proper search for the assassins was never carried out. There never was a post-mortem. In this paper we focus on the conspiracy as it might have unfolded between the two dates: April 9, 1865 (the day General Lee of the Confederacy surrendered at Appomattox to General Grant of the Union marking the end of the War Between the States) and January 1, 1879 (Resumption Day, when payment of the victorious Union's currency, the greenback was resumed in gold specie –but not in silver).

China has been on the silver standard since time immemorial. The Chinese did use coins for monetary purposes such as bank reserves until the end of the 19th century; in protest of U.S. and British colonial occupation attempts, they used the *sycee*, a boat-shaped bullion of approximate size 5x3x3 inches, weighing approximately 50 *taels* or about 5 pounds (avoirdupois). No one can pretend to know, however approximately, how much monetary silver has gone into hiding in China and in India, these two most populous countries of the world, over the millennia. In comparison estimates of monetary gold having gone into hiding over the same period of time are far more reliable. Be that as it may, the amount of monetary silver unaccounted for is probably greater than any estimate ever made.

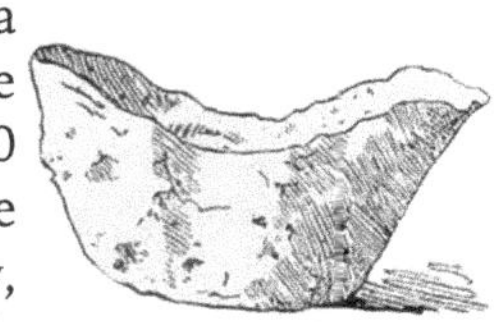

The 19th century found the world with silver coins doing most of the money-work. The turnover of silver coinage (the value of silver coins times their velocity) was at an all-time high, eclipsing the turnover of gold coinage. Inept governments did not follow the lead of Isaac Newton, and they tried to enforce a rigid exchange rate between the two monetary metals (called the Mint ratio). This system was called bimetallism – a stillborn idea.

What says the silver with her virgin hue? 'Who chooseth me shall get as much as he deserves.'

(Shakespeare, The Merchant of Venice)

Bimetallism (in its fixed ratio form) destabilised the natural monetary system based on silver and gold valued at a variable rate, just as Newton's monetary mistake of fixing the ratio in Britain did. Bimetallism was the disease, the demise of the silver standard (more precisely, the demonetisation of silver) was the unfortunate outcome. In the Western countries by 1879, in India by 1893, in China, the last stronghold of silver, by 1935, silver became demonetised. Between these two dates, 1879 and 1935, the world witnessed a most spectacular event: the collapse of the value of silver by more than 80% in a little over half of a century. Silver fell from $1.29/oz in 1873 to 25¢/oz in 1935.[1] Putting it differently, the gold/silver price ratio rose from 15:1 to 80:1. Never in history, ancient or modern, have markets put such fancy values on gold

Who Killed the Silver Standard?

All this can be neatly 'explained' in terms of the Quantity Theory of Money. 'The richest silver vein ever, called the Comstock Lode was discovered in Nevada in 1858. Surplus silver inundated the world and lost most of its value due to the oversupply and the lack of matching demand.' Or so the explanation goes.

But this explanation will not satisfy those of us who consider the Quantity Theory of Money as a mere mechanical metaphor. As a theory it is bound to fail because it is trying to give a linear explanation of highly non-linear phenomena.[2] January 1, 1879, Resumption Day, when the payment of the greenback in gold (but not in silver) specie was resumed **significantly coincided** with the date when the Latin Monetary Union in Europe closed its last Mint to silver – marking the end of the silver standard in the Western countries.

No satisfactory explanation has been offered in the literature for the fact that the closing of the Mints to the free coinage of silver was the starting point of an unprecedented destruction of wealth [of the middle class] world-wide, due to the relentless fall in the price of silver during the following 55 years. To make matters worse, it was destruction of liquid wealth. Not only did silver lose more than 80 percent of its purchasing power; it also ceased to be a monetary metal. As a consequence, silver became so much harder to sell. Worse still, the steadily falling price caused panic-mining of silver. Miners were anxious to sell before the price fell even more. As a result, almost all silver mines were mined out prematurely. Thereafter all silver output came as a byproduct of mining other minerals. These effects compounded and made the destruction of values so much worse.

The collapse of the silver price was a major historical event affecting the entire globe and all trading nations of the world. It caused the impoverishment of the indigent classes in India, China, and elsewhere in Asia. But it also wiped out the credit-worthiness of the middle classes in Europe that lost their landed wealth as a consequence. Monetary historians failed to treat this aspect of the demise of the silver standard with the seriousness it deserved. They also misdiagnosed the deflationary bias that the monetary system showed in the first half of the 20th century.

> The gold standard that arose on the ashes of the old monetary order in the wake of the destruction of the silver standard was less than satisfactory. Silver demonetisation has made all hoarding demand fall upon gold. This imparted a deflationary bias to the international gold standard that enemies of sound money were able to exploit with all consummate skill.

Following a vicious anti-gold agitation gold was also demonetised by the governments exactly one hundred years later, in 1973. The demonetisation process was no less unconstitutional than that of silver a hundred years earlier. It was also based on chicanery for good measure.

It should be noted that hoarding gold and silver is not an aberration. It is, in fact, part of the essential mechanism regulating the rate of interest. It will bar the banks from suppressing interest. When depositors realise what the banks are up to, they withdraw their deposits in the form of gold coin. The banks lose reserves and are forced to call in loans. It will also act as a deterrent against government profligacy. Ordinary citizens become disturbed by the government's overspending and serial budget deficits. In response they show a preference for holding their liquid wealth in gold coins instead of short-term government paper. Such hoarding demand previously fell upon gold as well as silver. Now it was falling upon gold alone. The deflationary consequences are obvious.

> There is no way self-destruction of liquid wealth of that magnitude could occur spontaneously.

It could not be explained on the strength of causality. We must invoke teleology if we want to understand it. Such an analysis was never carried out. Furthermore, speaking of destruction of wealth is not quite accurate. Value was not destroyed in the same sense of a house burning to the ground.

Clandestine Embezzlement

Rather, it was a clandestine embezzlement to benefit the world's Banking establishment at the expense of account holders. The value of account holders' assets was known, manipulated and ultimately taken over by the bank. Perpetrators were not worried that the disappearing liquid wealth would be missed and cause deflation. That was just the point of the entire operation of perpetrating it. They were confident that if they replaced the disappearing silver with bank credit based on debt, in particular, debt of the government, then there would be no deflation. This strongly suggests government involvement. In all probability there was 'an understanding' between an international Banking cartel (E.g. Morgan and its Rothschild networks in Europe, especially England, France and Germany) and some governments (e.g., the United States government acting either alone or in connivance with Imperial Germany).

Economic historians describe the Silver Saga as a natural evolution whereby gold monometallism gradually displaced bimetallism while strangling the silver standard. According to this reading of history, this process gradually eliminated silver as money, as it has so many others beforehand, challengers of gold's supremacy in the race for monetary hegemony. It was destiny. No need for a post mortem, still less for a search for the assassin. What would happen if every death due to natural causes was investigated as if it was due to violent causes? At any rate, they claim, the Quantity Theory of Money fully explains the market process eliminating silver from monetary circulation.

Upon closer examination the hypothesis that silver demonetisation was a market process rather than a collusion between governments and banks that killed the silver standard, appears untenable. There were powerful pressure groups pushing for the closing of the Mint to silver.

> One such pressure group representing special interest was that of international banking houses given their well-known penchant for monopolies.[3]

They avoided public debate. They acted behind the scenes. A 'monopoly of the gold standard' would mean, for them, a better handle on money-creation through their control of the gold mines, as well as their control of public credit. If this hypothesis is correct, then we know what has sealed the fate of the silver standard.[4]

A Short Silver Coin History of the U.K.

In Western monetary history, silver plays the leading role, even since antiquity. However, the story of silver's demise begins in Great Britain during the 16th century. Britain's silver coinage formed its monetary system for hundreds of years as evidenced by its name: the Pound Sterling. Early English Kings maintained their coins regularly throughout the ages. However, the practise of re-coining fell in disuse, and Britain's silver coinage became very worn, whilst coinage for small change (e.g. in copper) was so hard to come by, that private initiatives took over. In 1663 a new gold coin, the 'Guinea', was introduced, defined as 21 silver shilling. Since silver shillings were nowhere to be found, except worn or rejected, Britain managed to put itself on a de facto gold standard by this very introduction. [5] The exchange ratio's of gold and silver coins in terms of each other fluctuated as one would expect until 1717 when Isaac Newton, Master of the Royal Mint for decades, slipped up [6] and introduced a legally fixed ratio of 15½ :1 between silver and gold. That is what he thought. It is not what other people thought.

No sooner had Newton fixed the exchange ratio between gold and silver or Gresham came to say hello – that is: Gresham's 'law' (rather a natural economic habit) asserted itself. Nobody offered silver to the Mint, if and when they received better terms elsewhere – and they did in Amsterdam and Paris. Consequently, silver coinage stopped circulating in Britain. Britain's trading partners in Europe exchanged silver for gold on better terms. By 1816, the *de facto* gold Guinea standard forcibly became a legal gold standard. Britain's economic power coupled with its move to a gold standard was noted by its European trading partners, but they were not moved nor did they feel compelled to do likewise.

Silver Money in the U.S.

After the independence war of 1776 against Britain's King, the ex-colonists – now US – people used all sorts of coinage, mainly the already circulating Spanish real. In 1792 the U.S. Congress established a bimetallic dollar standard in the Coinage Act. Having learned by experience, they solemnly declared that both silver and gold extinguished debts private and public, to the exclusion of fiduciary or irredeemable paper issues. However, the U.S. Mint exchanged silver for gold at 15:1 correctly reflecting market ratio's at the time. [7] Having established the market ratio as a legal ratio, Gresham needn't remind the world of his existence. For the time being, that is. [8] Various territorial wars followed against Spain, Canada and others, financed with fiduciary currency that almost immediately and certainly inevitably went to a discount to specie; such caused monetary discontent in the early days of the U.S., hellbent on seigniorage as these early central bankers in spe were. Wartime expenses and railway construction were financed by trusts and banks engaging in illicit arbitrage between short term real bills and long term government bonds; they all faced insolvency and runs at one stage or another.

To make matters worse, Gresham ensured that the underweight silver dollar drove out fuller-bodied Spanish reals, but fuller bodied American small change (fractional dollars) were replaced by lesser quality fractional reals, only to be followed by an export of American silver dollars abroad. By 1820, no gold and few silver coins circulated in the U.S.; only the (discounted) greenbacks from insolvent banks were available: the dreadful, unintended result of positive law trying to alter economic reality waving a written note from Congress for its authority over reality.

> Debtors tried to abuse the time delay of repayment of principal (see hexagonal model and the wealth for income exchange) by repaying principal in inferior instruments, 'allowed' by law (greenbacks); creditors loaned inferior instruments (greenbacks) with the stipulation of repayment in superior instruments such as (gold) coin. Legal nominalism and its scion the greenback had contaminated natural justice and equity in the exchange of wealth for income paradigm, by abusing and distorting the time delay. And only one in a million people really understood how such abuse worked.

Not surprisingly, Andrew Jackson and the newly created Democratic Party won the 1832 election carried by ubiquitous popular discontent. The Coinage Act of 1834 sought to address the problem of silver exchange ratios in relation to gold and it changed the Mint silver/gold ratio terms to 16:1. But the 1850s brought new gold discoveries all around the world, and the increased production of gold changed the market exchange ratio for silver again, compared to the Mint ratio. Consequently silver rapidly disappeared from circulation. Coins were either hoarded (if interest rates proved too low) or melted down and exchanged for gold at the more attractive market ratio, which would be lower than 16:1. Despite its massive mining success the U.S. suffered from a shortage of small denomination silver coins, a direct consequence of a government decreed 'bi-metallic standard' at a government declared ratio. The same happened to Newton, famously, yet some people still refuse to read history books. To relieve the scarcity of silver coinage, created by themselves, Congress in 1853 Congress decided to use the legal 'atomic weapon' of positivism by artificially adding nominal value to silver coins (up to a maximum of $5). Silver coins with a nominal value of 5$ had less melt value in reality. It worked, of course, but it also turned out the first step in silver's demonetisation in the US.

The major European nations tried or suggested to follow Great Britain's lead by moving to a gold standard, away from bimetallism. (See below.) It would seem the Europeans had not read Newton or Gresham either and preferred reading Comte. (See below: international conferences) At the same time, large silver discoveries in Nevada (the Comstock Lode) and other western states in the US added to silver's problems relative to gold, but especially its problems relative to positivist declarations concerning the bimetallic ratio. Although parties had experienced and knew Gresham, they still invoked the 'legal ratio' for political purposes, if not for enrichment, either as creditor or as debtor, depending on election results, to the detriment of the other.

T'was silver for whom the bells tolled when in February 1873 Congress passed a law that discontinued the minting of any more silver dollars. **In other words, the US mint was no longer accepting silver for coining.** [9]

Silver interests labelled this law the 'Crime of 1873', followed a year later by another law ending the legal tender status of all silver dollars for payments larger than $5. While silver ceased to circulate completely, popular anger at the earlier Act's of Congress resulted in even more legal positivism getting thrown at economic reality. Ignoring Gresham, Congress passed the Bland-Allison Act of 1878 and the Sherman Silver Purchase Act of 1890. Both of these acts mandated that the U.S. Treasury to purchase silver at the old value equivalent to 16:1 instead of 35:1 in terms of gold – a euphemism for state subsidy of silver mining. In other words, privatise profits and socialise losses. Gold flowed out from the Treasury's coffers as silver and greenback dollars were exchanged for gold. Corruption in railway construction and subsidies and ongoing gold and silver tugs of war, between debtors and creditors, did not inspire foreign confidence in the U.S. dollar or the bonds that the US Treasury wanted to sell to foreigners.

A new government overturned these Acts and finally, in 1900, Congress passed the Gold Standard Act. This act provided for no retention of silver money except as token currency. The demonetisation of silver in the US and industrialised world was now complete.

Whodunit?

Meanwhile in Europe, Prussia obtained military victory over the French in a provoked war [10] called the Franco-Prussian war of 1870-1871. Bismarck proclaimed the German Empire unified at the Palace of Versailles on January 18; Paris fell to the invading German troops on January 28, 1871. Bismarck, anxious to join the gold standard club led by Britain and aware of possible silver demonetisation as a result of Pardieu's conferences in 1867, knew how to play poker. [11] On November 23, 1871, Bismarck exacted one thousand million dollars (five billion french francs) in gold reparation from France payable in four years, arguably the largest amount of gold ever changing hands directly, without involving promises to pay. One thousand million dollars in gold (at $19.39/oz!) is an incredibly huge sum of money by any standard. In comparison, the Louisiana Purchase in 1803 was consummated for a total sum of $15 million in gold. The Alaska Purchase in 1867 for $7.2 million in gold.

> This makes the French 'war indemnity' to Germany equivalent to 66 Louisianas or 172 Alaskas.

The temptation for the Germans to increase the value of their gold booty by fair means or foul may have been present as well. For example, it could be increased by demonetising silver, something Bismarck knew others had plans for. Such demonetisation of silver would increase the demand for, and thus also the purchasing power of gold. Predatory elements in society have no qualms about looking ahead at the possibilities for enrichment.

France paid the indemnity ahead of schedule. The new gold standard of the German Empire was inaugurated on July 9, 1873, when the new gold coin, the gold mark made its debut. This was preceded by **closing the German Mints to the coinage of the silver Taler in 1871**, the first overt step towards demonetising silver. [Remember that in Februari 1873, the US Mint closed for silver coining - the serendiptity !]

Some historians maintain that the demonetisation of silver and the subsequent sale of melted coins by the German government on the world market was the direct cause of the precipitous fall of the value of silver. [Ed note : a linear supply /demand argument] However, this is flatly contradicted by the fact that on February 12, 1873, the day when President Ulysses Grant signed the Coinage Act of 1873 into law, silver fetched a higher price in the market than the Mint price. [Although Grant closed the Mint for silver, silver fetched a better market price outside the Mint bid suspended by the law. Nobody flinched.]

No silver flowed to the Mint. Their bid did not match the market, despite the volumes from the U.S. and Germany selling its silver simultaneously. This was also the pretext used to drop the silver dollar from the list of allowed coins to be minted. Records of the minting of the standard silver dollar show that there has been no demand for the monetisation of silver on private account for years. This situation continued for some time afterwards. Silver mines continued selling their output on the free market. They seem to have been unaware that silver had been effectively demonetised in Germany in 1871 and in the United States in 1873, because the Chinese offered them a better price (in gold.)

The ultimate damage to the price of silver was not inflicted by the German demonetisation. Nor was it inflicted in the United States. People knew that demonetisation was coming and took it in stride. There was a ready market for silver in India and China, presumably for any amount, however large. American silver miners started to look at the U.S. Mint as a potential market for their production in 1875, as the price of silver in terms of the greenback was weakening. They were shocked to find that the Mint had been closed to silver 2 years earlier.

Anatomy of a Murder

Here is the step-by-step chronology of the passage of the bill that was to become the Coinage Act of 1873. It had the effect of eliminating the standard silver dollar unconstitutionally by failing ever to mention it. Since that coin was the only silver coin that could be struck in unlimited amounts for private accounts, it also meant the demonetisation of silver by the United States of America, following the example set by Germany.

(1) In 1868 senator John Sherman of Ohio sponsored a bill that, among other things, proposed that the Mint be closed to the coinage of the Constitutional silver dollar, thus demonetising silver in the United States. Although there was no opposition, the bill died in committee because the Senate was busy with other things, such as the greenback inflation struggle.

(2) Secretary Treasury Boutwell sent the bill (that was to become the Coinage Act of 1873 omitting the standard silver dollar) to Congress on April 25, 1870 with his strong recommendation for passage.

(3) The Senate passed the bill on January 10, 1871 by a vote

of 36 to 14. Among the ayes were the two senators from the silver state of Nevada. (At the time Nevada was the only silver state as it had been admitted to the Union in 1864. Colorado was the second admitted in 1876, followed by Montana, Idaho and Utah admitted between 1889 and 1896).

(4) The House passed the bill on May 27, 1872, by a vote of 110 to 13. Support among representatives from the silver state of Nevada was again overwhelming.

(5) President Grant signed the bill into law on February 12, 1873.

It is important to note that all the details, including the entire text of the bill, were in the public domain as early as April, 1870.

25 years later, in 1895, senator John Sherman, who was the sponsor of the bill in the Senate, in a famous speech of his entitled 'On the Crime of 1873' stated that, while the bill was pending in Congress for as long as three years, 'it was carefully considered in both houses and special attention was called to the omission of the standard silver dollar, and for the reasons for this omission…' It is strange that the very men who supported and urged this coinage law of 1873 and demanded the exclusive coinage of gold are the very men who now [in 1895] demand the free coinage of silver...

Later in that speech Sherman related that his colleagues, Senators Jones and Stewart of the silver states, were 'urgent and honest in saying that gold was the best and only standard of value'. However, they changed their minds when production from the Comstock Lode in Nevada [discovered in 1858] increased greatly, and the first signs of weaknesses in the silver price started to show ***after*** 1874. [12] Only then they wanted a market for their silver.

> They wanted themselves and their friends to pay existing debts and obligations, that had been contracted on a gold basis, in [devalued] silver; but took care in their own contracts to stipulate that debts owed to them were payable in gold.

International Monetary Conferences

While the United States fought out a civil war, first with arms in the field later with Acts of Congress, debtors against creditors, the French politician and statesman Félix Parieu [13] under Napoleon III, held international monetary conferences, the first on the occasion of the International Exposition in Paris of 1867. He did not do so on his own accord. Trouble had been brewing for a while. The Latin Monetary Union (See also Vol. IV) had been in operation since 23 Dec. 1865 and united France, Belgium, Switzerland and Italy in a common coinage agreement, with the intention of warding off collectively the international and intense silver speculation – enabled by the up and coming positivist movement (led by another Frenchman, Auguste Comte [14]) whose *animus dominandi* inspired French authorities to fix the ratio between gold and silver, in an attempt to 'control things.' The fixed ratio made arbitrage attractive and soon things spun 'out of control.'

As usual, the British press condescendingly named the Union 'Latin' (meaning Southern) opining the union could not possibly be extended to the Northern, obviously more civilised countries, such as the United Kingdom. The representatives of 20 countries met in Paris in June and July 1867 to discuss on unofficial terms how to achieve international monetary unification. The international conference was attended by all European countries, the U.S., Russia, China and the Ottoman Empire. Germany and the U.S. knew already in 1867 which plans others considered and that something was afoot. There was no conspiracy of a few against the rest of the world – it is all in the open.

> However... was the Franco-Prussian war of 1871 as a result of which a billion gold francs as indemnity were obtained, a coincidence, together with the Sherman-Boutwell sponsored Coinage Act passing the senate at the same time? One has to be politically naive, yet everything is possible.

Unwelcome Meddling

The international monetary conferences do not attract a lot of scholarly attention or study. An intense debate took place around this time and French ambitions showed every characteristic of an early European Monetary Union, although no credit ever goes to F. Parieu as one of the early founders... Nevertheless, the French proposals did not make it through Parliament. The French bureaucrats themselves, exercised in political side-tracking by way of employing special commissions, lingered on until the Germans stood in Paris, declaring the German unified Reich in Versailles. But even so, the French National Bank, a cartel of private banks amongst which we find Alphonse de Rothschild, objected to Félix Parieu's proposals, because French bankers knew that their French National Bank would be *de facto* the bank of last resort,[15] where all the silver and gold arbitrage would end up to their detriment, i.e. a gold outflow against the unlimited receipt of [by then superfluous] silver. For the keen observer: Banking houses knew something was afoot with silver, very visibly by 1871. Moreover, banks the world over made part of their money by the arbitrage in different national coins and by bimetallic arbitrage itself. Resistance to Parieu's plans of using gold only was massive and nationalism sabotaged the official plans of Parieu. France's ambitions of competing substantially against London went up in smoke, perhaps due to the family ties of the Rothschilds on either side of the Channel. In other words, if Parieu's scheme of s single gold standard (exit the bimetallic standard) would go ahead, there would be large inconveniences of getting rid of unsaleable silver and less profit opportunities, they thought. Some parties understood this better than others; the so-called dead idea became alive and very well executed during Bismarck's reign; he understood the card game of queen of hearts (ending up with all the silver) only too well. Germany and the U.S. demonetised first whilst the going was still good. I.e. the Chinese still accepted silver in unlimited quantities. It turns out that after the demoralising blow of the opium trade and wars, China imported almost the entire the world's silver. [16]

Smoking gun

In 1873 neither silver nor gold coins circulated in the United States, although the Mint was open to both metals. The country was on the 'greenback standard': irredeemable paper money issued by the Union to finance its efforts in the War Between the States, which circulated at a discount of about 13 percent to silver. It was understood, however, that gold payments on the notes would be resumed (as indeed it happened on January 1, 1879) and the greenbacks would ultimately be withdrawn from circulation pursuant to the Resumption Act of 1875. The question whether resumption was to be extended to silver payments as well was passed in silence.

The prospect of resumption could be the smoking gun prompting the international Banking houses to commit the crime. On April 9, 1865 (the day of Appomattox) and incredible opportunity to grab and usurp monetary powers presented itself. Obviously, resumption was coming, followed by a great increase in demand for gold and silver. This could be exploited most effectively for private gain if silver could somehow be eliminated as a monetary metal. The thing to do for the Banking houses and trusts was to initiate an arbitrage operation of selling silver mining shares against buying gold mining shares in anticipation of the demonetisation of silver.

Such an operation would take a number of years. By 1873, ten years later, following the German Empire, silver also had been demonetised in the United States through the back door, so to speak. Of course, speculators would start dumping silver in large quantities and selling it short, causing the price of silver to fall precipitously as early as 1868, when Senator Sherman first proposed silver demonetisation. [17] That never happened, making the whole affair very suspicious. The evidence appears to suggest that, far from being 'an honest mistake', the omission of the standard silver dollar to be minted was a deliberate act of destruction of individual property rights – possibly in collusion with Germany, but certainly silently so as not to forewarn short sellers. [18] These two start-up nations might have wanted to get the best mileage out of their respective victories in the battlefield. The indemnity of one thousand million dollars in gold exacted by Germany from France in 1871 would be that much more valuable, in view of the falling commodity price level in terms of gold.

> The banks in the North could greatly enrich themselves by making the mortgages they acquired on Southern land, denominated in silver, payable in gold. The extra value would come out of the hide of the victims of the War Between the States. The coincidence of interest of the two countries is telling. The would-be perpetrators of the crime had reason to make speculators behave differently from the norm. [19]

Circumstantial Evidence

The Banking houses in the North were apparently playing a duplicitous role. As observed above, there was profitable arbitrage possibility in the market for mining shares. The banks were betting against silver and were getting ready to profit from a prolonged decline in the price of silver. But it was not in their interest that the decline start immediately. They needed time to complete their arbitrage operations in mining shares. They wanted to get rid of their silver mining shares, without crashing the silver mining market, and replace them with gold mining shares, without overpaying for them. It is a plausible assumption, therefore, that the banks *temporarily supported* the price of silver (which they would have to do in the normal course of their business anyhow) but with the ulterior motive of preparing for the final assault on the silver price later. They succeeded to fool the speculators not to place their bets against silver. If the demonetisation of silver was not the result of a long-term market process (as suggested by virtually all economists) then the question is: what was it the result of? This question has never been satisfactorily answered. My answer is that it was the result of a collusion of banks and trusts secretly, perhaps, but silently for certain, manipulating the silver and gold market, as well as the carefully coordinated manipulating of the market for mining shares.

Leads and Lags

To prove (or disprove) my theory of a deliberate move on the part of some parties, I worked out a research program. It involved compiling the daily closing prices of eight series as follows:

(1) asked price of silver
(2) bid price of silver
(3) asked price of gold
(4) bid price of gold
(5) average asked price of silver mining shares
(6) average bid price of silver mining shares
(7) average asked price of gold mining shares
(8) average bid prices of gold mining shares

in the United States for the ten-year period from 1868, the year when the idea of demonetising silver first surfaced in Senator Sherman's committee, to 1878, the year when the Latin Monetary Union decided that the silver price has been mortally wounded, was beyond hope of recovering, and closed its last Mint to silver.

From the eight price series one can obtain four series of key price-spreads by taking differences as shown by tabulating them in the following table:

PRICE-SPREAD SERIES

series	arbitraging	
(4) minus (1)	from gold	to silver
(3) minus (2)	from silver	to gold
(8) minus (5)	from gold-mining shares	to silver-mining shares
(7) minus (6)	from silver-mining shares	to gold-mining shares

Next, one calculates the standard deviation from the means for each of the four price-spread series. By well-known theorems of mathematical statistics the standard deviation filters out 'noise', that is, random causes of price variations, but catches singular irregular causes (e.g., discovery of a major gold or silver ore deposit or, most especially, concentrated efforts to manipulate prices).

> One is looking for leads and lags. In particular, if arbitrage from silver-mining shares to gold mining-shares did lead arbitrage from silver to gold, and the latter lagged the former, then this would not be a random event. It would be conclusive proof that arbitrageurs were acting in unison to bring about a collapse of the silver price for maximum private gain.

When I wanted to carry out my research project, I found that it was beyond my meagre resources. Rather naively I assumed that most of the work had already been done, some of the price series had been compiled and some of the standard deviations from the means calculated.

> The collapse of the silver price after 1875 was so spectacular, it was such a precipitous and momentous event, involving the international monetary system, the wealth and welfare of so many people, literally changing the course of history, that some researchers at least could have questioned the 'conventional wisdom'. They could have rejected the market-process hypothesis. These researchers should have started looking for evidence of active connivance between governments and banks during the intervening 140 years.

This, however, does not appear to be the case. Everybody without exception has accepted the pat explanation [provided by Friedman] for the silver price collapse in terms of the QTM. Yet it is possible that 1875 marks the year when the conspirators completed their program of arbitrage from silver mining shares to gold mining shares; and started their follow-up program of arbitrage from silver to gold. It is not impossible to find out the truth about it some 140 years later. Researchers of today would have to start from scratch. This is a task I can no longer undertake, in view of my advanced age. But I would certainly encourage the younger generation to do it. I hope that my tentative research plan is going to be helpful to them. I have no doubt whatsoever that this would be a worthwhile project. I call attention once more to what above I have called 'circumstantial evidence' of monetary mischief. In the absence of mischief the silver price ought to have started its descent much earlier, several years before 1875 – possibly as early as 1868. Speculators (as distinct from bankers) must have been watching the political wrangle over silver starting in 1868. It appears that speculators missed their opportunity to sell silver short. This would be rather uncharacteristic of their trade, an assumption we can safely dismiss. A more plausible assumption is that the conspiring bankers met the speculators' short selling head-on. As pointed out already, they needed time to complete their program of arbitrage in the mining share market for monetary metals. Once it was completed, after they have sold their quota of silver mining shares and bought their quota of gold mining shares, they would be the first to dump their silver and let speculators do the rest. Of course, the duplicity of their conspiracy makes the detective work so much harder.

Monetary Mischief

There is no doubt that the U.S. Congress grossly exceeded its authority when it passed the Coinage Act of 1873. In signing it President Grant shared responsibility for making the unconstitutional bill the law of the land. The Act nowhere mentions the Constitutional standard silver dollar, the only coin cited by the Constitution – as if no such coin has ever existed. Consequently the interpretation arose that there was no authority for coining it by anyone after the Act became law. The contrast with the logical interpretation of the Constitution is striking. According to the Constitution the standard silver dollar can be minted in unlimited quantities for the account of anyone tendering the silver to the Mint. Not only is the standard silver dollar to serve as a yardstick but, even more importantly, it is there to test the material, silver, out of which the yardstick is made. If you eliminate or obstruct its availability, then the standard silver dollar obviously cannot discharge that function. It makes no sense to tie the access to it to permission from Congress, from the President, from the Secretary of the Treasury, or anyone else. This is a clear case of usurpation of powers. The standard silver dollar had to go because the public was to be deprived of a means to test the monetary quality of silver.

The Constitution guarantees the right of the individual to take silver to the Mint in unlimited quantities. Only in this way can we be certain that silver is sufficiently inelastic to serve as the yardstick of value. If the flow of silver to the Mint was orderly, then the yardstick would be satisfactory. But if the Mint were inundated with silver and could not be kept open for that reason, it would be proof that silver was no longer suitable to serve as material out of which the monetary yardstick can be made. It would show that silver had a rubber-like quality: it was far too elastic. It would show that silver has failed the test. It hasn't got the indispensable quality a monetary metal must have. As a matter of historical record, silver has never been put to the test. There has never been a run on the Mint by owners of silver bullion wanting to turn their metal into silver coin before it's too late. In every instance the run on the Mint occurred not because people feared that the price of silver will collapse, but because inane government policies made silver-to-gold arbitrage risk-free. People bought silver abroad in exchange for melted U.S. gold coins. They wanted to get more gold coins at the U.S. Mint for their silver – as was their right to do under bimetallism. Then they wanted to export the gold coin, since it was worth more abroad, and they wanted to continue this arbitrage indefinitely for the risk-free gain it afforded them. When the Mint was closed to silver, it was a protective measure taken by the government in trying to prevent further losses to its gold reserve. It was not a failure of silver. It was a failure of bimetallism, or better the fixing of a bimetallic ratio by positive law. The solution was not the demonetisation of silver: it should have been the abolition of the bimetallic ratio by statue law.

Whatever Happened to the Chinese Silver?

The most populous country, China has one of the oldest civilisations on earth. It had been on a silver standard since time immemorial before the Communists overran the mainland. Nobody knows how much silver was involved in running China's monetary system, but the amount must be mind-boggling. In addition, China was forced to absorb enormous amounts of silver (both through legal channels and through smuggling) after silver was demonetised by the rest of the world and the price of silver collapsed. We do know that this addition to the Chinese money supply created an inflation horrible enough to cause the fall of the Kuo-min-tang regime and the ascension of the Communists to power in 1949. When the entire world supply of silver ends up in one country, such exceptional situation suspends the autonomics of a market process. We do not know what proportion of the monetary silver the Communist government left in the hands of the people while confiscating the silver in the banks with characteristic ruthlessness. Finally, we have no idea whether or not China was buying silver clandestinely during the twenty-year period between 1980 and 2000 when the price was falling. Be that as it may, the silver left over from the silver-standard days, plus the silver subsequently flowing into China, is largely unaccounted for. The question is: where is this Chinese silver?

> It appears that China does hold the silver wild card, and hasn't played it yet.

We cannot blithely assume that China will play it stupidly. The possibility exists that China will play it intelligently. For all we know, China may already be active, if only clandestinely, in the silver market and has been deriving handsome profits from it. The alleged naked short positions in silver may in fact be genuine hedges for Chinese-owned silver. In other words, China may have decided upon a strategy to derive a steady income from her silver treasure, at least for as long as prices remain low, in preference to the alternative strategy of driving up the price of silver and then cashing in. We haven't examined the evidence and we do not suggest that this is the case. All we are saying is that there is another possibility that could explain the anomalous market behaviour for silver. One reason why we find the theory of inordinate and growing naked speculative short positions unattractive is because it assumes that the insiders are either stupid or suicidal or both. It is dangerous to underestimate one's opponents.

Serial Crimes of 1871, 1933, and 1971

The right of the people to free and unlimited coinage of silver at the Mint is carved into the corner-stone of the U.S. Constitution. This right was abolished with a sleight of hand in 1871. 'The Crime of 1871', as William Jennings Brian called the unconstitutional demonetisation of silver, may get its just punishment after a 130-year hiatus before our eyes. It wasn't an isolated crime. It was a serial crime through which politicians deprived the American people of all their Constitutional rights and prerogatives pertaining to money, that started even before 1871. The crime was repeated on a bigger scale in 1933 when a Democratic president tricked the American people out of their gold. The crime was crowned in 1971 when a Republican president tricked the rest of the world out of its gold, while inflicting a regime of irredeemable currency on the American people and everybody else. Although through the betrayal of the economists the people were left in darkness about what has happened to their money, these crimes cry to high heaven for justice. While we are somewhat doubtful about the theory of conspiring private parties, we find the theory of a secret government plot to suppress the price of silver plausible. It will become even persuasive if evidence of unloading silver and silver mining shares has taken place, as suggested in our research plan above. This plot may also include collusion between the governments of the United States and China to fend off a price explosion. According to this scenario China would supply cash silver to deliver against futures contracts, in return for the right to collect the income flowing from her short positions in silver. Even the obvious delivery problems cannot serve as conclusive proof that the insiders (also called 'silver managers') have rigged the silver market in an effort to cap the price. After all, the silver to be delivered may have to be brought in from China. That takes time. Silver analysts would do well to compile intelligence as to what percentage of the delayed deliveries to the Central Fund of Canada and other longs has originated in China. If it was a large percentage, then we would have evidence that the silver managers were neither stupid nor suicidal. They merely acted as the agents of the government China.

Conclusion

We have never been conspiracy theorists. We never joined latter-day crowds crying 'stop the manipulation of the silver and gold price by unlimited short sales!' We know full well that the present low price of silver is a remnant of the tragic outcome of the Silver Saga that started some 145 years ago at Appomattox. The prospect of Resumption of specie payments after the War Between the States created an incredible opportunity for monetary mischief. The circumstantial evidence suggests that the opportunity was fully exploited by an international banking cartel to 'sabotage' – at the very least profiteer from – the international monetary system. This observation does not make us conspiracy theorists. We are offering a detailed plan to find out, some 145 years after the event, using the method of standard deviations from the means borrowed from mathematical statistics. We owe it to ourselves to do the necessary research. The world economy, sagging under the weight of its debt tower and fast depreciating irredeemable currencies, is clearly on its way to self-destruction. The forcible elimination of, first, silver and then –a hundred years later– of gold from the monetary system removed the only ultimate extinguishers of debt we had. In consequence, total debt can only grow, never contract. The process is concealed from scrutiny since the unpaid and unpayable debt accumulates as sovereign debt of governments. The world deludes itself that sovereign debt can increase indefinitely as governments can extend its maturity indefinitely. In 2008 we had the wake-up call that it cannot.
Unless we stop the proliferation of debt, the world faces prolonged deflation, depression, continuing capital destruction, bankruptcies and unprecedented unemployment. It leads to a breakdown of law and order. It could spell the end of our civilisation.

Endnotes to Chapter 33

[1] The use of the $ indicates here that silver's exchange value is expressed in terms of a gold $, as defined by the U.S. constitution and not an irredeemable dollar, which would make an exchange value pointless.

[2] The prince of linear thinking, after Kemmerer, must be Milton Friedman, still widely read, and before him Fisher. Friedman succeeded in reviving a populist line of thinking, with positivist philosophy, although positivism had died out at the time of and with Max Weber. Positivism is a form of gnostic dualism, a dangerous deformation of thinking.

[3] In Germany, the monopolies in power at he last quarter of the 19th century are mostly Prussian state monopolies and cartels concerning the railways. Werner von Siemens and Krupps Steel stand out as private companies and still exist today. In France, the situation with monopolies looks very much like the German situation. A particular concentration can be found in Banking families like those of Rothschild (Paris), de Wendel, Millerand, Mirabaud etc. In Belgium, the largest and most infamous monopolist and slave owner used to be King Leopold II, whose private possessions included the Congo; his daughter Stéphanie married the Austrian-Hungarian Crown-Prince Rudolph; Turn & Taxis still exist; they used to have a the postal services monopoly in Europe; in the UK, we have Cecil Rhodes, de Beers, Rothschild and in the U.S. the Vanderbilts, Rockefeller, J.P. Morgan, Schwab, Carnegie, Gould, Field, etc. However, monopolies have existed worldwide, including China, Japan and Russia and not all monopolies came about as the result of connivance.

[4] Since most 'anti-capitalists' use the argument of what has happened under 'a gold standard' to disparage the latter, it is safe to assume that the anti-capitalist camp equally upholds the existence of criminal actions at a high level.

[5] George Selgin, *Good Money: Birmingham Button Makers, the Royal Mint and the Beginnings of Modern Coinage* (1775-1821), Institute of Economic Affairs, 2008.

[6] Some historians believe Newton inadvertently fixed the ratio, for it had been stable for a long time. This brings us to Murphy's law, which is another story.

[7] Alexander Hamilton preferred gold over silver for being less 'subject to change', recognising the better marginal utility of gold. But in democratic fashion, he accommodated other views and adopted a bimetallic standard, suing the correct market ratio's of the time. But if anything can be learned from history is that things change over time...

[8] L. Laughlin, *The History of Bimetallism in the United States*, p. 14, sums up the difficulties in adopting a monetary standard.

[9] Congress of the U.S. had sent a delegate to the French monetary conclaves of 1867 in Paris. Some people knew something was afoot with silver. Germany and other countries with large silver circulation ran the risk. The U.S. techni-

cally also, but there was no mass circulation at that moment. In fact, due to Gresham, silver obtained a better exchange ratio outside the Mint.

[10] Not all historians agree, but not all historians are equally naive.

[11] Germany had engaged its state railway enterprise in constructing a railway from Berlin stretching all the way to Bagdad. (See Morris Jastrow, *the Berlin to Bagdad Railway*), supra.

[12] Probably the silver was exported to China and perhaps India, who still accepted silver without question in payment for exports. Let us not forget that both China and India were under British influence.

[13] The French economist, politician and statesman Félix Esquirou de Parieu initiated French policy regarding monetary matters. Since all civilised countries were *de facto* using gold in trade, though each with their own coins, Parieu argued for a unification. He presided as vice-president and as Minister of the Council of State under Napoleon III over three international conferences and several national commissions where he set out his arguments and cause.

[14] Comte A. occurs in the endnotes of our Vol. II. Positivism or the brain child of Comte, is treated in Volume II, Chapter 16. For a full philosophical analysis of Comte see E. Voegelin, *From Enlightenment to Revolution.*

[15] Luca Einaudi, *Money and Politics : European Monetary Unification and the Gold Standard (1865-73)*, Oxford , 2001.

[16] This holds a lesson for the extreme, greedy gold collector: once all the gold ends up in one hand, the owner of the hand is not as 'rich' as he would think. Collecting gold in one place may demonetise gold...(temporarily, for holding on to the gold is not a given).

[17] Like Parieu in France, who had political and economic motives for unification, Sherman resembled the Frenchman, except the Civil War had already been decided. The monetary unification was not between the Unionists and Confederates, but about gold or silver.

[18] It would seem that a lot, if not all legislation where a public debate is 'undesirable' for its promotors, gets introduced in an 'oblique' way, that is under a title or section where one would not expect it. The U.S. silver demonetisation was arrived at, not by direct 'law' or 'statute' but rather by *not mentioning it* on the list of pieces allowed to be struck by the U.S. Mint, which is on a lower or administrative - technical level. Another modern way of 'Jekyll and Hide' games legislators play, is burying an innocuous looking provision with large consequences (those that are aimed for by the lobbyist) beneath thousands of other 'rules and regulations' having no connection with it and or introducing it on the last working day of Parliament or Congress when everyone is in a hurry to leave and in no mood for reading or discussing it ...

[19] Perhaps people ought to discard their naive belief in the noble aim of getting rid of slavery as the 'cause of war'...

Chapter 34

Act II: Giving Gold A Bad Name

" Gold legalisation will cause a major catastrophe, of the same magnitude as a Martian invasion or a nuclear attack...

Treasury Deputy Undersecretary Jack F. Bennett

Economic Hit Men

Whether or not the silver demonetisation in the U.S. was an accidental occurrence through omission, one may wonder. Equally so, the result of the above defined forensic analysis of the murder of silver, is not known. It may still be a coincidence. However, what followed after silver demonetisation in 1873, could not possibly be misunderstood or explained as accidental. Untangling United States political developments completely, would be outside our scope. But focussing on relevant monetary and Banking developments we notice that both the United States and Britain *systematically* dismantled the silver standard in other countries in the world, by hook or by crook, as well as by colonising. And they used the gold standard to do it.

The presidential election of 1896 provided a rallying opportunity and national opinion platform on the gold standard, resembling the 1810 currency vs Banking school debate in England. William Jennings Bryan in the U.S. enamoured the Democratic Party at its 1896 convention; he recognised what New York bankers in Wall Street (his own Morgan faction) had been doing so far: arbitrage between the greenback and the gold standard by abuse of legal positivism. The Republican Party on the other hand, backed by Ohio's Rockefeller, proposed William McKinley with a populist move of their own: ditching prohibition, with stood in the way of obtaining the vote of German and other immigrants. The Morgan faction, previously dominant in the Democratic Party struck a voting deal with the Rockefeller faction. The Morgan faction within the Democratic Party would support McKinley for president provided that McKinley left Wall Street (The Morgan faction) and the greenback-gold standard carry trade and its protectionist tariffs untouched. Elections are hardly about the purported issues such as prohibition or silver. It is all about the bigger interests, not hidden, just not talked about.

With McKinley safely elected, the united Morgan-Rockefeller forces started working on their own agenda. Going gingerly about their ultimate purposes, such move had to be concealed behind a respectable front like a 'broad grass-roots movement', very much like today's 'green movements' which, when scratched, will reveal different underlying motives – and colours…

Lo and behold, 1897 saw the U.S.'s own monetary convention hosted by the Indianapolis Board of Trade, but presided over by the Morgan-Rockefeller lieutenants. To the one-in-a-million who can see clear, any organisation featuring Henry Payne and George Foster Peabody meant but one thing: J.P. Morgan. All this happened in the aftermath of yet another bank panic (of 1893), during which all financial institutions had yet another close shave when confronted with their illicit interest arbitrage, reflected by an inverted yield curve. Determined not to be embarrassed again, the idea of a Bailout Bank, a.k.a. Reserve bank became urgent. Addressing illicit interest arbitrage did apparently not enter their minds.

At the opportunity of this crisis, in January 1898, the Morgan opinion engineering machine demonstrated its abilities buying or using countrywide newspapers and magazines, orchestrated by A. Conant *et al.*,[1] riding on the general discontent of the U.S. panic of 1893. The Banking and currency reform (the Morgan and Rockefeller version, that is) had arm-wrestled itself to political prominency.[2] Many of its delegates consisted of academics like Jenks, Taussig, or Laughlin, but the whole congregation affaire seemed to have taken over the role of the earlier Monetary Conventions held in France. One of the commissioners writings in nominal support of the gold standard, but nevertheless expressing the strong wish for a bailout bank, found its way to the library of Carl Menger. [3] The U.S. Gold Standard Act provided for a single gold standard, without role for silver money except a token role and buried deep within the legislative bill, clauses will be found allowing for more national banks – the precursor of the Federal Reserve Bank – providing credit to farmers at harvest time, to counter the rigidity of currency at times of need. [4] Of course, this was only a small step, reformers said. One professor even branded the U.S. Banking system as the world's worst, comparing the U.S. to Britain and France, who did have a (Rothschild controlled) central bank.[5]

Meanwhile, U.S. Marines paid an unannounced visit, to Cuba and to the islands around the United States. The spanking brand new U.S.S. Maine warship somehow managed to blow up; it sank in Havana harbour, probably the result of living too close to gun powder and the 1898 revolt of the islands against colonial Spain turned into a U.S. war against Spain – for retribution in the form of territorial concessions:

Cuba, Haiti, Dominican islands, Puerto Rico, Panama, Philippines etc. J.P. Morgan bankers followed on the heels of the Marines: Arthur Conant, a J.P. Morgan lieutenant, orchestrated the entire operation of financial annexation aided by later Edwin Kemmerer, both nicknamed 'money-doctors'; they 'convinced' these new territories to move from their Spanish silver reals to a 'gold-exchange' or dollar standard. [6] Perhaps U.S. bankers had learned how to transfer exchange value from silver to gold in the mean time? These country's currency, would henceforth consist of 'token' silver coins of low value, yet tied to the dollar (or for the U.K. territories: the pound sterling), both in turn redeemable for gold on demand. All transactions in the old silver currency would be taxed out of existence and the U.S or Britain put an import ban on the old silver coins. The new U.S. 'conant' coins of low silver content (and much higher nominal value) were soon followed by copper and irredeemable paper money.

In this way countries tied themselves into the US monetary system. A gold exchange or dollar standard (rather than a true gold standard) ensured these countries used paper dollars as their reserve currency, nominally exchangeable for gold at par, except for the colonies, that is.

First in line to adopt the US doctored system after the US took over control from Spain in 1898 happened to be Puerto Rico. Many followed. The Philippines, the last Spanish colony, in 1905. However, the Philippines used the Mexican real, well known for its soundness and widely used as money outside Mexico. The cunning US plan called for replacing the Mexican silver dollar with a debased American silver coin 'tied to gold'. After implementation, the immediate fall off in purchasing power would have been absorbed in seigniorage booty by the U.S. Banking cartel. The Philippines however, would not fall for such chicanery. Not willingly, so the U.S. Marines 'convinced' them instead.

Mexico and China, both mentioned in Conant's paper since they sent a representative to his monetary conference, had a strong silver standard ingrained in the public psyche and China was indeed a major user of the Mexican real just as well. Mexico converted to the proposed U.S. gold standard (i.e. seigniorage for the Morgan cartel) with 'relative' ease; China refused the British proposal though, having not forgotten the Sassoon family, known as the 'Rothschilds of the East', but notorious for aiding the British trade surplus with China in the form of contraband opium smuggling. [7] The British Marines helped to change the Emperor's mind nevertheless. China soon replaced the Mexican silver dollar in public protest with their own currency called the tael. The same fate befell India in 1898 already, under British 'influence'.

Gold Crisis or Illicit Arbitrage?

Meanwhile in Europe, to quote C. Kindleberger: 'Gold discoveries in California (1848) and Australia (1851) led to exports spurts to those countries…' [8] which does not surprise us, for *that is exactly the practical result of the theory we insist on in Vol. II.* Moreover, C. Kindleberger adds : '...and enlarged the credit bases in Europe and the United States.' which can only mean illicit interest arbitrage between the real bills market and the bond market to finance other projects than international trade, but with the social circulating fund as source instead of saved capital. It is that vast body of silver or gold circulating coin that fuels daily living and it circulates permanently: from paper boy, shoe shiner to grocer, taxi driver and butcher, etc. The propensity to consume necessarily operates on a very short time basis. Tapping into the social circulating fund to finance projects not driven by any propensity to consume, will necessarily cause shortages in the circulating fund to manage daily living. Not surprisingly then, bankers speak of shortages of coin or even fiduciary money, since all of it has been sunk into long term projects and its reflux into the Banking or deposit system proves inadequate to replenish the social circulating fund. Aided by substandard credit standards under the stock broking houses, such shortages crystallise into an inversion of the yield curve. Inevitably it will soon lead to panics and bank runs that Carl Menger would have experienced and known about: black Friday, 11 May 1866, which coincided for good reason into the Prussian victory over Austria at Königgrätz. Various panics and bank runs occurred on both sides of the ocean, some inter-connected like dominoes, but all reducible to illicit interest arbitrage (maturity mismatch – see Vol. I and II) and resulting in yield curve inversion with panic & bank run. A significant crisis occurred again in the year 1873, during the opening days of the Vienna International exhibition, two years after Menger published his Principles. Whilst expecting to draw in financiers from abroad by its prestige, the exhibition opened on the day the markets suffered liquidity anxiety and instead of prestige and attracting foreign investments, Viennese expectations suffered a bloody nose. Economists explain this panic of 1873 with various ad hoc reasons, such as 'rampant speculation' or silver demonetisation by Germany. All remedies offered call for the same solution: let the central bank provide liquidity...[9] Hence, since the string of panics did occur both in Europe and the U.S., one finds that the charters of various central banks were systematically adapted to accommodate more treasury debt in their portfolio as reserve or backing, instead of real bills maturing into gold. [10] Central banks started out as private banking cartels having real bills, maturing into gold (or silver) in portfolio, to having less real bills and more government bonds, until they only had government bonds in portfolio as backing for their coins (mostly token) and notes (entirely fiat). In the U.S. which did not have a central bank until 1913, the credit expansion was fuelled by territorial conquests and seigniorage shenanigans performed by the Morgan and Rockefeller cartels, who monetised Treasury bonds with their own notes.

Illicit Arbitrage Across Borders: Sovereign Debt Crisis

Barings Bank worked itself into the newspapers more than once. The first time with baron Edward Baring, having used short term credit from its London branch (real bills discounting) into speculative South American ventures (bonds) that went belly up. Barings London failed in 1890 and won the dubious award of first bank causing a sovereign debt crisis. Unfortunately for Britain, the City of London never again played the same role after 1890. J.P. Morgan in the U.S. did not get where he was by sitting idly on his hands: he filled the power vacuum that the British were vacating.

But Britain was far from knock out. Like the U.S., Britain installed a reserve currency system in their colonial possessions. Its satellite central banks in India, Hong Kong, Australia or South Africa used the pound as reserve currency, entitling the colonial reserve banks to nominally profit from the good standing the British pound enjoyed under its nominal gold standard. Of course, playing 'acceptance bank' all over the world, whilst financing both merchants and governments, railway projects and more of this type of maturity mismatching, does give rise to liquidity crises at various inconvenient intervals. American Austrian economists prefer to talk of 'inflationism' whilst they actually mean maturity mismatching [11] causing reserve banks to 'expand the monetary base' once [12] the inverted yield crisis hits the proverbial fan. Nominally the pound and the dollar could be redeemed on demand on a one for one basis for a unit of gold designated by these concepts. That is, until people in droves start insisting on redeemability.

Currency School vs. Banking School debate – An Evergreen

Today's economics students do not have to nor want to study economic history intensely. One such historical debate that one ought to know nevertheless if one is to call oneself an economist, would be the debate mentioned above and held in England around 1810. A full background may be obtained from reading the eminent French professor Charles Rist [13] – translated into English as well. The entire debate had been engendered by a crisis, (again) after specie payments in England had been suspended on the occasion of a French revolutionary invasion of England. However, the ensuing bank runs did far more damage than scaring the inhabitants of Fishguard in Wales for an entire two days. [14] The nation's best and most eloquent entered the debate from which two sides may be grossly distilled: the Currency School and the Banking School. Ricardo and Thornton led the Currency School. The proponents of the Currency School proposed and pleaded for a strict limit on on the expansion of the money supply to curb price inflation. A proposition that sounds too good to be true especially because it sounds so simple. The adherents of the Banking School argued that Real Bills could not be inflationary as both goods and money existed all along and at the moment of the payment by the consumer, the real bill will be removed together with the goods. Such 'expansion' is temporary and elastic enough to allow for seasonal peaks. Menger's notes and remarks on Ricardo enlighten us on why exactly he rejects Ricardo's position and sides with Adam Smith and the real bills 'doctrine'. However, neither side in the above debate laid the finger upon the real wound: interest arbitrage from the cheaper bill market with the more expensive bond market. Discounters using short term funds to feed into the longer term market, causing a maturity mismatch also known as a liquidity problem. [15] That indeed forms the crux of the problem of bank runs that do not end very well. Everyday, in a commercial bank's portfolio 1/90th of the portfolio value falls due and can be paid in specie without a glitch. Unless...

Imperial Toolbox

At the end of the 19th century, Britannia ruled the waves, but also the financial world, at least up to around 1890, when Barings brought The City ill repute ... To the British public, the French foreign office was attempting to attack British financial hegemony with the International Monetary Conferences of 1867. In other words, the issue became politicised and ideologues always lurked behind every move. Whilst U.S.

trusts exploited through monopoly and state privileges the general public, bypassing the sovereignty of the consumer under a gold standard, Mr. Marx agitated British, French, German and Russian masses with dubious pamphlets. Privileges and monopolies in the U.K. and on Continental Europe equally bypassed the sovereignty of the consumer under a gold standard. All parties, and that included the Japanese, abused the gold standard, or at least the illicit interest arbitrage perpetrated under its cover, to suppress real bills in the portfolio of issuance banks, which had to be replaced by acceptance bills and Treasury bonds as 'backing' to enlarge their monopolistic green cheese production, a.k.a. manufacturing paper money and synthetic credit. Most of which went into dousing the fire of illiquidity and bank runs/panics, caused by maturity mismatching and lax credit standards.

British shipping continued to rule the waves. [16] It needs to be remembered that Rudolph Diesel, a German engineer, developed a marine diesel engine, put to work in the Danish MS Selandia in 1912. The British Admiralty followed developments and could not have ignored Germany's efforts for building, not only the first marine diesel engine, but also a railway straight to the diesel source: Bagdad. The British Admiralty did not like this one bit. Imperialism around the turn of the century ran at its extremes. The U.S. 'civilised' ex-Spanish territories, in the name of 'humanity,' if not J.P. Morgan. China's Qing dynasty succumbed to internal strife after the Chinese had to prostrate themselves to all sorts of foreign influences, especially Japanese colonisation. The City of London lost a major source of income, having to share China with the U.S., Germany, France and Russia. Germany, Italy and the U.S. were late-comers to the imperial game of colonisation. Think again why World War I followed ...

As usual, in anticipation of the war, specie payments in Europe were lifted, in 1909 in France and Germany. The French legislation can only be found by scrutinising social laws that allowed major changes under cover of darkness: in casu the French social law of forcing any employer of paying the worker's wages, no longer in kind, but in specie or its equivalent at the option of the employer. French wages and salaries were paid in bank notes, issued by the Rothschild's *Banque Nationale*. In Germany, the twenty and fifty mark notes, issued by the *Reichsbank* became legal tender; the use of cheques and postal orders were introduced with the aim of reducing the demand on specie, which was hoarded by the *Reichsbank*. [17] German military planned an invasion of Belgium as early as 1905.

Across the Atlantic, the U.S. fared no better. U.S. bank notes flowed from its National Banks system, which legally forced all other state or municipal banks or discounters to keep their reserves with the National banks. **In other words, the National Banks belonged largely to J.P. Morgan companies** and its state monopoly subjected all other banks to itself. The same happened in its colonies obtained from Spain: Haiti, Cuba, etc.

Lest one thinks the world was not perfectly divided yet, the Japanese Empire expanded its power over territories we now know as Manchuria, Taiwan and Korea. All western countries had some form of financial system in place like a Reserve or national bank, exploiting seigniorage and, though nominally on a gold standard, all of them hoarded gold instead of enabling its circulation. Germany, thanks to Wilhelm von Humboldt's 'education' policy, gave rise to a massive boost in the hard sciences such as chemistry as well as mechanical and electrical engineering. Germany's universities attracted students from the U.S., Great Britain, France Russia and even Japan. The French attitude of positivism, promoted by Auguste Comte, still managed to dominate the humanities, but the success of the hard sciences made the humanities, such as literature, culture, art and philosophy less attractive. Except for economics as part of sociology. It strangely managed to combine positivism and mechanical engineering logic in a linear Quantity Theory of Money and equilibrium wizardry. Although dead as a doornail, mathematical economics is propped up by hook or crook. Remember Bacon and his hall of fame for meritorious scientists in the service of their country ?

Serfs of the Leviathan

Legal tender legislation made the impression on the minds of some people that the government had the power to create value out of nothing by stamping a higher value on a lower-valued piece of metal.

> They saw the legislation, not as an obligation imposed on the government in accordance with the original intention but, rather, as an obligation imposed on the citizens.

Out of this misrepresentation of the original legal tender legislation, which in no way intended to limit the freedom of the individual, grew the Leviathan. It disenfranchised the savers and labourers. If legal tender legislation can make worn gold coins and cheap silver coins circulate at a face value higher than that of metallic content, then it can also make paper circulate at *arbitrary* values.

Enemies of monetary freedom [18] argued thus: making paper money legal tender [19] could be used to subjugate a free people, reducing them to the status of serfs in the service of the Leviathan, without their realising just what is happening to them.

Badmouthing Goldsmiths

Nevertheless, a problem had to be overcome. All the bank notes in circulation were issued in large denominations. They were used only by people knowledgeable about the market, the condition of the banks, and about the credit of the government. The goldsmith did not issue bank notes of small denominations. His clients would have no use for it and would not take them either. If the 'Great Fraud' [allegedly the over issuance of goldsmiths' receipts as circulating money] was to succeed, then it was necessary for the government to pull off a coup. Small bank notes should be put into circulation, and the labouring classes had to be mesmerised into accepting them.

Small and Ugly

The introduction of bank notes of small denomination was inextricably intertwined with the granting of special privileges by the government to the banks of issue (banks authorised to issue bank notes). Invariably, these special privileges were highly detrimental to the public interest, and should have never been granted. The patent (monopoly) was reward for the favour of banks to monetise government debt. In practice, this meant that the banks were allowed to have a fiduciary issue of bank notes against government paper in addition to (but indistinguishable from) bank notes issued against gold and self-liquidating bills of exchange. The paper backing the fiduciary issue included government bonds and notes that the Treasury was unable to sell to the general public. These bonds and notes were automatically reissued upon expiry – that is: rolled over. In effect, the bank was carrying a perpetual government debt. This it could do only because the bank was able to pass the burden on to the shoulders of the general public in the form of non-interest-bearing paper: small bank notes. Thus fiduciary currency, far from being a present good as suggested by Mises, is the worst possible type of future good one can have! The burden was passed on to the public, and the banks pocketed risk-less profits in the form of interest payments by the government, not passed on to the note-holders, obviously. They had no idea...

Please note that it would not work with the issue of large bank notes. Holders of large notes would hang on to them for as short a period of time as was absolutely necessary, and then would pass them on to others, or would return them to the bank – for redemption. Small is beautiful from the bank's point of view, but it is certainly ugly from that of the public.

A case in point is the establishment of the Bank of England. King Charles II had borrowed gold from the goldsmiths of London who held it on deposit from some 10,000 depositors. In 1672 the King refused to repay the loan and, naturally, the crown was having great difficulties in borrowing money thereafter. The goldsmiths presented their claims against the King in 1691 and, out of the agreement hammered out, the Bank of England was born. William Paterson, a Scotsman, offered to advance 1 million pounds to the government against its bonds on the following conditions:

(1) the bonds were to pay interest at 6½ percent per annum,
(2) there was also a management fee to be paid,
(3) the government granted the bank monopoly to issue bank notes in the London area.

The notes of the Bank of England became legal tender in 1694, and the intervening three centuries did not afford an opportunity for the government to retire the bond against which the original 1 million pound worth of bank notes were issued. It will probably be retired only when the pound will have lost the remainder of its value.

Mises also considers the problem of small bank notes. 'For reasons which were connected with certain views on the nature of notes it was thought that the circulation of notes of small denomination ought to be opposed. The battle against the one pound note in England ended with the complete victory of the sovereign – the one pound gold coin'. [20] 'Old British banking doctrine banned small bank notes (in their opinion, notes smaller than five pounds) because it wanted to protect the poorer strata of the population, supposed to be less familiar with the condition of the banking business and therefore more liable to be cheated by the wicked bankers.' [21] There appears a disturbing misprint on p. 494 where Mises talks about his proposed new gold standard for the United States (apparently not a translation error, for Mises wrote in English himself in 1952). 'It does not require any special mention that the new-stock legal-tender notes to be issued by the Conversion Agency must be issued only in denominations of one dollar or fifty dollars and upward'. For this to make sense, I think, the words 'one dollar or' should be deleted. That is to say, Mises in 1952 advocated a new gold standard for the United States which would have excluded small bank notes. Unfortunately, he did not exclude 'legal-tender status' for the larger ones.

Special Privileges Granted to Banks

It should be clear at once that under the pact between the government and the banks of issue the smooth redemption of bank notes has been seriously undermined, if not made outright impossible. It was no longer true that one-ninetieth of the banks assets matured every single day of the year, bringing in plenty of gold coins to satisfy normal demand. Nor was it likely that the banks could meet abnormal demand through liquidating assets.

Whereas real bills were highly marketable and could be easily liquidated through discounting at any time on short notice, government bonds had low marketability and their liquidation could involve the bank with losses. In fact, these losses could be quite substantial, in some cases they would wipe out the bank's entire capital. The banks were no longer in the position to operate on the same basis as before. They could no longer make good on their promise to redeem their notes in gold coin on demand.

The banks could continue operation only under special dispensation from the government. The dispensation was designed to protect the banks against the ire of their creditors in case of insolvency. The banks were given special privileges in the form of a patent which made it virtually impossible for their creditors to have legal recourse in forcing liquidation in case the banks failed to perform on valid contracts and obligations. But for the patent, should the bank fail to live up to its promise to pay, creditors would satisfy themselves from the proceeds of the liquidation of the banks' assets.

In effect the new dispensation meant the establishment of a double standard, one for the banks, and another for everybody else, in adjudicating cases that involved contract law. The banks, under the protection of the patent, enjoyed special privileges. They could disguise their breech of faith with creditors under solemn-sounding euphemisms. They could declare a 'bank holiday' or a 'suspension of convertibility', they could 'stand still' or 'go off gold' – and the use of any number of linguistic innovations to cover up the fact of fraudulent bankruptcy. By contrast, other firms had to face the music if they could not perform on their contracts: their creditors could force their liquidation. Banks have grown traditionally out of large traders that grew even larger with a little help from their friends in the bureaucracy or governmental bodies. [22] Like a heat-seeking missile, they have **a natural penchant**

for financing election campaigns (any and all side), governmental protection, monopoly and sole trading or other privileges. [23]

Mesmerising the Labouring Classes

Still, the conspiracy between the government and the banks of issue would have been transparent and easy to expose if it wasn't for the trick that was employed to throw dust into the eyes and confuse the minds of the people. The trick was to maintain the pretence that there was a great unsatisfied demand for bank notes of small denomination out there. It was the government's responsibility to mint gold coins for circulation, so it had to provide a substitute in case of a dearth of gold. The idea was to put over on the public the notion that the fiduciary issue was necessary in order to meet the demand for small bank notes. The argument is disingenuous.

The allegation that gold coins would be in short supply if they were dispersed in the hand of the saving and consuming public is spurious. As we have seen, the producers of consumer goods did not need gold to finance their operations. They could use real bills as a means of exchange. Every urgent and legitimate business transaction in the service of the consumer gives grounds for drawing bills. The greater the urgency, the easier it is to discount commercial paper drawn against the movement of merchandise destined to satisfy consumer demand. Long-term business investments, on the other hand, should be financed by appealing to the saving public for accommodation, and the going rate on long-term funds should be paid. As long as these guidelines were followed, there could be no dearth of gold coins.

> There was no genuine demand for bank notes of small denomination. Had there been such a demand, the goldsmith would have put them into circulation. The idea of a dearth of gold is a red herring. The issuance of bank notes of small denomination was clearly a ***ploy to fool labour***. Gold and silver coins were drained from the pockets of labourers and other people of small means. When wage earners lost their right to demand gold and silver in exchange for their services, and dust was thrown into people's eyes in the form of bank notes of small denomination, the stage was set for the Great Fraud.

Thou Shalt Not Press down upon the Brow of Labour This Crown of Thorns!

We may paraphrase Daniel Webster as follows:

> *'Of all the contrivances for cheating the labouring classes of mankind, none has been more effective than that which deludes them with small-denomination paper money.'*

It was not the bank note per se, but the bank note of small denomination, that was instrumental in cheating the wage-earner out of his fair wages. The distinction is significant.

> The wage earner is supposed to be paid in gold or silver coin. This is his Constitutional right. With gold and silver coins jingling in his pocket he was the unquestioned master of the market place. His wishes were sacrosanct to all vendors and producers. He was the proverbial boss who was 'always right'. Bereft of his gold and silver coins he was reduced to the station of a serf. Important decisions such as what to produce, when, and how much, are now made without consulting him.

He's inundated now with obnoxious merchandise from unhealthy food through gimmicks with built-in obsolescence, to the lowest quality entertainment including pornography. As pointed out above, the excuse of a dearth of gold is lame. But even if we assume, for the sake of argument, that there had been a dearth of gold, for that the blame belongs to the government and the banks. A dearth of gold is always an indicator of one or both of the following:

(1) the banks are pursuing unsound credit policies, such as constructing a debt-pyramid upon a slim or non-existent gold base, or conducting illicit interest arbitrage in borrowing short to lend long.

(2) the government is trying hard to monetise its debt, that is, make the banks buy the bonds it could not sell to the public.

The dearth of gold is merely a reflection of public distrust in the unsound and dangerous policies of the banks and the government. William Jennings Bryan, fiery orator, populist politician, and unsuccessful three time presidential candidate said at the National Democratic Convention in Chicago in 1896: 'Thou shalt not press down upon the brow of labour this crown of thorns. Thou shalt not crucify mankind upon this cross of gold.' Bryan thought that gold was the *enemy* and silver the *friend* of the working people, and the gold standard was the rich man's ploy to enslave labour. Unfortunately, in looking for adversaries he missed the real enemy of the labouring classes: paper (i.e. the greenback) [24]

Thou Shalt Not Crucify Mankind upon this Cross of Paper!

The Constitution of the United States provides for a metallic monetary standard for the country. This still stands. Those who run the monetary system of the country could not face a Constitutional debate to change that (although they forced Switzerland to change her Constitution). This is indicative of the bad faith that permeates our present monetary system. Its managers would sooner open themselves to charges that theirs is an unconstitutional monetary regime than muster the necessary courage to propose changing this provision of the Constitution. They obviously have something to hide.

The Constitutional provision for a metallic monetary standard was not a rich man's ploy. It was grounded in the Founding Fathers' genuine regard for the welfare and advancement of the labouring classes. The gold and silver coins are the protectors of the wage earner.

The rich man can usually protect himself against monetary mischief even without them. But collective agreements and wage contracts are not worth the paper on which they are written, if gold and silver coins in circulation do not give them substance. History proved the wisdom of the Founding Fathers. In 1971, as the Republic was approaching its bicentennial, there was nobody to cry loud and clear: 'Thou shalt not crucify mankind upon this cross of paper money!' The world had quietly submerged in an ocean of worthless paper. The debasement of the dollar that started in 1971 had reached unprecedented proportions in American history. As a side effect, the labour movement in the United States was greatly weakened, unions getting decertified as bargaining agents by the hundreds, in no small measure because labour leaders have failed to stand up for the monetary provisions of the Constitution. This was a betrayal not only of the Constitution, but also the traditions of the labour movement, as shown by the leadership of Ely Moore, the first union official ever to have been elected to the Congress in 1834. The ploy of turning the Constitutional monetary regime into a paper-mill aimed at depriving wage-earners of their right to wages payable in silver and gold coins has succeeded beyond the wildest dreams of its authors. There was not one single labour leader, in 1971 or since, to protest and to initiate a public debate exposing the unconstitutionality of this high-handed and arrogant way of trampling on the people's most elementary rights.

CHAPTER 34

Understanding the Gold Market

Before the United States defaulted on its obligations in 1968 and subsequently demonetised gold in 1971 all economists, including the arch-conservative Ludwig von Mises, predicted that demonetisation would send the price of gold [25] way down. They pointed to the episode of silver demonetisation one hundred years earlier, followed by the collapse of the price of silver. They also adduced a pseudo-theoretical argument that the disappearance of the lion's share of demand, namely the monetary demand, cannot help but make inroads into the gold price.

Of course the economists fell on their face when gold was demonetised yet its price, instead of falling, rose more than twenty-fold in less than ten years. Nobody dared to confront the economists with their embarrassing failure. Why did they fail so miserably? I shall now give the answer to this so far unanswered question. The economists fell victim to one of the most elementary fallacies known as *post hoc ergo propter hoc* (after this, therefore because of this). When silver was demonetised in 1871, no government default was involved. Owners could continue to redeem their silver certificates without let or hindrance. Since its price showed a falling trend, a lot of people rushed in to sell silver. Even the silver mines redoubled their efforts to produce all the silver left in the shafts, before they had to be closed down and abandoned for good. Genuine silver mines have all but disappeared. Whatever silver production survived was byproduct from the gold and copper mines. It was not *demonetisation* that caused the price of silver to fall but *dumping*, official and unofficial, that followed it.

By contrast, the demonetisation of gold a hundred years later was a default on the gold obligations of the U.S. government. Nobody has ever seen a dishonoured promise to go to a premium. Yet this is exactly what the economists were predicting that would happen to the dollar. The gold obligations of the U.S. were internationally recognised. By the Bretton Woods Treaty of 1944 that was responsible for hatching the IMF, foreign governments could treat their dollar balances as gold-equivalent at the rate of $35 to one oz of gold. These gold obligations were solemnly reconfirmed by three sitting presidents. Browbeaten by Washington, foreign governments wouldn't dare to protest the breach of faith and the unilateral abrogation of international obligations. They meekly swallowed the loss that arose. They pretended that nothing much happened and the dollar was still as good as gold. They ignored the market and continued to count their dollar balances at 'the official price at which the U.S. Treasury refused to sell gold'. They called it the 'two-tier monetary system'. Of course, that hare-brained scheme could not endure. The market trumped the governments, as it always does when they do something foolish. It is interesting to note that the financial annals are silent on the biggest default in history. Well, you can get away with it if you are the paymaster of the annalists. As there was no point in pretending any more that the dollar was as good as gold, the U.S. government put measures in effect designed to drive down the price of gold or, at least, to prevent it from rising further. IMF gold auctions were followed by U.S. Treasury auctions. Both backfired badly. The market obliged in bringing down the price of gold temporarily to allow the IMF and the US Treasury to unload the bothersome surpluses. But no sooner had the auction been completed than the price of gold returned to its pre-auction level to resume its upward march.

It is hard to find another example of such an inane market action in the long catalog of government blunders. If a bank needs to sell an asset, then it does so discretely in order that it may fetch the best possible price. Fanfare and the Dutch auction method were used for their propaganda value in demonstrating how the price falls when gold is put on the block. It is clear that these gold auctions were not an exercise in high finance but one in low propaganda. More recently the Bank of England auctioned off more than half of her gold reserves at record low prices, to replace it with U.S. government securities at record high prices. In doing so the Bag Lady of Threadneedle Street was replacing her best asset gold, that is nobody's liability, with the worst, obligations of a default-happy government. This made the portfolio of the bank weaker, not stronger. Once again, the completion of the auction gave the green signal to gold that it may resume its upward move.

It should be abundantly clear that in sacrificing their remaining ordnance governments are fighting a desperate rear-guard action in an effort to fool the public. In this situation it is puerile to call for a free market in gold and to go to court accusing the government of price manipulation. Once more without trying to refute the conspiracy theory I wish to point out that, given the idiosyncrasies of the regime of irredeemable currency, the uniform action of 'the shorts' may find a spontaneous explanation. The gold mining executives, the bullion bankers, and other speculators may read the mind of the government and central bank manipulators in the same way.

Endnotes to Chapter 34

[1] Charles Conant set forth his theory of surplus capital in *A History of Modern Banks of Issue* (1896) and in other writings, such as 'The Economic Basis of 'Imperialism'' (1898), *The North American Review* vol. 167, pp. 326-340. Curiously, Keynes in 1934 **does not ever refer to Conant as a source**. Perhaps he not only 'borrowed' Conants' concepts of surplus capital but he studiously avoided reference to 'Imperialism' especially because the British in the person of Cecil A. Rhodes and others knew a thing or two about imperialism...?

[2] With a self-made panic at the expense of the public.

[3] See C. Menger Library housed in Hitotsubashi University, Japan : *Stability of International Exchange: explanations and opinions on the proposals of the Mexican and Chinese governments to the government of the United States transmitted to Congress by President Roosevelt on Jan 29, 1903* - prepared for the Commission on International Exchange. By Hugh H. Hanna, Charles A. Conant, Jeremiah W. Jenks, commissioners. Washington D.C. Gibson Bros, 1903. We have not studied this volume for remarks of Carl Menger. It is outside our possibilities, but it would nevertheless be interesting to know if he made any notes in this publication and what his position was at the time. It would be interesting to know if Menger were supportive of the gold standard as proposed by the new International Monetary Commission and or whether or not he could see through the veil of manipulations orchestrated by the Morgan-Rockefeller factions.

[4] How noble of the National Banks, under J.P. Morgan and Rockefeller. Since time immemorial, harvests have been financed with appropriate instruments such as cooperatives, (grain) elevators, futures and forward contracts. The U.S. Gold Coinage Act, despite its name, lay the groundwork for more illicit interest arbitrage between bill market and bond market.

The National Banks had obtained privileges granted by the administration to subordinate all other banks under the National banks, owned by large cartels run by J.P. Morgan, Rockefeller etc, with the monopoly of issuing paper dollars against its assets: gold (not silver), Treasury bonds, merchants real bills and others. By 1900 not a single real bill, maturing in gold coin, was to be found in the assets column of these National banks, issuing de facto partially backed (or is it half-baked?) dollar notes against Treasury debt.

[5] See Joseph F. Johnson, 'The Currency Act of March 14, 1900' Political Science Quarterly 15, 1900, pp. 482-507. In fairness, of course, European bank runs did exist and how. That will be treated under the next heading. Morgan would not achieve his ultimate goal of a central bailout bank until 1913, on the eve of World War I.

[6] Everything known about these men reads like John Perkins, *Confessions of An Economic Hit Man*, Berrett Koehler, San Fransisco, 2004. The economic hit man is charged with paving the way by hook or crook, propaganda or intimidation. The first 'recognised' function of economic hit man, a.k.a. 'special advisor,' seems to be Kermit Roosevelt, a son of Theodore Roosevelt, sent to Persia. The gold-exchange dollar worked on the same basis as the later gold bullion-exchange after Bretton-Woods, some forty years later.

[7] The U.S. ran a deficit trade with China whilst the British traded at a deficit with China

[8] C.P. Kindleberger and Aliber, *Manias, Panics and Crashes, A History of Financial Crises*, 5th ed. p. 116.

[9] Menger was in possession of the volume: *Die Spekulationskrisis von 1873*, by Joseph Neuwirth, Leipzig, Duncker & Humblot, 1874. In it, Von Neuwirth describes the illiquidity that overcame the Vienna Stock Exchange and which would call for central bank intervention, in the same vein as C.P. Kindleberger. Again, it would be instructive to know what Carl Menger remarked, if anything, inside or upon this volume. We have to leave this question to historians.

[10] That must have been a serious limitation on credit expansion or speculation. Maturity matching means one cannot live beyond one's means...and brings credit standards in line with best credit practises. Obviously, the frustration can be overcome - be it temporarily- with more treasury bill backing (based on taxation) instead of real bills maturing into gold.

[11] The American Austrian School choose the Currency School side in the debate of the Currency v. Banking School, held in the 19th century. They follow von Mises, whilst we have indications that such a position cannot be maintained if one follows Adam Smith or Carl Menger's logic. Since we do our own research and think for ourselves, we tend to discover support in Menger and Smith and point out that mainstream Keynesians, Friedman monetarists and contemporary Austrians have taken a doctrinaire and wrong stance, without much sense of history or reality. To be sure, both sides in the debate had salient points. A proper scientist separates science from opinion or doctrine.

[12] A typical monetarist phrase, the meaning of which seems to point to inflation. The 'monetary bases expansion' means the basis of backing for the redeemable note issue. Redemption of notes should at all times consist of gold, whilst in the case of the monetarists, the backing is provided, not by real bills maturing into gold, but by Treasury bills (debt)- a negative value, which may or may never mature into gold, unless by gold taxation, a redistribution of someone else's value; Moreover, the difference with bills as a proof of value added may be opposed to taxation as proof of value diminished....

[13] Charles Rist, *History of Monetary and Credit Theory From John Law to the Present Day*, (Transl. J. Degras), New York, 1966.

[14] From February 22-24, 1797.

[15] Charles Rist, *A History of Monetary and Credit Theory*, p. 40.

[16] The British Marine had a policy of keeping itself twice as large as the two next competing nations together. This expensive policy could no longer be kept up by 1914, when the German and U.S. war fleet combined became too large too keep up with.

[17] See note 14 on page 86 for details of sources.

[18] The Social Darwinistic streak of certain parts of the population around the turn of the century knew no bounds. It is no invention of ours, we have several un-suspect sources. E.g. The parents of writer J. Perkins, (bibliography), on page 3 and 4. As such, it is no big leap from social Darwinism to Malthusian eugenetics, as in the case of Keynes.

[19] See glossary for an explanation of the term and its implications.

[20] von Mises, *Human Action*, p 321.

[21] von Mises, *ibid*, p. 494. Again another expression of condescending social Darwinism

[22] The traditional large bankers such as the Rothschilds or J.P. Morgan are known for financing election campaigns on more than one side.

[23] One known example concerns the Parisian Nathan Rothschild who offered the first Belgian King, Leopold I, to provide him with the necessary finance in 1831, in exchange for opening the Banque Générale who would act as cashier for the fiscal revenues of the new State. See. Walter de Bock, Cahiers Marxistes, De Twaalf Werken van Walter De Bock, 2005. (In Dutch) Another example concerns the American Red Cross mission to Russia in 1917, with 16 of 31 people consisting of J.P. Morgan appointees, under command of William Boyce Thompson, U.S. Federal Reserve Director, handing out bribes for future contracts, in the hope they could outcompete the Germans from establishing profitable positions in Bolshevik Russia.

[24] Actually, we think he knew well enough, but wanted to profit from the greenback - silver arbitrage in extracting metal money from debtors but insisting on paying their own debt with greenbacks at the nominal value. But that would be speculating on his state of mind. In any case, never assume stupidity. Or immorality for that matter.

[25] There is no proper 'price of gold' except in terms of silver. A price of gold in fiat dollars is tantamount of expressing a measurement of lenght in terms of an elastic band.

Chapter 35

Act III: Frankenstein's Impoverishment Machine

The following piece of history, known as the Portuguese bank note case, instructs the gentle reader about the nature of 'forgery' but more so on the nature of seigniorage. In the late 1920s an astonishing and ingenious crime led to a fascinating civil suit that was not without its ironic side. A gang of international swindlers succeeded in convincing the well-respected London firm Waterlow & Sons, engravers of postage stamps and bank notes, that they represented the Bank of Portugal and placed an order for the printing of a large quantity of fresh Portuguese bank notes. The order was duly filled and the bank notes were delivered to the swindlers. Upon discovery of the fraud, the Bank of Portugal was forced to call in all its extant notes, replacing them with a new issue. The criminals were never apprehended, but the Bank of Portugal sued Waterlow & Sons in British courts, demanding compensation for losses resulting from the issue of fraudulent notes. In listening to expert testimony the Court discovered that the case involved issues of unusual subtlety and complexity. The Court admitted evidence of negligence, but the question of damages was another matter. If it had been postage stamps instead of irredeemable bank notes in which the swindlers had trafficked, it would have been clear that the loss incurred by Portugal was equal to the face value of the fraudulent issue. With respect to bank notes, however, no such simple assertion could be made. Among the questions that troubled the experts the following stood out as particularly relevant to our study:

> *'Would the Bank of Portugal have issued the same amount of bank notes even if the swindlers had not done so?*
>
> *If not, was the increase in the supply of paper currency resulting from the fraudulent notes beneficial or detrimental to the Portuguese economy?'*

Some experts even testified that the swindlers may have done an unintentional favour to Portugal in helping fend off an imminent deflation. At any rate, why should the face value, rather than replacement value of a counterfeit bank note, govern considerations for damages, if the bank note is irredeemable anyway?

These and other considerations led the high court to award only a small fraction of the damages claimed. [1]

The Yellowback Saga

My next example will, more than any other, demonstrate the difference between a present good and a promise to deliver a present good to bearer on demand. A U.S. $20 gold certificate (nicknamed the 'yellowback' in order to distinguish it from the 'greenback') and a U.S. $20 gold coin were both present goods, in the sense of Mises, on Saturday, March 4, 1933, the day of the inauguration of F. D. Roosevelt as the 31st president of the United States. The new president was elected to office in 1932 on a platform which contained the following preamble:
Believing that a party platform is a Covenant with the people to be faithfully kept by the party when entrusted with power, and that the people are entitled to know in plain words the terms of contract to which they are asked to subscribe, we hereby declare this to be the platform of the Democratic Party . . . and this declaration:

'A sound currency is to be preserved at all hazards.'

During the election campaign of 1932 Mr. Roosevelt chastised president Hoover for endangering the integrity of the dollar by uttering irresponsible remarks about the possibility of going off the gold standard. There appears to be no evidence that Mr. Roosevelt favoured the debasement of the dollar prior to his election. But debasement began very soon after inauguration. By the Emergency Banking Act, passed by Congress and signed into law on March 9, 1933, the president was empowered to prevent the hoarding and exportation of gold. Next day the Administration took the first step by refusing license to exporters of gold. With that refusal the dollar and the yellow backs with it declined sharply in terms of gold and foreign exchange abroad. For all intents and purposes the yellowback ceased to be a present good. Lest there remain any doubt about the matter, on April 5, 1933, an Executive Order was issued requiring the owners of gold coins, gold bullion, and gold certificates (yellow backs) to deliver these items to a Federal Reserve bank against replacement in the form of Federal Reserve notes (greenbacks) on or before May 1, 1933. The Executive Order specified heavy penalties for non-compliance.

Deliberate Dollar-Debasement

Actual debasement of the dollar was authorised under Section 43 of the **Agricultural Adjustment Act** of May 12, 1933, the 'Thomas Amendment', empowering the president to reduce the gold content of the dollar. On June 5, 1933, Congress passed a 'Joint Resolution to assure uniform value to the coins and currencies of the United States'.

This recited that holding and dealing in gold affected public interest and were therefore the object of regulation; that the provisions of obligations which purport to give the obligee the right to require payment in gold coin obstructed the power of Congress to regulate the value of money and are inconsistent with the policy to maintain equal value of every dollar coined or issued. It then declared that 'every provision in any obligation purporting to give the obligee a right to require payment in gold is against public policy, and directed that every obligation, heretofore and hereafter incurred, whether or not any such provision is contained therein or made with respect thereto, shall be discharged upon payment, dollar for dollar, in any coin or currency which at the time of payment is *legal tender* for public and private debts'.

The final status of the yellow backs remained unclear until 1935, when the U.S. Supreme Court decided against the creditors of the U.S. government (Nortz v. the United States). In this landmark decision the high court ruled that the government of the U.S. did not act unconstitutionally in breaking its promise, stated on the face of the gold certificate:

> 'This certifies that there have been deposited in the Treasury of the United States of America twenty dollars in gold coin of present weight and fineness, payable to bearer on demand.'

In the opinion of the Court:

> These gold certificates were currency . . . Being currency and constituting legal tender, it is entirely inadmissible to regard the gold certificates as warehouse receipts. They were not contracts for a certain amount of gold as a commodity. They called for dollars, not bullion.

However, in the words of Justice McReynolds who formulated the *minority opinion* of the four dissenting justices:

> These were contracts to return gold left on deposit; otherwise to pay its value in currency.

The majority of the Court argued that the Constitution granted monetary powers to the *government*, including the power 'to coin money and regulate the value thereof'. Therefore, the breaking of this promise fell within the power to regulate the value of coin. The Court side-stepped the issue whether another provision of the Constitution, denying the power to the government to deprive citizens of property without due process of the law, was violated or not. Incredibly, the high court even argued that no loss accrued to the citizens in consequence of the arbitrary action of the government, because the domestic purchasing power of the Federal Reserve notes remained identical to that of the yellowback which it replaced. In saying this, the high court ignored the immediate and sizeable losses of individuals under the jurisdiction of the United States who had obligations payable in foreign currency, as well as losses of citizens living in or visiting foreign countries.

Appalling Legal and Moral Chaos

Justices McReynolds, Van Devanter, Sutherland, and Butler disagreed with the majority of the court. The dissenting opinion was delivered by Justice McReynolds. It should be taught in American schools along with the Emancipation Proclamation.

> "*We conclude that, if given effect, the enactments here challenged will bring about confiscation of property rights and repudiation of national obligations. Acquiescence in the decisions just announced is impossible; the circumstances demand a statement of our views. To let oneself slide down the easy slope offered by the course of events and to dull one's mind against the extent of danger . . . that is precisely to fail in one's obligations of responsibility.*
>
> *Just men regard repudiation and spoliation of citizens by their sovereign with abhorrence; but we are asked to affirm that the Constitution has granted power to accomplish both. No definite delegation of such power exists; and we cannot believe the far-seeing framers, who laboured with hope of establishing justice and securing the blessings of liberty, intended that the expected government should have authority to annihilate its own obligations and destroy the very rights which they were endeavouring to protect. Not only is there no permission for such actions; they are inhibited. And no plentitude of words can conform them to our charter.*
>
> *The federal government is one of delegated and limited powers which derive from the Constitution. It can exercise only the powers granted to it. Powers claimed must be denied unless granted . . . The fundamental problem now presented is whether recent statutes passed by Congress in respect of money and credits, were designed to attain a legitimate end. Or whether, under the guise of pursuing monetary policy, Congress really has inaugurated a plan primarily designed to destroy private obligations, repudiate national debts, and drive into the Treasury all the gold within the country, in exchange for inconvertible promises to pay of much less value. Considering all circumstances, we must conclude they show that the plan disclosed is of the latter description and its enforcement would deprive the*

> *parties before us of their rights under the Constitution. Consequently the Court should do what it can to afford relief . . .*
>
> *The end or objective of the Joint Resolution [of June 5, 1933] was not 'legitimate'. The real purpose was not 'to assure uniform value to the coins and currencies of the United States', but to destroy certain valuable contractual rights . . .*
>
> *These words of Alexander Hamilton ought not to be forgotten: 'When a government enters into contract with an individual, it deposes, as to the matter of its Constitutional authority, and exchanges the character of legislator for that of a moral agent, with the same rights and obligations as an individual. Its promises may be justly considered as excepted out of its power to legislate, unless in aid of them. It is in theory impossible to reconcile the idea of a promise which obliges, with a power to make a law which can vary the effect of it . . .'*
>
> *It was not intended to give Congress the power under the law to repudiate the obligations in question . . . No such power was ever granted by the framers of the Constitution. It was not there then. It was not there yesterday. It is not there today. We are confronted with a condition in which the dollar may be reduced to 50 cents today, to 30 cents tomorrow, to 10 cents the next day, and to 1 cent the day after . . .*

Under the challenged statutes it is said that the United States has realised profits amounting to $2,800,000,000. But this assumes that gain may be generated by legislative fiat. To such counterfeit profits there would be no limit; with each new debasement of the dollar they would expand. Two billions might be ballooned indefinitely to twenty, thirty, or what you will.

Losses of reputation for honourable dealing will bring us unending humiliation. The impending legal and moral chaos is appalling.

Congenital Disease of All Paper Currencies

Thus did the yellowback cease to be a 'present good' at the stroke of a pen in 1935. At any rate, the market had long recognised the true state of affairs: it treated the yellowback as a dishonoured promise. By contrast, the $20 gold coin was still a present good after the Supreme Court decision as it is still today. So is the gold Napoleon. They continue to be a present good on the same terms indefinitely, whatever fate awaited the issuer. Paper money issued under the authority of Napoleon III, of course, no longer enjoys present-good status. They and the yellowback have suffered from the same congenital disease of all paper currencies: their status is tied up with the fortunes and integrity of the issuing authority.

> Any gold coin is free from this congenital disease precisely because, unlike the paper currency, it is a present good, not a promise.

I treated the saga of the yellowback at length because it shows, I think, that Mises' concept of a present good is untenable. The yellowback lost its status as a present good, as the term is understood by Mises, for no cause more substantial than a stroke of the pen. This not only violates one's intuitive idea of a present good, but also obscures the real state of affairs. It appears to condone the mischief involved in the prestidigitation. There is no need to stretch the meaning of the term 'present good'. A perfectly satisfactory term to cover bank notes and other varieties of paper currency redeemable in gold already exists: they are promises to pay bearer a definite quantity of gold on demand. The value of a present good can be protected against physical deterioration by its owner in taking precautions to prevent it. The value of a promise cannot be so protected: it depends on the integrity of the other party and that of the prevailing legal system. A promise can be broken, no matter how carefully one protects the paper on which it is written. Nor does it matter who the promisor is and what what resources are at his disposal. As our example shows, even if the promise has been issued by the government of the richest and 'most democratic' country on the face of the earth, with vast economic and military resources at its command, and even if the promise is backed up by Constitutional guarantees, a promise is still just a promise, and not a present good. Greater economic and military power won't make a country less likely to stoop so low as to have recourse to fraudulent bankruptcy, in order to destroy the contractual rights of weaker countries or individuals.

Gold needs no endorsement. It can be tested with scales and acids. The recipient of gold does not have to trust the government stamp on it if he doesn't trust the government that had stamped it. No act of faith is called for when gold is used in payments, and no compulsion is required. Gold is gold, and paper is paper. A present good is a present good, and a promise is a promise. Finally, whether the highest of high courts admits it or denies it, a broken promise is just that: a broken promise.

The Deep Cause of the Great Financial Crisis

> The Great Depression of the 1930s, in particular, the un- precedented world-wide unemployment was caused by the decision of the victorious Entente Powers to return to the gold standard after World War I, but without allowing the clearing house of the gold standard, the international bill market, to make a comeback.

This decision was made in secret. It has never been made public. But there can be no doubt about the fact that in 1920 everybody, even Keynes himself, admitted the desirability of an expeditious 'return to the gold standard.' Since all political parties and their backers, like J.P. Morgan and Rockefeller had always officially supported a gold standard, all noses pointed in the same direction. Or so it seemed. Had there been no decision to curtail it, world wide bill trading would have re-started spontaneously.

This 'decision' resulted from the effects of the British sea-blockade (under the Anglo-French Alliance Treaty and their own 1909 declaration [2]) reducing multilateral world trade by brute force to bilateral trade- if any. At first, British interests and free trade spirit still reigned and imported food did reach the belligerent parties, but one year into the war and lots of propaganda later, [3] the naval blockade turned strict under total warfare. The blockade of Germany, including the Mediterranean, did not win the war for the Entente but it exhausted the Germans. If no goods came through during the war, why keep the blockade after the Germans had surrendered? Blockade of ships entails no imports nor any exports from Germany or its industrial products. And no payments or bills either [4]... Why did the victorious Entente powers decide to keep the blockade from 1918 until well after the signing of the Treaty at Versailles in 1919? Choking trade would hurt their own producers and consumers, and hinder reconstruction and therefore: repayment? Some wags suggest Great Britain or France wanted to curtail German competitors... At any rate, history reports they did it because they wanted to punish Germany over and above the provisions of the Versailles peace treaty. They wanted to maintain the wartime blockade under a different name. [5] They wanted to monitor, and control if need be, the move of goods in and out of Germany. In peacetime such action would not have been possible, but under war-conditions the opportunity arises by way of replacing multilateral with bilateral trade – under military control or under control of the War Office, staffed with... bankers, their lawyers and their elected politicians. They possess intimate knowledge how to block the financing of world trade with short-term commercial bills, also known as real bills. To put it differently, the Entente powers phased out self-liquidating credit, under no-one's control, and replaced it with artificial bank credit, the creation of which they could control through their central or commercial banks. Their short term aim was self-enrichment at the expense of Germany, its colonies, Austria-Hungary, Bulgaria and the Ottoman empire. Even the Allies competed amongst each other for the spoils of war.[6]

World trade prior to 1914 was multilateral. By this we mean that imports were paid for by issuing, endorsing, and accepting bills of exchange payable in gold at maturity no more than 91 days after shipping the underlying merchandise. With three good signatures: that of the exporter, that of the importer, and that of a recognised acceptor the bill of exchange went through a most remarkable metamorphosis. It became money. Ephemeral, to be sure, but money nevertheless. The exporter could use it to pay for his imports by passing it on, after endorsing it, to the exporter in a third country. This exporter could likewise use it to pay for his own imports, and so on and so forth. Only in the light of this fact can one explain the unprecedented expansion of world trade during the 100-year period between 1815, marking the end of the Napoleonic War and 1914, marking the outbreak of World War I. Such a record level of world trade would not have been possible without the clearing house for the gold standard, the bill market. Geographically, this clearing house was located in the City of London. It was the great London trading houses and banks on which bills of exchange, covering merchandise shipped from country A to country B, were drawn. It was the great acceptance houses in London that accepted them. Once so endorsed and accepted, these bills started to circulate on their own wings and under their own power, as only monetary gold could circulate: without friction.[7]

It was this great clearing house of the gold standard in London that was blocked, nay, sabotaged, by the decision of the Entente powers at Versailles in their vindictive moment of victory. They never examined the broader economic implications of their move, beyond the obvious effect of putting the foreign trade of Germany on a leash. They utterly failed to see the wider consequences of their folly.

To show just how short-sighted the decision to block the circulation of real bills was, consider the argument of the German economist Heinrich Rittershausen (1898-1984) that he presented in his monograph entitled Unemployment and Capital Formation, published in 1930, but obviously written before the Great Depression has become a reality. Rittershausen predicted that, hard on the heels of the collapse of the gold standard, a horrendous wave of world-wide unemployment would prostrate the world economy.

Under multilateral world trade financed by real bills there was something we may, in want of a better term, call the Wage Fund — out of which the wages of labourers producing merchandise demanded most urgently by consumers could be paid. Please remember that these goods during their gestation period of up to 91 days could not be sold to the ultimate consumer. He was the only one to pay for his purchase by handing over the gold coin. Neither the producers of semi-finished goods that go into the merchandise, nor the wholesale and retail merchants would ever pay gold: they would issue or endorse bills. It could take 91 days (or 13 weeks, or 3 months, or a quarter) before the real bill matured into the gold coin with which wages could be paid. But labourers have to be fed, clad, shod and sheltered in the meantime. They cannot wait for 3 months till the merchandise will have been sold to the ultimate gold-paying consumer. Wages have to be paid weekly, not quarterly.

> Thus the Wage Fund is absolutely necessary for the maintenance of world trade and full employment on a scale it has reached prior to 1913. Such a Wage Fund could only exist by virtue of the bill market. So much of the 'float' of real bills in the world was earmarked for paying wages; the remainder was earmarked to pay for supplies. The system worked extremely well: 'structural' unemployment was unheard-of before World War I.

This Wage Fund was unwittingly destroyed by the victorious Entente powers at the moment they decided to block the financing of world trade through real bills circulation as it existed before 1914. The result was that world trade never really recovered. In fact it took the better part of the twentieth century for the volume of world trade to reach its 1913 peak level again. In the meantime it was touch-and-go. Bilateral trade, barter, or direct payment of gold and gold exchange replaced self-liquidating credit, as the credit represented by real bills was called.

The destruction of the Wage Fund was not immediately noticed. The great inflation due to World War I imparted sufficient stimulus for a full decade to cover up the complete absence of a reliable fund out of which wages could be paid. In due course, however, the surplus money was siphoned off by an extraordinary explosion of speculative activity in financial bills, real estate, and in the shares of joint-stock companies. Real bills were conspicuous only by their absence.

When money became scarce after the bubbles burst one after another: the bubble in US Treasury bonds in 1920, the Florida real estate bubble in 1925, and the stock market bubble in 1929, the absence of the Wage Fund, destroyed a decade earlier, immediately became obvious. There was no money to pay the wage earner. Workers were laid off. They had to be put on the dole. [Ed. note: For the first time — ever since the industrialisation !]

> An unprecedented wave of unemployment, like a tsunami, engulfed the world. Dictatorships could escape the curse of unemployment by destroying civil liberties: Lenin's under the banner of international socialism, Hitler's under the banner of national socialism. Welfare states and its version of corporate (some call it Wall Street) socialism,[8] hidden behind the veil of democracies followed on its heels.

The only economist in the world who saw what was coming was **Rittershausen**. But he was treated by the international community of economists with the same contempt as the German delegation was at the Versailles peace conference. A new economic gospel was promulgated by the prophet John Maynard Keynes who made a complete *volte face*. He was a most vocal opponent of Britain's return to the gold standard in 1925. Not because he realised that Britain's 'newly-born-again' gold standard was not viable as it grievously lacked a vital part: the clearing house. Keynes opposed the gold standard on doctrinaire grounds. According to him the gold standard was obsolete, contractionist, an obstruction to progress. The new dispensation called for flexible foreign exchange rates that could be easily manipulated in the service of a hidden political agenda. Keynes was the *enfant terrible* of economic science. He was a perfect antithesis of Rittershausen. He was a master of *demagoguery*. He made economics stand on its head. For thousands of years the problem of economics was the scarcity of savings as well as over-consumption, especially during princely wars. Keynes dreamt-up oversaving and its twin brother, underconsumption. These notions are as obnoxious as they are preposterous. Yet the world, desperate for getting out of the depression, bought them. This was just what Keynes has been waiting for. He was hell bent on manipulating the whole world through clever verbiage, but which *utterly lacked any substance*.

Rittershausen, on the other hand, had no ulterior motivation. He just wanted to find the truth. And, indeed, he found it by pointing to the destruction of the wage fund in the wake of blocking the circulation of real bills. It is a great tragedy that Rittershausen was born in Germany rather than Britain, and Keynes was born in Britain rather than Germany. If it had been the other way around, then Keynes would have been totally ignored, as was his desert and Rittershausen would have been elevated to international fame, as was his. He would have been made the object of world-acclamation and admiration. History may not be repeating, but it certainly is strongly echoing itself. The Great Financial Crisis of 2008 is such an echo of the Great Depression of 1930. Or could it be that the Great Depression of 1930 was the harbinger of something far worse: the Great Financial Crisis of 2008 and its aftermath, still to be visited upon the world? The last remnants of the gold standard were abolished in 1971 when the Republican president Richard Nixon defaulted on the international gold obligations of the US – almost 40 years after the Democratic president Franklin D. Roosevelt defaulted on its domestic gold obligations. It triggered the fast-breeder of money, originally envisaged by Keynes, later dressed up academically and made palatable politically by Milton Friedman. At first, the going was great under the catch-word: 'you have never had it so good'. But then, just as during the 'roaring 20's', speculators grabbed the money spun out by the fast breeders and ran with it. Once again, bubbles were blown and started bursting one after another. Now the world is confronted with the worst prospects for unemployment ever. At any rate, far worse than the one Rittershausen had predicted in 1930. We can, using his methodology, predict Great Depression II in the making. The world still is lacking a Wage Fund. A vastly expanded army of unemployed people will have to be fed, clad, shod and sheltered. The money to do it is not there. Once again, governments will have to create it out of nothing to pay the dole.

The obvious way out of this corner is the resuscitation of the Wage Fund through allowing the spontaneous circulation of real bills that were last used in 1914. Lest anyone suggest that this feat could be accomplished under the regime of irredeemable currency, beware: real bills can only work if they mature into gold. It is unthinkable that they could mature into irredeemable paper currency. A real bill is an IOU promising to pay gold, and it offers a return to boot. An irredeemable banknote is an 'IOU nothing' and it offers nothing – an inferior instrument at best, a fraud at worst. A real bill, to be meaningful, must mature into a superior financial instrument. Otherwise it refuses to circulate. Therefore the rehabilitation of real bills assumes the simultaneous rehabilitation of the gold standard. The two go together as hand and glove. The way to return to the gold standard is for the US government to open the US Mint to gold – as ordained by the American

Constitution that has been violated by power-hungry presidents such F. D. Roosevelt and his successors, every one of whom swore to uphold it, only to turn around and trample on it. It would be an extraordinary act of statesmanship if a new president reinstated the monetary provisions of the American Constitution.

No State shall...make any Thing but gold and silver Coin a Tender in Payment of Debts...

United States Constitution, Article One, Section 10.

There is no other way to prevent the collapse of the debt tower, or to fend off the tsunami of unemployment and the global breakdown of law and order.

The Bag Lady of Threadneedle Street

It is commonplace to badmouth the Bank of England for her role in the corruption of the gold standard of Sir Isaac Newton, the Master of the Royal Mint from 1699 to his death in 1727. But whatever one can say of the low circumstances of her birth in 1696, and of her most recent role as the 'Bag Lady of Threadneedle Street' in selling her gold reserve to the drumbeat from the paper mill on the Potomac, we must give the Bank of England credit for financing Pax Britannica for a period of one hundred years between the close of the Napoleonic Wars and the outbreak of World War I. Authors often wondered how the Bank of England could run the international gold standard on a shoestring of a gold reserve. The mystery readily finds its solution if we contemplate that the Bank of England acted as the clearing house for real bills financing world trade between 1815 and 1914. This was history's most successful episode demonstrating the power and the potential of the RBD. By 1913 world trade in consumer goods had reached a high mark that was not surpassed until the 1990s. In whichever countries they were domiciled, the exporter billed the importer and the terms of the bill '91 days net payable in London' were standard. The importer endorsed the bill, attached shipping and insurance documents, and sent it back to the exporter. Thereafter the bill circulated world-wide in lieu of gold till it matured. Hardly ever did a default occur, and even then it was in consequence of violations of bill trading rules. Gold was shipped only to the extent of the difference between imports and exports. The modest size of the gold reserve of the Bank of England was no fetter on a most prodigious increase in world trade, a monument to the triumph of clearing. Goods in bottoms did not have to sail anywhere near England to be eligible for financing through bills drawn on London.

It is incumbent on the detractors of the RBD to explain how the phenomenal increase of world trade in consumer goods, on which the remarkable prosperity of the world before World War I depended, was possible with only a negligible amount of gold changing hands.

The Permanent Crisis of the World's Monetary System

The outbreak of World War I in 1914 put an end to international bill circulation and wiped out world trade in consumer goods almost entirely.[9] When the war ended, the garrison states that emerged did not allow real bill trading to recover. [10] Bill trading assumes that the gold is outside of the banks, in the hands of the people. Strategic imperatives called for the concentration of monetary gold in bank vaults. [11] People had to be weaned from the gold coin. Nor was the reintroduction of real bill trading considered an option [12] at the Bretton Woods conference in 1944 that was charged with the task to regenerate the world economy and trade after the ordeal of World War II. The world is still doing without the benefits of real bills. Trade has been placed under the direct control of governments. Political, not economic considerations govern the flow of consumer goods across international boundaries. Government regimentation of the lives of the people has become virtually complete. The expulsion of real bills and the failure of world trade to recover after World War I, together with the advent of 'cash and carry' mentality, was one of the main causes of the failure of the international gold standard and the Great Depression about a dozen years after the cessation of hostilities. A strong case could be made that if bill circulation had been allowed to return, then world trade would have quickly recovered, too, and the international gold standard would not have collapsed. Collapse it did because, without the clearing mechanism provided by real bills, it could not cope with world trade, much reduced though it was. People were talking about an 'acute shortage of monetary gold'. Money doctors rose with a phoney diagnosis that the malady was due to the increase in the price level that was not accompanied by a commensurate increase in gold reserves. This diagnosis holds no water. It is based on the Quantity Theory of Money, a flawed theory that is applicable only in a world where all changes are in a linear relationship with their causes. In reality, however, changes in our world are a non-linear function of causes. There is no way of telling how much trade a given amount of monetary gold can support at any given price level. The volume of trade depends, not on the stock of monetary gold, but on the clearing system which can be improved to meet the challenge. Instead of improving it, governments conspired to sabotage the clearing system by blocking international trade in real bills that had worked so efficiently before the war. The proper prescription should have been the restoration of the clearing mechanism through real bills. Please remember that you have seen it here first: the main cause of the Great Depression of the 1930s was government sabotage of the Real Bills Doctrine of Adam Smith. The world's monetary and payments system is still limping from crisis to crisis, and will continue doing so until the RBD is fully rehabilitated.

The Revolt of Quality

The idea that the monetary regime based on irredeemable currency can endure indefinitely is the stuff of which the dreams of dictators are made. The list of attempts to translate that dream into reality is very long. Yet every one of those attempts in history failed, and did so miserably. There is no shred of scientific evidence that the substance of the present attempt is any different from that of the previous ones. It is true that this experiment has so far survived longer than previous ones. This proves nothing, nor is it necessarily an improvement, for it only prolongs the agony, and makes the end-game even more painful. The paramount fact is that the depreciation of currencies is continuing year in and year out, in good times and in bad, albeit at a varying rate. The linguistic innovation of introducing the euphemism 'price inflation' and the official pretence that monetary depreciation is a 'natural' phenomenon rather than the direct result of dishonourable dealings, will not make the outlook for the present experiment any brighter. Nor is there any reasonable hope that some significant scientific discovery, or a break-through in data processing and information technology, will change the pessimistic long-term outlook for the regime. It cannot be emphasised too strongly that longevity of a monetary regime is a matter decided not on the basis of the quantity of money or the rate at which it is increased, but by the quality of assets in the balance sheet of the monetary authority. It is futile to pretend, as the Friedmanites do, that restricting quantity makes for quality. Restricting the quantity of a dishonoured promise cannot make it more valuable. If the regime of irredeemable currency could be perpetuated, it would be tantamount to the overthrow of the fundamental principle of double-entry book-keeping. This principle demands that an item must appear either in the liability column, or in the asset column of the balance sheet, and it cannot be shifted from one to the other at pleasure. It is not possible to create a liability in the balance sheet of the government and pretend that, by increasing this liability at the 'optimal rate' one can, somehow, increase the assets in the same balance sheet, as the Friedmanites do. If the revenues of the government consist exclusively of its own liabilities, as is the case today, then the implication is that the citizens are mere slaves of government authority with no power over their own affairs. It means that the citizens, their children, their chattels, their produce, all belong to the government. In order for them to buy food, shelter, medicine, etc., they have to get permission, in the form of a piece of government debt (itself subject to unilateral cancellation) to do so. Elections are meaningless. They are about deciding which party will collect the tithes, not about the question whether tithes should be abolished altogether. The pretence is maintained that the government is in debt to its citizens, and it is the destiny of the debt to be retired. This has no basis in fact. The government debt will never be retired: it is to keep growing indefinitely. It is the citizens who are in fact in debt to the government. It is no longer true that the government belongs to the people: rather, the people belong to the government. In the words of the currency expert, the late Dr. Franz Pick, government bonds are 'certificates of guaranteed confiscation'.

> Tax revenues can, in theory, reduce the rate of increase in government debt. However, to the extent that the government wants to translate tax revenues into tangible goods and services, the debt reduction is immediately canceled.

In order to have command over real goods and services the government has to borrow, and borrow it must at an accelerating pace. The burden of debt can only be lightened through ongoing currency depreciation. This depreciation must occur in fits and starts. Otherwise people would see clearly what is going on, and would refuse to hold the currency, causing it to lose its value, as it were, overnight. The unstated premise underlying the regime of irredeemable currency is the proposition that it is possible to keep borrowing with the right hand while destroying the value of the resulting obligations with the left. Governments trying to perpetuate the regime of irredeemable currency will ultimately find that they are destroying their own credit and their ability to borrow in the process. They will, sooner or later, reach the point where they can no longer borrow because they are no longer trusted. This is the revolt of quality. Even with the most drastic quantity controls of money-creation, the destruction of the regime of irredeemable currency is inevitable.

Gold Demonetisation

In the late 1960s quantity theorists widely predicted that the de-monetisation of gold would seriously undermine the exchange value of gold. Ludwig von Mises was among them: 'The important thing to be remembered is that with every sort of money, demonetisation, i.e., the abandonment of its use as a medium of exchange must result in a serious fall of its exchange value.' [13]

To a quantity theorist, the disappearance of the lion's share of the demand, the monetary demand, couldn't help but make gold cheaper. It is a source of endless amazement for us that a quantity theorist could be so blinded to the other side of the de-monetisation coin, namely the effect it has on the *irredeemable bank note in which gold is quoted.*

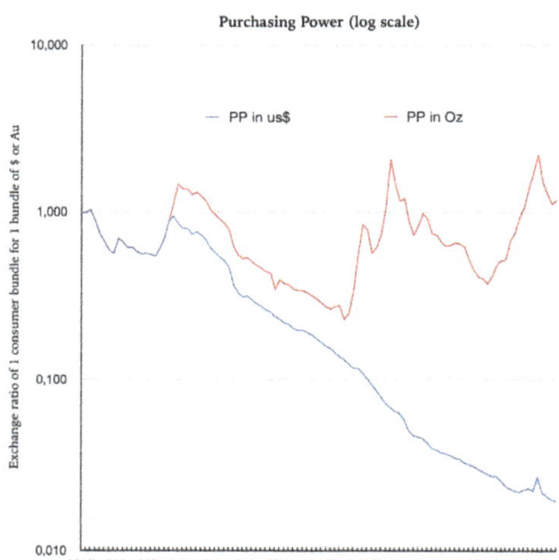

It is not known whether these views of the quantity theorists had any influence on the thinking of the decision-makers who demonetised gold on August 15, 1971. Be that as it may, the idea that dishonouring promises to pay gold on demand would, somehow, cause the dishonoured paper to go to a premium in terms of gold is preposterous. It is true that insolvent bankers have in the past tried to promote their discredited paper (sometimes using extreme measures such as the death penalty to punish the owners of contraband gold, as proposed by John Law of Lauriston and, later, by the issuers of the assignats and mandats), to no avail. Logic and history prove that dishonoured promises to pay gold always and everywhere go to a discount, never to a premium. Indeed, this is exactly what happened after gold was demonetised world-wide in 1971. In less than a decade the U.S. dollar went to a 90 percent discount in terms of gold. Moreover, the discount was commensurate with the 90 percent loss in purchasing power that the dollar suffered during the same period. There is no use to blame that loss on the conspiracy of Arab sheiks and the gnomes of Zurich. The huge loss in the value of the dollar during the decade of the 1970s was due to one cause only: the de-monetisation of gold. The hope that the discount on the dollar would ever disappear is a forlorn one. Domestically and internationally, a deflation of that magnitude is unthinkable. Furthermore, the disarray in America's budgetary and trade accounts suggests that the currency depreciation is likely to continue, if not accelerate. The only way to stop the rot would be the adoption of a reasonable plan to resume gold redeemability of the dollar. Neither party has so far come up with a platform embracing the idea. The use of the word 'demonetisation' in connection with gold is inappropriate. It is but a euphemism for debt-abatement (partial debt-repudiation) inflicted upon the foreign creditors of the United States of America. These foreign creditors were deprived of a valuable property right: the right to a fixed amount of gold per dollar. This unilateral and capricious act has done nothing to benefit the citizens or the government of the U.S. On the contrary, the debt abatement had one predictable consequence: harsher terms on future borrowing, as measured by the higher and unpredictable rates of interest which the government and the people of the United States had to pay on new borrowings abroad. It is true that the burden of debtors who had contracted debt prior to the abatement was lightened but, insofar as they were the same borrowers on whom the harsher terms on further borrowing fell for the indefinite future, there were no beneficiaries, only losers. In particular, the big losers were the taxpayers. The international credit of the U.S. government was grievously damaged as manifested by the unprecedented interest rates (e.g., 16 percent per annum on the 30-year bonds) the Treasury was forced to pay on its obligations.

From Greatest Creditor to Greatest Debtor

> The stubborn denial that the credit-standing of the U.S. has been damaged in any way by the de-monetisation of gold of 1971 is the centrepiece of mainstream economics.

We must realise, however, that gold de-monetisation is just a euphemism for the crime of pauperising the labouring classes here and abroad, who are the main holders of the irredeemable dollar. Ironically, the 'moneyed classes' have the habit of holding irredeemable currency for as short a period of time as necessary. Then *they get rid of it by investing their funds in something more reasonable.* [14] This is a world of crime and punishment. No one, not even the government of the mightiest nation on earth can exempt itself from the numerous and onerous consequences. One of them is the fact that, in an incredibly short period of time, America turned itself from the world's greatest creditor into its greatest debtor country. Another is that that part of the American industry which is not in the process of dismantling itself, is losing international competitiveness, just at the time the country would need a strong export industry to help pay for its burgeoning foreign debt. Due to volatile interest rates in the 1980s, a large part of America's park of capital goods has become submarginal. Producers were either unwilling or unable to maintain capital by replacing worn and obsolete equipment with new ones. As capital was becoming submarginal under a rising interest-rate structure, so were the producers. They were forced to sell their business at a loss, and invest the proceeds in high-yield Treasury bonds. This was a textbook-case how the government can despoil its own taxpayers.

> In printing high coupon-rates on Treasury bonds, instead of collecting taxes from the productive members of society, the government is now obliged to pay them for holding its debt.

A large segment of the producers found themselves unable to compete with the high coupon rates the government so cavalierly printed on its bonds and, from producers of new wealth they became coupon-clippers. [15] The consequences of wholesale destruction of capital are camouflaged by the burgeoning import of consumer goods.

> Foreigners accept the U.S. $ for the time being, as in their judgment the dollar depreciates more slowly than their domestic currency.

Such a situation cannot continue indefinitely. The most visible sign of the progressive deterioration is the ever-growing trade deficit, the flip-side of the accumulation of U.S. Treasury paper in foreign hands. At one point, the world market will get saturated with the U.S. dollar. When that happens, another convulsion in the world's commodity and financial markets will follow. It is not widely understood that the dollar was given a stay of execution by the 'fortuitous demise' of the Soviet Union and its 'Evil Empire' in 1990. [16] This unforeseen historic event [17] turned the dollar-glut into a fresh dollar shortage. All of a sudden a new market, counting some 400 million souls, was thrown wide open to dollar-penetration a market that had earlier been hermetically sealed off by the threat of the firing-squad. Huge though this market for dollars may appear, it is not unlimited. At one point it would also become saturated as were markets in Western Europe in the late 1960s. Predicting that the present dollar-shortage would never turn into a dollar glut, appear useless. Similar predictions were also made during the dollar-shortage of the 1950s at a time when America's trade advantage over the rest of the world appeared unassailable. When the dollar-glut of the late 1960s hit the unsuspecting world, those predictions were totally discredited. Today America's trade position is incomparably weaker, and getting weaker still. And, remember, America is no longer the world's greatest creditor. Now, it is the world's greatest debtor. Accordingly, the effects of the dollar glut, when it comes, will be that much worse.

The Swing of the Wrecker's Ball

Another great danger has unexpectedly appeared on the horizon, the blackhole of zero interest. It turned out that the volatility of interest rates, that was unleashed through the demonetisation of gold, also has a long cycle measured in decades. At first, the pendulum was swinging towards infinite interest, threatening the dollar with hyperinflation. Right now the pendulum is swinging to the other extreme, to zero interest, spelling hyper-deflation. This is just as damaging to the producers as the swing towards infinite interest was in the early 1980s. It is impossible to predict whether one or the other extreme in the swinging of the wrecker's ball will make the world economy to collapse. Hyperinflation and hyper-deflation are just two different forms of the same phenomenon: credit collapse. Arguing which of the two forms will dominate is futile: it blurs the focus of inquiry and frustrates efforts to avoid disaster. In the meantime, the wrecker's ball keeps swinging, with ever wider amplitude, and ever greater force. The credit of the U.S. government suffered its greatest setback in history, as a result of the 1971 devaluation of the dollar, even though it was only by a relatively insignificant amount (the official price of gold was increased from $35 only to $38). The deterioration of the credit of the U.S. still continues, with unforeseeable consequences. This is not generally acknowledged by financial writers at home and abroad. The gross mismanagement of credit in the U.S. and in the rest of the world has created intractable problems for which there are no painless solutions. Such are the consequences of the confusion between present and future goods, between capital and credit, between assets and liabilities deliberately fostered in the minds of the people by the proponents of mainstream economics. Such NewSpeak forms the pillars of academia to bamboozle the next generation. The people have no idea what ship wreck is coming their way.

Endnotes to Chapter 35

[1] See: C.H. Kisch, *The Portuguese Bank Note Case*, London, 1932, and Wilhelm Röpke, *The Economics of Free Society*, Chicago, 1963.

[2] The 1909 Declaration concerns the Law of War - a most meaningless positivist point of view- and relates supposedly to maritime law during war times. Most European heads of State signed the declaration that reiterated existing maritime rules but now included more rules of engagement under a blockade; it dealt with how the spoils of contraband were divided and how the neutral countries were to behave or be treated. Although signed, the treaties were never ratified by the parliaments of the respective states. Only then would the treaty be binding.

[3] All belligerent parties used propaganda. The first casualty of war, as the saying goes, is the truth.

[4] See e.g. Col. I. L. Hunt, *American Military Government of Occupied Germany 1918-1920* – Report of the Officer in Charge of Civil Affairs, Third Army and American Forces in Germany, U.S. Government Printing Office, Washington, 1943, p. 234-235.

[5] The armistice was asked for by Germany in 1918, on the basis of the 14 point plan of the U.S. president W. Wilson and after the German high command realised that, although the war was not lost by defeat or physical destruction, they failed in their plan to move swiftly and were bogged down for 4 years instead on the Western front. In the mean time, the German activist Kerensky managed to stop Russia from fighting Germany after the February Revolution. But William Boyce Thompson, Federal Reserve Bank Director of New York, financed the Bolshevik revolution in 1917 in the hope of capturing the very large Russian market. No more fighting took place after 1918, yet the war time sea-blockade was never lifted until well into 1919. Armed forces occupied parts of Germany thereafter.

[6] Tzar Nicholas II had mobilised the Russian Army, before any war had been declared. His aim was to capture Constantinople. But things turned out different for the Tzar. The U.S. openly declared war on Germany after the sinking of the Lusitania. However, Germany has sunken other U.S. ships before and regarded the U.S. as a neutral, whilst by the British declaration, all ships providing the enemy were contraband. That makes the Lusitania and its cargo contraband and open to capture or destruction in the eyes of Germany, just as the British had been doing with German and other ships providing – perhaps – Germany. The Hoover plan provided *'Belgium'* with relief shipments, whilst all ships, other than those sent by Hoover, were sunk, ended up in neutral *Rotterdam*, from which the goods were distributed via the Rhine, that only flows to *Germany*, not to *Belgium*. Hoover, therefor, obtained a trade monopoly with Germany, just as William Boyce Thompson opened up the Eastern front for the U.S.A. with a monopoly agreement between the U.S.A. and Bolshevik Russia.

[7] To be sure, the great discount houses had degenerated to acceptance houses under an adulterated gold standard, as witnessed by the several bank runs in the U.S and elsewhere.

[8] See A. Sutton, *Wall Street and the Bolshevik Revolution*, Arlington House, 1974.

[9] See the British sea blockade above and Belgian Relief monopoly above. The multilateral trading was entirely disrupted by the war and due to legislation such as 'Trading With the Enemy Acts' (TWEA) trade nearly stopped.

[10] See Col.I.L. Hunt, American Military Government of Occupied Germany 1918-1920, p. 234-235; Treaty of Versailles - Note the language: the representatives from many countries, being a mixture of military personnel, bureaucrats and BANKERS, call themselves Allies and Associated POWERS. Note also how the Treaty of Versailles differed entirely from Wilson's 14 point plan for armistice and how it sneaked in the establishment of the League of Nations. This League of Nations will later be replaced by the United Nations, but its role was to be a 'Power over Powers' or some sort of 'Final Godlike Judgement Panel' in true nihilistic and Nietzschean style. Obviously such conceited approach invites disaster. However, from an economic point of view, these international leagues, bodies, etc. democratically supported or not, do cost the tax payer in return of very dubious results and a boatload of bureaucratic jobs.

[11] That is: restricting its circulation and making it 'scarce' so it invites printed note making instead – 'backed' by the gold in the vault. Obviously, this extraction out of circulation and sight invited mischief.

[12] At least not in specie payment as it would defeat the purpose. The withdrawal of printed war money, even gradually, would result in a loss of control of the interest rate and discount rate 'management'. To be avoided at all cost in the eyes of the banking oligarchies: gold had to GO ! Cfr. B. Eichengreen, 'Fetters of Gold and Paper' who considers the gold standard supporters 'ideologists'.

[13] *Human Action*, ibid., p. 428.

[14] Whatever that something 'more reasonable' may be, it pays at least some interest instead of no interest.

[15] The exact opposite of what Saint Keynes had planned for the world. Too bad.

[16] We nevertheless sympathise with the plight of the people of Russia who carried the burden of the Bolshevik madness of international communism.

[17] The fall of the Russian Tzar provided ample opportunity for international conniving in carving up Russia. It would appear the Bolshevik revolution was financed by **William Boyce Thompson and many of his colleagues at the Federal Reserve of New York**, not because they were communist ideologues, but they recognised Banking and financing opportunities in fresh and large territories. With the demise of the Communist Empire, financiers have the know-how and the network necessary to fill the vacuum. Irredeemable currency has the characteristic of being one of many tools in imperialism.

Chapter 36

Act IV: Fast Breeders Of Extinction

Gulliver In the Land of the Mad Scientists

Jonathan Swift described the strange island of Balnibarbi and its capital city Lagado, governed by a committee of mad scientists, in his satire *Gulliver's Travels*. The Grand Academy of Lagado, the citadel of arts and sciences, was more advanced than anything Gulliver had ever seen. Thousands of scientists were engaged in hundreds of research projects believed to bring great benefits to the island nation. In one studio a painter employed blind helpers for the task of blending paints by smelling and tasting them. In this manner the olfactory and gustatory faculties could take their proper place in defining the spectrum of colours, a place long usurped by the faculty of vision. There was a studio where an ingenious architect was perfecting a new method to build human abodes from top to bottom. This was said to be justified by the kindred practice of those prudent insects, the bees and spiders.

What puzzled Gulliver most was an invention that the Balnibarbians hailed as the 'floating system of timekeeping'. The inventor, the island's greatest astronomer, replaced the rigid hand of the sundial by a flexible one, and attached it to the Great Weather Cock of Lagado's town hall. In this manner the annual and diurnal movements of the Sun could be properly modulated by local conditions such as the twists and turns of the wind. The government was so impressed with the new timepiece, and still more with the fine research behind it, that it made the use of floating time mandatory throughout the land. Reactionaries opposed the measure calling the new timepiece capricious and misleading. They argued that you cannot keep regular time by an irregular timepiece. But these people were roundly denounced as conservative belly-achers with a visceral contempt for progress. The great astronomer took pains to convince the incredulous Gulliver that floating was light-years ahead of that 'barbarous relic', the rigidly fixed standard of time-keeping.

> '*The main excellence of floating time is in its ready adaptability to changing conditions*', *he said.* '*The importance of this innovation is not to be seen in the role it assigns to the wind in time-keeping, but in the newly-found*

> *freedom of mankind in guiding its own destiny', he added. 'We can now appoint competent managers who will direct an array of fans towards the weather-cock whenever stretching or shrinking time is deemed to be in the national interest by the government'.*

He also explained that workers would strenuously object to lengthening the working day from 8 to 9 hours. 'Naturally, we want to please them, so we shall shorten their working day from 8 to 7 hours. Their unions are too dumb to realise that each work-hour has been stretched by one-quarter through floating time.'

The great man concluded: 'There is nothing more absurd than trying to make local time synchronous with global time. We have learned, at great cost to us, that our complex world can brook neither simplistic explanations nor rigid standards.'

The Integrity of Standards

Absurd though the idea of throwing the unit of time-keeping to the winds might be, something equally absurd did indeed happen to the unit measuring values. In 1971 the government of the United States threw the international monetary unit to the winds, and embraced the regime of floating exchange rates. It solemnly declared that the old unit was obsolete, rigid, as well as reactionary. Above all, it was irrational as it denied the advantages of rational management of the dollar. At the long last, the government was now in a position to assume full power in the discharge of its sacred duty unfettered by petty superstition, namely, managing the currency in the national interest.

Please note that this is not fantasy taken from Gulliver's Travels; this is history. The essence of floating is the denial of standards. The folly of the exercise can be seen in its true colours if we consider that Western Civilisation was built upon the foundation of integrity of standards. By the same token, civilisation is endangered if that foundation is allowed to decay. In an earlier less enlightened age the unit of linear measure, the foot, was adjusted every time the king died, in order to match its length to the foot of the newly anointed king. If he happened to be an infant, woe to the consumers and cheers to the producers of lace and fabric. The former just had to absorb the losses concomitant with the shrinkage of the foot, while the latter enjoyed an undeserved windfall. Later more enlightened monarchs stabilised the length of the foot thereby promoting trade and strengthening contract law. Modern technology is unthinkable without a rigidly fixed standard of weights and measures. What would happen to safety of travel on land, sea, and air, if tolerance standards could be compromised in response to political pressures? Efficiency of production is unthinkable without rigidly fixed standards. What would happen to industry and agriculture if the length of the meter and the weight of the gram were made subject to manipulation by the government? What would the effect on world trade be if the bushel and the barrel, units of measurement whereby grain and crude oil are bought and sold, were made subject to floating?

Fixity is the most basic characteristic of any good standard. We pride ourselves on being more scientific in defining units of measurement than were our predecessors. We have refined the definition of the meter several times. Originally intended to be one ten-millionth of the length of a meridian from the pole to the equator, the meter was later redefined as the distance between two marks on a platinum-iridium bar kept in Paris. The reason for the change was that the original definition proved to be too imprecise for measurements calling for greater accuracy. The choice of the material of the bar was guided by considerations that the alloy used was less prone to changes in response to heat influencing length than other substances known to man, and therefore less open to manipulation. The length of the meter was redefined again in terms of the wave-length *in vacuo* of the orange radiation of the krypton 86 atom. The purpose of this change was to make the unit more accurate, not less. Since 1983 the meter is defined in yet another way. The International Bureau of Weights and Measures in Sèvres, France, keeper by treaty of the world's standard units of measurement, has decreed that the meter is the distance that light travels through vacuum in 1/299,792,458 of a second. The increased degree of precision matters. If astronomers treated a meter as most Americans do ('y' know, 'bout a yard'), the resulting inaccuracy would be prodigious. Just between Earth and Mars you would get an error in measurement four million miles long.

If draught depleted the water reservoir of Madrid by one half, the quickest way of restoring volume would be to cut the size of the unit of cubic measure by one half. Demagogues would advocate this course of action arguing that in this way anxiety of city-dwellers about water shortages would be assuaged. Yet we would resist the temptation to follow their advice as it would do nothing to restore water level in the reservoir. Worse still, it might encourage further waste in the use of water just at the time when greater economy would be the wisest course of action.

Exactly the same logic dictates that the government should ignore demagogues and refrain from tampering with the monetary standard in cutting the size of the unit of value at a time when wealth is being dissipated as a result of waste and collapse of savings. Such a foolish course of action would encourage further waste and profligacy just at the time when greater economy and higher rate of savings is called for. Here, however, demagogy gains the upper hand. As profligacy depletes the reservoir of wealth in the country, guardians of the Treasury and the central bank find it expedient to reduce the unit of value in an effort to conceal the disappearance of wealth and the drying up of savings, while masking the dire consequences of extravagance. The amazing thing is that we meekly accept such official tampering with the monetary unit, even though we would reject similar tampering with linear and cubic measures. The explanation of this peculiar inconsistency cannot be compressed sufficiently for presentation here. As if struck with some sort of mass madness, academia and the media are parroting the official propaganda line to the effect that a country with falling value of the monetary unit is better off than the country with a stable one. Consequently the worst currency is the best, and the best currency is the worst. Should this perversity lead to even greater imbalances, waste, and destruction of wealth, then remedy is sought in more of the same: further devaluation of the monetary unit, never in its stabilisation. The profligate country is digging itself ever deeper in the hole. Governments in their wild intoxication with this idiocy have never settled down to face the logical consequences of their position. If a debased currency is better for the nation than one based on a fixed monetary standard, then the best currency of all would be the one having no value at all, and that country would gain most in trade which simply gave away its goods and services in exchange for nothing.

A Milestone in the History of Money

1971 was a milestone in the history of money. Previously in the world's most advanced countries money and credit had been tied to a positive value, that of a well-defined quantity of a good of well-defined quality. In 1971 this tie was severed, the fixed unit of value discarded and replaced by a variable one. Today the value of currencies is no longer tied to a positive value; it is now defined in terms of negative values, the value of debt instruments. Through this stratagem governments have quietly seized the most pervasive power over the lives of their citizens: the power of disposal over their savings, and the right of first refusal to the fruits of their labour.

The innovation of linking the currency to negative rather than positive values had one immediate consequence, seldom recognised and studiously ignored in the technical and scholarly literature on the subject. The power to reduce total debt in the world through the process of orderly retirement has been lost. Henceforth total indebtedness could only be reduced either through default or through monetary debasement. As the tide of unpaid and unpayable debt grows, so ebbs the value of the monetary unit. This must ultimately spell disaster: the collapse in the value of the monetary unit, inflicting great economic pain and distress on the people.

That we have lost the facility of reducing total indebtedness short of default or monetary debasement can be demonstrated with absolute clarity through the example of the dollar. A debt of one dollar can no longer be extinguished. If it is paid by a check (or a Federal Reserve note) drawn on a (Federal Reserve) bank, the debt is merely transferred from one debtor to another: the liability of the bank has been increased by one dollar. The situation is no better if the debt is paid in coin. The coins of the United States have no intrinsic value. They are mere tokens and as such they, too, represent debt. When paid in coin, a debt of one dollar becomes the liability of the U. S. Treasury itself. It should be clear that substituting one debtor for another is not the same as extinguishing debt.

What we are facing here is an elaborate scheme to cover up default and making mockery of the full faith and credit of the United States. Since the 1971 repudiation the Treasury has not paid any part of its debt in any meaningful sense of the word. Instead it keeps piling new debt upon unpaid debt by juggling interest-paying and non-interest-paying debt instruments. When old debt matures, the Treasury simply replaces it with new, usually on inferior terms. Interest-paying debt is replaced by non-interest-paying debt. In particular, for the first time in history, the U.S. Treasury arrogates itself the power to sell debt to foreign creditors without assuming any responsibility for its redemption. It is issuing liabilities to foreigners which it has neither the intention nor the means to honour. This is a particularly dangerous confidence game, since foreigners are not subject to the jurisdiction of the United States and cannot be taxed as residents can. Foreign creditors are in better position to refuse to be victimised by the prestidigitation that consists in debt-retirement by paying out certificates of 'IOU nothing'. If and when they stop buying U.S. government debt, as at one point they most assuredly will, the Ponzi-scheme will come to a halt and a world crisis will ensue. 'Dollarisation' of the world economy is the next step. Treasury officials aim at promoting the dollar abroad as the ultimate extinguisher of debt. However, this is no more possible than turning stone into bread. In the absence of coercive legal tender provisions foreign creditors cannot be forced to accept the irredeemable dollar in repayment of debt.

Ever since the make-believe arrangement for retiring debt by paying irredeemable dollars to foreigners was introduced in 1971, the United States has been running persistent trade deficits with the rest of the world. This is entirely natural and there is no need to look further for causes and explanations. It is a safe bet that these deficits will continue unabated and the foreign indebtedness of the United States will increase exponentially. The very notion of 'debt maturity' has lost all reasonable meaning previously attached to it. At maturity, creditors are coerced into extending their original credit plus accrued interest, in the form of new credits (possibly to another debtor).

Disenfranchisement and Exploitation

It is true that, for the time being, the creditor has the option to consume his savings at the time the debt matures. But is it not a strange monetary system, to say the least, which forces savers to consume their savings whenever they are not satisfied with the quality of available debt instruments, or with the terms on which they are offered? More to the point: what is the guarantee that creditors will always have that option? Of course, there is no such guarantee. The option is available as long as only a handful of the creditors exercise it. Should their number increase, the option will fast lose its value, and if the rest of creditors get scared and try to exercise their option simultaneously, the music stops and the game of musical chairs will come to a screechy halt.

Creditors to the United States will be holding the bag.

To put it differently, creditors and savers are presently being lulled into believing that their savings exists somewhere, in one form or another, and will be available when they need it. In truth, these savings exist only as the irredeemable promise of a government that has defaulted on its promises to pay as contracted twice in a generation. For the time being, doubting savers are allowed to cash in and consume their savings. But when a sufficiently large number of claimants try to assert their claims simultaneously, the ugly truth will dawn upon the world. The drying up of savings in the United States is a natural phenomenon.

It means that savers are not as stupid as the government would like them to be. [1]

The international monetary system has been turned into a system of massive disenfranchisement, exploiting the world's saving public, the ultimate providers of credit. The power of control over savings is being usurped by the U.S. Treasury. This is also a system of depriving the world's producers of the uninhibited right of disposal of their products. As they are forced to grant first refusal to the issuer of irredeemable promises to pay, producers are disabled in the exercise of the right of free disposal of the fruits of their labour. The two pillars of world prosperity, savers and producers, are thus placed under permanent duress.

It is not possible to defend these arrangements as a paternalistic system benevolently guiding the destiny of the world in the best interest of the people. It is these same arrangements that expose the people to the threat of untold sufferings at the end of the road. The coercive nature of the regime of irredeemable currency is fully commensurate with the coerciveness of similar systems, long since discarded by history: slavery and serfdom. To the extent that coercion and bondage today is covert, whereas they were overtly admitted and practiced under slavery and serfdom, the present regime is even more odious than its historic forerunners. The consensus it represents is akin to that of the drug addict and his pusher. By playing off people's propensity to consume against their propensity to save, and by promoting instant gratification, the regime of irredeemable currency makes people addicted to compulsive consumption in exchange for their acquiescence in coercion and pilferage.

Sweet Dreams, Rude Awakening

Dire predictions were made in 1971 about the future of the irredeemable dollar. It was predicted by many that its value would collapse and all paper currencies would become worthless in a matter of a few years. Events unfolded differently. After the international monetary system adopted dollar-debt as the standard of value, quite predictably, a fast-breeder of debt started operating in earnest. Theoretically, total dollar-debt must increase at least at the same rate as the dollar rate of interest, in order to make debt service possible. In practice, total debt has been increasing much faster than that. Rising commodity prices forced an increase in the stock of money, and the increase in the stock of money gave occasion to further price increases. A vicious circle has been engaged which is reflected in the increase of total dollar-debt.

The propaganda machinery of the government, the media, and academia shifted responsibility for the price-explosion to the oil-sheiks and to the 'gnomes of Zurich'. It was considered impolite to suggest that the cause could, perhaps, be found in the flooding of the world with unwanted dollars. It was considered a sign of paranoia if anyone questioned the wisdom or legitimacy of tying money to negative values, the value of debt.

There were other consequences, too. The interest-rate structure in the world was destabilised, reflecting unprecedented volatility in the bond market. This was also explained away using ad hoc arguments such as crop failure and other natural disasters. Once more, the international monetary system escaped scrutiny, and the dollarisation of the world economy could continue apace, putting ever more creditors as vassals into permanent bondage to the United States. By 1981 it was the turn of other currencies to decline in value. Thereby the dollar regained a semblance of stability. An optical illusion was created that the dollar was 'strong' again, even though it continued losing value in absolute terms. But a dollar appreciating in relative terms was poison in the international monetary system. It made the servicing and the repayment of the dollar-debt well-nigh impossible for foreigners. A debt-crisis engulfed the world. In 1985 governments declared that a 'strong' dollar was against public policy. The value of the dollar had to be clubbed down. Thus, then, a monetary cycle has evolved: the dollar went from weak to strong, and from strong to weak again. It appeared that the value of the dollar was subject to a cyclical pattern, ergo, its fall meant no threat as it was bound to be followed by a rise soon enough to correct it. In reality, however, all currencies were falling in absolute terms, albeit at a variable rate.

The crisis of the international monetary system is concealed under a thin veneer of prosperity. The world is consuming more. A wealth of new products is brought to the market year after year. The world's stock markets have, after being overrun by the tide of newly created dollars, soared to unprecedented heights. People are lulled into a false sense of security. They don't understand or care what is happening to the value of their currency and savings. They act as if they have arrived to the land of Cockaigne where more consumption and less saving combine to bring greater prosperity.

The rude awakening in Japan did not disturb sweet dreams elsewhere. Yet it should be clear that the world economy is a big life-boat which, if leaking water in one corner, will endanger the lives of all occupants regardless where they may be seated. The original doomsday scenario of a dollar losing its purchasing power in one fell swoop has not materialised. The world goes on merrily constructing the Debt Tower of Babel, unmindful of the consequences. But the wise should guard themselves against concluding that the narrow escape of disaster has brought security. The debt crisis is far from over; in fact, it is more threatening than ever. Once the dollar has been destabilised, the path of least resistance is downhill. The roller-coaster ride should not conceal the fact that, when it comes to a stop, it will be at the bottom, rather than the top. All in all, the wild and mindless experimentation with debt money has been an unmitigated disaster, the full extent of which remains to be seen.

The Wisdom of Redeemability

Throughout the long and sometimes painful evolution of civilisation, coined money has always been linked to a metallic monetary standard, and paper currency has always been made redeemable in coin made of the standard metal. To be sure, sporadic experiments with irredeemable currency have occurred but, in every instance without exception, these experiments ended in a humiliating fiasco. Ultimately, sanity and monetary rectitude always prevailed as the deviant currency was made redeemable. Self-styled experts ridicule the requirement that debt be made redeemable in the monetary metal as hopelessly antediluvian. But the requirement to make currency and debt redeemable was not the outcome of backwardness, ignorance, or superstition on the part of our grandfathers. On the contrary, it reflected great practical wisdom as well as the spirit of freedom. It showed a deep understanding that debt was an indispensable pillar of civilisation which, if abused, could cause its collapse.

The great creative role of debt is found in the fact it makes human enterprise possible, irrespective of the accident of birth. In this sense, debt is an agent of freedom. But it must also be well-understood that debt is a double-edged sword. If used improperly, it could do more harm than good. When allowed to accumulate, debt could become an instrument of enslavement. In this sense, debt is also an agent of bondage. For this reason debt ought to be handled with utmost circumspection, and its orderly retirement ought to be promoted by every available means. Only if extinguishing debt was within the power of every individual of character and industry could debt bring its great blessings to mankind. Conversely, if extinguishing it proved to be difficult or impossible, then debt would become a great curse to society.

Inevitably, debt would become an enemy of freedom and an instrument of bondage.

I have already discussed why irredeemable currency makes the reduction of total debt impossible, and how it leads to the snow-balling of debt, a process that is bound to end in a disaster. By contrast, under the regime of a gold standard, debt is reined back and men of character and industry may greatly benefit from it without facing the danger of permanent bondage. It is not surprising that enemies of freedom are inevitably enemies of redeemable currency. It was not an accident of history that the very first act of both the Soviet Bolshevik and the Nazi Socialist governments was the abolition of redeemable currency and the imposition of the most severe foreign exchange controls.

Take the Current When it Serves, or Lose our Ventures

In 1971 the largest holders of dollar balances abroad were the members of the European Economic Community (EEC). A large part of the savings of the prosperous burghers in Europe was invested in dollar-denominated debt. When the U.S. government refused to honour its promise to pay its debt in gold as contracted and in doing so it defaulted on its obligations to overseas creditors, the central banks of the EEC countries were hit with huge losses, the size of which was unprecedented in the annals of international finance.

Determined that they will not be victimised again in this fashion, the EEC countries decided to create a new international currency of their own, the euro. On January 1, 1999, outstanding debt in most of the EEC countries was converted at a fixed rate into euro-debt. It was hoped that the new currency would be based on a thorough and careful analysis of the dollar-debâcle. Indeed, there was much to be learned from the ill-starred experiment with the fast-breeder of dollar-debt which has saddled the world with mountains of unpaid and unpayable debt.

As reflected by the volatility of the interest-rate structure, the value of debt has been destabilised and was subject to unprecedented fluctuations. In consequence, the seeds of deflation have been spread in the world. It is already consuming the economic vitality of Japan, and sapping the energy of other countries in Asia and Latin America. A low and falling interest-rate structure is no less dangerous than a high and rising one. One sucks businesses into bankruptcy just as readily as the other. There is no way to assert with any degree of certainty whether the deflationary or the inflationary danger is greater, as the pendulum is swinging from extreme high to extreme low interest rates. In spite of the deflationary threat, the spectre of an inflationary collapse has not disappeared. It is still very much alive. The world's hunger for dollar-debt could reach the saturation point at any time without prior notice (those old enough may recall that this saturation point was once reached in 1974 already). If and when the demand for dollars dries up, the debt-markets will be thrown into a tailspin. This explains why the Year of the Euro has been hailed as a great historical opportunity:

There is a tide in the affairs of men
Which, taken at the flood, leads on to fortune;
Omitted, all the voyage of their life
Is bound in shallows and in miseries.
On such a full sea are we now afloat,
And we must take the current when it serves, Or lose our ventures.
(Shakespeare, Julius Caesar, 4–iii–217.)

Have the EEC countries taken the current when it serves? If they have, they could rid the world of the servitude of bad debt. They could disengage the fast breeder of debt sprung upon the world by the United States in 1971. They could enable people of character and industry to free themselves of bondage. In order to bring these great benefits the euro, unlike the dollar, is supposed to be defined in terms of positive rather than negative values.

Robin Hood Money in Reverse

That did not happen. The tide was missed, and a great historic opportunity to deliver the world from evil has been lost. The voyage of people's life is now bound in shallows and in miseries. The euro that has been introduced is just another irredeemable currency, designed to entrench the Moloch of debt. It contributes nothing to the stability of the international monetary system. It merely replaces one kind of bondage with another. Authors of the euro expect that the new currency will be as strong as the German mark used to be. They forget that no chain is ever stronger than its weakest link. They hope that people will be more confident to lend and borrow euros than dollars. Given the fact that the euro is not tainted with repudiation, defaults, broken promises, bad faith, monetary mischief and duplicity as is the dollar, they are confident that they are making a positive contribution to the world economy.

Regrettably, this is not so. 'The mountain has gone into labour and gave birth to a mouse'. The euro, another 'Esperanto' currency, was conceived in sin. It is grounded in the belief that it is possible to fool all the people all of the time. It is trying to perpetuate the myth that a durable international monetary system can be constructed on the foundation of irredeemable promises. The euro, in competition with the dollar, may succeed in plundering the savers and pilfering the producers. It is not Robin Hood money. It is Robin Hood money in reverse.

Previous historical experiments with irredeemable promises to pay had been local and temporary. It was the refuge of weak governments living in monetary backwater. Whenever they exhausted their credit lines, they defaulted on their promises to pay and declared their dishonoured paper 'money'. These episodes, designed to cover up the fact of repudiation, were ephemeral. Other countries with self-respecting governments refused to listen to the siren-song. They continued to deal with their creditors honourably. They paid their debt according to the terms of contract, that is, surrendering positive values at maturity. Wayward countries would feel obliged to return to the fold sooner or later, resuming redemption of their outstanding debt.

The euro represents a new adventure in bad faith. Its authors were promising emancipation from dollar-slavery. What they gave the citizens of EEC and the world instead is a choice between euro-debt slavery and dollar-debt slavery. We are treated to the spectacle of some of the richest countries offering competition to the United States in flooding the world with make-believe currency. They issue obligations that they have neither the intention nor the resources to pay. They cover up the deceit by maintaining that their irredeemable promise to pay is 'money', the ultimate means of payment. They are coercing their domestic and foreign creditors, producers and savers, into accepting the irredeemable euro in final payment of debt.

The extent of corruption is clearly shown by the fact that there is not one court of law in Euroland with sufficient wisdom and moral fibre to challenge this fraud making mockery of debt-retirement. Nor is there a university in Euroland with sufficient courage to establish the fact that the practice of issuing irredeemable promises to pay fully exhausts the definition of the crime commonly called fraud, regardless whether it is committed by an individual, by a government, or by a group of governments. Even those members of the EEC that declined to join the euro-scheme, namely the United Kingdom, Sweden, and Denmark, are guilty of deceit. They have failed to criticise the euro on grounds that its issuance violates the principles of common decency. They have failed to point out that the euro is a prescription for the pauperisation of people at home and abroad through deliberate currency debasement.

Authorship of the Policy of Deliberate Currency Debasement

The three decades since 1971 is not a great length of time when measured in historical terms. But it is sufficiently long to warrant an examination of the deliberate policy of disenfranchisement and exploitation, the experiment with irredeemable currency in the light of its practical consequences. Has this policy served the people well? Or, perhaps, the negative results of the experiment justify a more careful examination of the principles involved than hitherto carried out? The question is not raised, and the euro-scheme is launched without the slightest attempt at soul-searching in this regard. A great deal of obfuscation surrounds the issue. Officialdom has declared the topic off limits to scholarship and research. Anyone who dares to question the legitimacy of irredeemable currency, anyone who dares to challenge the official tenet that the paper monetary standard represents 'progress' over 'obsolete' metallic standards, is browbeaten and subjected to ostracism. Professional standing in the monetary field is reserved for those sycophants who pay lip service to official propaganda, to the dogma that metallic monetary standards 'have been swept away by the progressive forces of history' and any effort to restore them is tantamount to trying to turn the clock back.

Let us bypass the question whether standards of honesty and upright dealing can ever become 'obsolete'. Let us refrain from asking why the surrender of positive rather than negative values in discharge of obligations has become antediluvian just at the time when the United States was ready to default on its debt. Let us disregard the question what is the justification for double standards of justice allowing the United States and the EEC to issue promises to pay that they have neither the intention nor the means to honour, while the same conduct would constitute criminal fraud if committed by private parties. Instead, let us examine who the original authors and apostles of the 'progressive' monetary system involving irredeemable currency were, and what their original intention was in proposing the disenfranchisement of the saving and producing public.

The euro is a leap towards the realisation of the aims of The Communist Manifesto. In 1848 Marx and Engels published this document describing their design for a step-by-step transformation of the system of production based on free and voluntary cooperation into a command economy. The proletarians should 'win the battle of democracy' and thus raise themselves to the position of ruling class. Then they should use their supremacy to wrest, by degrees, all capital from the bourgeoisie. Marx and Engels gave detailed instructions for the measures to be adopted, including the centralisation of credit and the issuance of legal tender banknotes. [2] They were fully aware that the measures recommended were destructive to social cooperation *in the extreme.* They meant, in their own words, 'despotic inroads on property-rights and on the conditions of capitalistic production', moreover, they were 'measures economically insufficient and untenable but which, in the course of the movement would outstrip themselves, necessitating further inroads upon the old social order, and are unavoidable as a means of entirely revolutionising the mode of production'. Undoubtedly, the blueprint for the irredeemable dollar and euro were copied straight out of the Communist Manifesto.

It is noteworthy that the adoption of the monetary provisions of the Communist Manifesto in 1971 and 1999 was not received by public outcry and protest, nor was it resisted in any significant way by the people as, for example, the abolition of the freedom of press and assembly could have been. This lack of interest finds its explanation in the simple fact that the public still does not understand, even after the miserable record of the dollar during the past thirty years in losing nine-tenth of its purchasing power, that we are facing a gigantic scheme of embezzlement of savings. It also shows the extent of decay and corruption in the media and academia. Those not in thrall to the Communist Manifesto have been muzzled through bribes, blackmail, and other administrative measures. Their voices are not heard, so their arguments can safely be ignored. In the words of John Maynard Keynes (written before he joined the forces of destruction):

> " *Lenin is said to have declared that the best way to destroy the capitalist system was to debauch the currency. By a continuing process of inflation governments can confiscate, secretly and unobserved, an important part of the wealth of their citizens. By this method they not only confiscate, but they confiscate arbitrarily and, while the process impoverishes many, it enriches some. The sight of this arbitrary arrangement of riches strikes not only at security, but at confidence in the equity of distribution of wealth.*

Lenin was certainly right. There is no subtler, no surer means of overthrowing the existing order of society than debauching the currency. The process engages all the hidden forces of economic law on the side of destruction, and does it in a manner which not one man in a million is able to diagnose. [3]

Timeo Danaos et Dona Ferentes

The introduction of the euro must be considered as a victory for International Communism. It is an intriguing question to contemplate whether, in the final analysis, the 1991 defeat of communism will turn out to be less important than its 1999 victory. More intriguing still is the question whether or not both events are an organic part of the same grand strategy. Communism had only defeats to chalk up in every open contest. Its successes were confined exclusively to the field of clandestine operations and conspiracy. **A hopeless bungler of construction, communism is a brilliant master of destruction.** We may safely assume that this verdict of history was not entirely lost upon the the communist leadership that by 1991 was ready to cut its losses. If it felt forced to abandon enterprises where constructive skills were indispensable, by the same token, it must have felt encouraged to retain or even expand projects in the execution of which its expertise was unsurpassed. The Bolshevik leadership may have been eager to imitate deceit employed by the ancient Greeks. After laying siege to the city of Troy for ten years in vain, the Greeks decided that where brute *force* fails, *cunning* may go a long way. They pretended to give up their plan to destroy Troy and sailed away in their ships. But they left behind what has come to be known as the Trojan Horse, with Greeks in its belly armed to the teeth. In vain did the high priest of Troy, Laocoon, warn his compatriots: '*timeo Danaos et dona ferentes*' (I fear the Greeks, and those bearing gifts). The jubilant people of Troy dragged the horse inside of the walls of their city to celebrate what they thought was their victory. But after nightfall the armed Greek soldiers climbed out of the Trojan Horse and murdered the city-dwellers, tired of celebration, in their sleep.

The Bolsheviks ended the siege of Western Europe in 1991, pretending to give up their almost 75-year experimentation with command economy. However, they left behind the Trojan Horse in the form of **Lenin's monetary legacy**. By 1999 the Trojan Horse was firmly implanted in the inner *sanctum* of the citadel of Western Europe, in the form of the newly created euro.

It is naive to suppose that the people promoting and financing inter-national communism accepted defeat and gave up their luciferian lust for world-domination without a fight in 1991. It is more likely that they considered that Western Europe was fully capable of destroying the basis of its own prosperity. In discarding the principle of *pacta sunt servanda* (contracts are made to be honoured), it would let the constitutional order be subverted. All the Bolshevik leaders [4] would have to do now is to sit back and watch the drama as it unfolds. In the fullness of time the Trojan Horse will regurgitate the contents of its entrails. In fulfilment of Lenin's prophecy the debauchery of the currency will eventually overturn the existing basis of society. Western Europe, softened up by currency debasement would fall, like a ripe apple, into the lap of Communism, just as Germany did fall into the lap of Nazi Socialism, after it had similarly been softened by currency debasement. The Bolsheviks must be superbly confident that, with the economic resources of Western Europe at their disposal, they will succeed where their predecessors have failed.

It is a cruel joke to suggest that 'Capitalism is burying Communism', and that 'the philosophical tenor of our time is democracy and the free market, to the exclusion of totalitarianism and the command economy', unless the world is willing to dump not just Lenin's statues, but Lenin's monetary legacy as well, in order to emancipate the savers and the producers of the world from their present servitude.

Double-entry Book-keeping and the Euro

In order to assess the future prospects of the euro we have to reach back to basic principles. It is not good enough to present ad hominem arguments to the effect that the world is facing a monetary collapse as politicians and bankers, freed from the fetters of the gold standard, could not resist the temptation and would enrich themselves through monetary manipulation. We must have a scientific argument that would apply even if politicians and bankers were saints imbued with altruism.

I shall argue that the euro does indeed face an eventual collapse because its authors have recklessly ignored the basic principles of double-entry book-keeping. The euro is designed to confuse the concepts of liability and asset. It is true that the dollar also operates the same way, however, it was not so designed at inception. The collapse of the euro may take the form of an implosion of debt through default (deflationary scenario) or through depreciation (inflationary scenario) or, possibly, through a mixture of both.

Since the value of the monetary unit is defined in terms of debt,

and debt is bound to implode after reaching a certain threshold,
the world is inexorably driven towards monetary collapse.

Double-entry book-keeping is one of the main pillars of society. Without it progress, indeed, production and distribution of the means of preserving human lives at present levels of security, health, and comfort, would be unthinkable. Double-entry book-keeping is based on the clearest possible distinction between an asset and a liability. It is true that a particular item may be a liability in the balance sheet of one while serving as an asset in the balance sheet of another. What monetary cranks are advocating is an arrangement whereby governments are enabled to shift items freely from the liability to the asset column of the same balance sheet. Like alchemists of old, they could create wealth out of nothing (better still, out of less than nothing).

The job of the illusionists and the conjurer is to deceive the audience into believing that something contrary to the laws of reality has been accomplished before their very eyes. The essence of irredeemable currency is the same. The monetary unit is defined in terms of government debt. What has been a liability, through monetary prestidigitation and machination, is turned into an asset. The illusionist has succeeded in deceiving the public. Pretence can be maintained for varying lengths of time. People are lulled into a false sense of security. They are made to believe that their savings are there, and could be drawn upon any time when needed. From time to time they may even test this assumption and withdraw larger or smaller amounts. When they do, they are happy to conclude that their savings are safe.

But are they really? The harsh reality is that the government has long since spent their savings and would have to tax people to get it back if a sufficiently large number of savers tried to withdraw it simultaneously. This number may not be reached for a year, for a decade, or even for a generation. The supply of fools in the world is very great indeed. But it is not inexhaustible. Eventually, after many false starts, the truth will dawn upon everyone. But then it will be too late to withdraw the savings that were never there in the first place, except as an irredeemable promise.

Inflationary and Deflationary Phases

While the ultimate outcome may not be in doubt, the course of history is impossible to predict. The inflationary phase of currency depreciation is well-understood. Less well understood is that it alternates with a deflationary phase. This will reinforce the illusion that the purchasing power of the currency, while it obviously fluctuates, is not really in danger of collapsing. Indeed, the government will be quick to take credit for the feat of 'controlling inflation' every time another deflationary phase starts and, likewise, of 'controlling deflation' when a new inflationary phase sets in. Needless to say, the government performed no feat of any sort. The only way to control the real value of the currency is to tie it to positive values. It may take a long time to find out this elementary truth, but the value of a promise promising nothing is exactly that, nothing. As long as the currency is tied to negative values, depreciation will be the inevitable outcome.

It is only to be expected that the process of depreciation will be opaque. It is hardly ever a one-way street. Currency debasement moves by fits and starts. It is never clear-cut nor easily understandable. It is always confusing. If it wasn't, the party would be over before it got started. Producers would refuse to exchange real goods and services for irredeemable promises to pay. Savers would refuse to allow their savings to be denominated in a depreciating currency. But precisely because the process of currency depreciation is opaque, and because it moves by fits and starts, it will be prolonged and agonising.

We can make another broad-brush picture of the shape of things to come. Apart from minor leads and lags, the price level and the rate of interest are going to move in tandem. A rise in the price level (hinting at currency depreciation) will be accompanied by a tendency of the rate of interest to rise as well. Likewise, a fall (hinting at a remission of currency depreciation) will be accompanied by a tendency of the rate of interest to fall. There is a simple explanation for this puzzling phenomenon called 'linkage'. The process of currency depreciation can be pictured as an oscillating money-flow to-and-fro between the bond market and the commodity market. When fearful of the safety of their savings invested in debt, people move it *en masse* from the bond to the commodity market. This move makes the interest rate and the commodity price level rise together (inflationary phase). When stockpiles become so large that saleability at exaggerated prices becomes problematic, people grow fearful of the safety of their savings invested in commodities. There follows a reversal of the tide: exodus of money from the commodity market and into the bond market. This makes the rate of interest fall together with the price level (deflationary phase). This is known as the Kondratiev long-wave cycle, that may take 60 to 70 years to repeat itself. The last inflationary phase started in 1947 and ended in 1980; we are apparently still in the deflationary phase that started in the early 1980s.

The oscillating money-flow between the commodity and bond markets, caused by the savers making the tide flow in one and ebb in the other before changing roles, is further aggravated by speculators who understand the dynamics of the Kondratiev cycle. They go long in commodities and sell bonds short during the inflationary phase. Just before the tide turns, they take profit by selling commodities and by covering their short positions in bonds, and get ready for the deflationary phase in going long in bonds and selling commodities short. Of course, speculators know full-well that the onset of the deflationary phase does not mean the end of currency depreciation. The wild roller-coaster ride is going to continue and get even wilder. Just as a coin has two sides: heads and tails, currency depreciation has two phases: the inflationary and deflationary phase. Neither phase can be understood without understanding the other. A one-phase currency depreciation (inflation without deflation) is just as unthinkable as a coin *missing one side*.

The Hot-Money Cycle

We have seen how people try to protect their savings and in doing so they induce an oscillating money-flow to-and-fro between the bond and commodity markets. This pendulum-like swing conceals the underlying phenomenon of currency depreciation. But there is also a second pendulum: that of hot money jumping from one currency depreciating relatively faster to another that, for the moment, is considered safer as it is depreciating more slowly.

I do not hesitate to predict that the hot-money pendulum will focus on two currencies: the dollar and the euro. To begin with, the dollar will be preferred while the euro is considered an unknown entity. As the dollar-debasement will continue unabated, hot money is going to jump from dollars into euros, making the former fall and the latter rise. Then the pendulum turns, and hot money will jump back from the euro to the dollar. When it does, the illusion is created that the dollar is strong. In truth both the dollar and the euro are falling in absolute terms, albeit at different rates. Since the 'rise' is measured in terms of a falling standard, it is not a rise at all. The hot-money cycle, of course, has a different frequency from that of the Kondratiev long-wave cycle. I predict that it will be shorter, but we have to wait and see how events unfold before we can say more. Foreign exchange speculators aggravate the hot-money cycle just as bond speculators aggravate the Kondratiev cycle. It goes without saying that both cycles aggravate the process of monetary destruction.

The Metamorphosis of Speculation

It is important to note how the nature of speculation has changed since 1971. Beforehand bond values and the rate of interest were stable, along with foreign exchange rates, precluding speculative activity in the bond and foreign exchange markets. Speculation was confined to agricultural commodities where it had a stabilising effect. All the risks were nature-given, none were man-made. Speculators were forced by the 'invisible hand' to resist the formation of price-trends. Bull-speculators had to sell as prices rose; bear speculators had to cover their short positions as prices fell.

The nature of speculation changed dramatically when the monetary unit was redefined in terms of negative values. Bond prices and foreign exchange rates were destabilised. In response, for the first time, speculation emerged as a permanent feature of the bond and foreign exchange markets. However, significantly, speculation never had a stabilising effect in the bond and foreign exchange markets. The reason for this is simple enough. The risks are not nature-given. They are man-made. Speculation in these markets has the character of a wager. One set of gamblers (the speculators) is setting their wits against those of another (the central bankers and treasury officials). Speculators are freed from their obligation to resist the formation of price trends. They are now inclined to ride price trends rather than oppose them. They jump on the bandwagon, thereby making volatility soar. Their job is no longer to compensate for nature's fickleness, but to outwit central bank and treasury officials. And they usually do.

Central bank officials as a rule are very smart people. But they are civil servants on fixed salary. Their personal stake in the outcome of the wager is limited. This is in contrast with that of the speculators, who risk their own wealth. Also, central bank officials were trained in a different school. Their mindset is different. They don't risk their own money. They have virtually unlimited access to the public purse to cover their losses. Speculators must quit playing when they have exhausted their capital. Ever since currency devaluation was made 'respectable' by the governments in the 1930s, a staggering amount of public money has been lost to speculators in the foreign exchange markets. After 1971 bond speculation made its debut and the losing streak of central bankers has continued.

It is not possible to understand the dynamics of currency depreciation without understanding the metamorphosis of speculation, from benign to malignant. It is noteworthy that this topic is off limits as far as subsidised economic research is concerned. The metamorphosis has been made 'taboo' in the media and academia by the powers that be. Financial writers and researchers must parrot the official propaganda line that interest-rate speculation that drives the derivatives markets, and foreign exchange speculation that determines the relative values of the dollar and the euro, are a stabilising factor in the economy, the same way as speculation in agricultural commodities, which is an absurd lie. The derivatives markets are programmed to self-destruct through explosive growth.

The Rubble of the Ruble

The Ruble is a reminder what is happening to all currencies based on debt. The savings of the Russian people has been wiped out. Job opportunities in the country, one of the richest in natural resources, are disappearing. Private foreign investments are going up in smoke choking off the flow of new capital. Russia is drowning in debt. Great economic hardship is visited upon hundreds of million innocent people. Life expectancy is on the decrease, infant mortality is on the rise. A similar scenario is unfolding in other parts of the third world. The self-immolation is due to a single cause: the mindless experimentation with currency tied to negative values. Opinion-makers blame the disaster on a plethora of loosely related *ad hoc* causes. However, they all have a hidden agenda: that of propping up the regime of irredeemable currencies, the most pervasive single corrupting factor of our times.

Exactly the same forces that devastated the Russian ruble will ultimately threaten the dollar and the euro. It is not inconceivable that the dollar may at one point lose half of its purchasing power within a month, as did the ruble. Self-styled experts dismiss this saying 'it can never happen here'. But it could and did. America in the 1770s and 1860s, France in the 1720s ands 1790s, Germany in the 1920s and 1940s had gone through the same harrowing experience. More recently the currencies of these and other countries lost up to nine-tenth of their purchasing power during the 1970s. We may say categorically that the cure of cancer has not been discovered in the intervening years. Our money-managers have not acquired the know-how, if such exists, to avert similar disasters in the future.

Millennia come and go, but man still gains his bread by the sweat of his brow, and not by clever tricks in trying to shift entries from the liability to the asset column in the balance sheet of the government.

Self-Destruction of Irredeemable Currency

The explanation of hyperinflation in terms of the quantity theory of money is untenable. You cannot explain non-linear phenomena in terms of a linear model. The proper explanation must be sought in terms of a non-linear model. Such a model can be developed using the concepts of basis and backwardation. If applied to the monetary metals, we shall see the cataclysmic conflict that will bring about the end of the regime of irredeemable currency. No one can predict the future, but science makes it possible for us to find the most likely course of events. It is in this spirit that I offer the following observations.

As the regime of irredeemable currency threatens to crumble under the weight of the inordinate debt tower of Babel, people increasingly take flight to gold. Supplies will get tight and the gold basis will fall. The gold futures market may even go to backwardation [5] briefly at the triple-witching hour, i.e., the hour when gold futures, as well as call and put options on them expire together. Later, flirtation with backwardation may occur even more often, at the end of every month when gold futures expire. Gold will get caught up in a storm.

Backwardation in gold has a perverse effect. In the case of agricultural commodities backwardation provides a most powerful incentive for traders to sell the cash commodity and buy the futures. Not so in the case of gold. Rather than bringing out deliverable supplies of gold, backwardation tends to remove them. The more the gold basis falls the less likely it becomes that owners will exchange their cash gold for futures. Please remember that you have seen it here first. This perversion of the gold basis constitutes the self-destroying mechanism of the regime of irredeemable currency. The longs tend to take delivery on their gold futures contracts in ever greater numbers, and refuse to recycle cash gold into futures, regardless how low the gold basis may go. As it is not set up to satisfy demand for delivery on 100 percent of the open interest, the gold futures market will default. Exchange officials will declare a 'liquidation only' policy to offset long positions in gold. At that point all offers to sell cash gold will be withdrawn. Gold is not for sale at any price. The shorts are absolved of their failure to deliver on their gold futures contracts.

Previous descriptions of hyperinflation purporting to explain the descent of a currency into the abyss of worthlessness do so in terms of the quantity theory of money. My explanation of the hyperinflation that is staring us in the face is very different. I dismiss the quantity theory of money as a linear model that is not applicable. Every previous episode of hyperinflation took place in the context of a war replete with shortages caused by the destruction of stockpiles and productive facilities. In this situation it is not possible to sort out the effects of an increasing demand (due to a flood of printing-press money) and a decreasing supply (due to the destruction of stockpiles and production facilities). We want to show that prices may also explode in the presence of unsold stockpiles and ongoing production.

Moreover, previous episodes of hyperinflation affected isolated countries which had embraced the regime of irredeemable currency out of desperation, while the rest of the world stayed the course of monetary rectitude.

> In the present situation the entire world has been inflicted with irredeemable currency. There are no gold standard countries around that could lend a helping hand to countries that want to stabilise their currency.

My description of hyperinflation is not in terms of the quantity theory of money, but in terms of a model where the relentlessly declining gold basis leads to backwardation destroying the gold futures market. When all offers to sell cash gold are withdrawn, producers of essential commodities such as grains and crude oil refuse payments in dollars, and demand gold in exchange for their product. The dollar and other irredeemable currencies will go the way of the assignat.

Backwardation in gold should therefore be considered the self-destroying mechanism for the regime of irredeemable currency that 'only one man in a million may identify and understand'(my thanks to Keynes for the felicitous phrase). This is where supply/demand analysis is utterly useless. The huge stocks of monetary gold are still in existence, yet zero supply confronts infinite demand.

The only way to fend off this outcome is for the government of the U.S. to come up with a credible plan to stabilise the dollar in terms of gold. Presently there is no hint that contingency plans for the rehabilitation of the gold standard exist. It doesn't matter. Any country, e.g., China, India, Iran, could do it through the back door by opening the Mint to the free and unlimited coinage of gold and silver. The alternative may be mass starvation in the midst of plenty as world trade comes to a halt for want of a universally acceptable medium of exchange.

Here is a question for the U.S. President and Treasury Secretary to contemplate: How many innocent lives are they willing to sacrifice on the altar of doctrinaire purity in defence of their untenable gold policies?

To understand how thoroughly unsound the present monetary system is, it is helpful to revisit its early advocates and examine their arguments. The names John Maynard Keynes (1883-1946) and Milton Friedman (1912-2006) come to mind. But we could do no better than start with Irving Fisher (1867-1947), American statistician and economist of Yale University. In 1936 he published an small book with the title *100% Money*. [6]

The proposals presented in this book could have served as the blueprint for the world's global monetary system as it exists today. Briefly, Fisher proposed to hurl the world headlong into thorough-going inconvertible paper money. The presumably good assets of banks and the presumably good bonds issued by the governments of the major powers, above all, by the government of the United States of America are to be converted into inconvertible paper money — the most effective and ruthless device for defrauding innocent and helpless people that (some) human beings probably have ever devised. [7]

Once the Fisher plan is adopted, the currency is 'reflated' (a word devised to remove one's fear of inflation) until the price level reaches a presumed 'optimum'. [8] Thereafter the stock of money is managed in such a way as to perpetuate this optimum.[9]
History is strewn with the wreckage and record of human suffering caused by 'ingenuous devices' to issue inconvertible paper money and to 'remedie' the consequences flowing from the issue. These efforts to create wealth out of paper, to make something out of nothing, are a species of black magic, and they have always failed.[10]

The Fisher proposal and the present global experiment with inconvertible paper money differ from earlier experiments principally in their intricacies, ingenuity, and the cleverness with which the hocus-pocus involved is covered up. [11] The operation of the monetary system is shrouded in technical details to the effect that the average observer experiences considerable difficulty in forming a clear picture of its nature and implications, and putting his finger on the fallacies and dangers involved. [12]

These dangers appear as a consequence of the principle of causality. However, there is an unknown lag between cause and effect that greatly confuses the issue.

There are great advantages (from the point of view of the perpetrators) in having a plan so intricate and technical in nature to explain and understand, that it remains a mystery to all but a small number of specialists in the field. [13] To add insult to injury, the system uses bribes and blackmail to silence those specialists who demur. Through an incestuous incentive system research grants and official favours are available only to those who approve of the plan. Mystery attracts people and its author always has the advantage. He can talk in broad terms, he can speak of admirable objectives. He can dodge embarrassing questions. He can hide behind labels that hypnotise and elicit approval, such as 'restoring prosperity,' 'prevention of depressions', 'supplying people with the money to meet their needs', and so on.There are hardly any politicians who have the proper training in monetary theory and history who could recognise the fallacies in Fisher's and the managed money advocates' plan, and who could see the dangers. During the twentieth century universities and research institutes were purged, both by passive means (such as natural attrition through retirement) and by active (such as denying research grants, and withholding promotion) with the result that monetary scientists equipped with a proper understanding of the dangers are now few and far between.Concerning these dangers that the global monetary system has in store for countries, while inflation is generally recognised, the same cannot be said of the deflationary danger that is ever present because of the insidious capital destruction, [14] the inevitable consequence of managed money, the Achillean heel of the new millennium of fiat money.Advocates of managed money insist that they are opposed to inflation. They also shout from their rooftops that they have all the tools needed to control 'deflation', the latter they simplistically identify with a 'falling average price level'. 'Just print as much money as it takes'. However, they never examine the question to what extent this 'control' is or could be counter-productive: instead of curing deflation it might make it worse. The Quantitative Easing program, the Zero Interest-Rate Policy and the creation of trillions of dollars in new money throws into gear an engine that may not be possible to stop except at the cost of a terrible crash, loose talk about 'tapering' and 'exit strategies' notwithstanding. Considering these facts, it does not change the picture in the least, nor is it of the slightest consequence (except in so far as it misleads people), for the policymakers of the monetary regime to call themselves 'stabilisers' and 'experts in the art of money-management'. Their good intentions (if any) amount to nothing in the face of the consequences of uncorking the bottle and letting the genie out to roam around the world creating chaos in its wake.Fisher's book on 100% Money says on its title page that it is designed to keep bank deposits 100% liquid to prevent bank runs, both inflation and deflation; it would cure or prevent depressions; and it would wipe out much of the government debt. [15] The purposes and assumed advantages of the Fisher-plan and also those of our present global monetary regime to make money independent of loans by divorcing from the banking business, that is, creating and destroying money; to make Banking safer and more profitable; to prevent booms, bubbles and depressions, by ending chronic inflations and deflations. The 'fractional' reserve banking business model, Fisher says, in contrast with his 100 % reserve banking business model:

> " *impels bankers to make and unmake money not according to any criterion at all, but by a sort of mob rule, guided fitfully by reserve requirements and other factors, and, in a depression, by the instinct of self-preservation, followed blindly and individually, regardless of what the effect may be on the value of the dollar, the welfare of the public, or even on the collective welfare of the bankers themselves.' (p 99).*

The essentials of the Fisher 100 % plan and of the current global monetary regime are as follows. Through the open market committee of the U.S. Federal Reserve, or through the monetary council of the European Central Bank or that of the Bank of Japan, governments are to turn into cash enough of the assets of every commercial bank to increase the cash reserve of each bank to up to 100 % of deposits. Fisher complains that the assets (other than cash reserves held by the banks) cannot be employed to meet the demand liabilities of the bank. His plan would convert these assets into cash that can be so employed. The banks would be authorised to pay out these promises of the government, although the government could not and would not redeem them. Stated in another way, the assets of the banks – promises of others to pay the banks – would be converted into promises of the government to pay on demand, although these promises of the government were made in bad faith, with the knowledge that it would not and could not redeem these notes on demand. [16] Thus the Fisher plan leads into an inconvertible currency scheme, and rests upon the doctrine that it is wise and proper for the government to enter into agreements that it knows it cannot fulfil. [17] The same doctrine is also at the heart of our present global monetary regime. The unsound nature of this doctrine runs through the experience of nations throughout the entire history of money.The conversion of interest-bearing government debt into inconvertible paper money involves a confusion of an investment instrument and a medium of exchange. It is a check-kiting scheme whereby one arm of the government (the Treasury) issues unlimited amounts of promises to pay (Treasury bonds) while the other arm (the Federal Reserve, hereafter F.R.) also issues unlimited amounts of promises to pay (F.R.

notes and deposits). Neither arm makes provision for meeting the liability at maturity. The two arms then swap promises. The Treasury uses the F.R. notes and deposits to retire its bonds at maturity; The Fed uses the Treasury bonds as reserves for issuing more F.R. credit. Such a shuffling of vacuous promises to pay is a conspiracy dealt with by the Criminal Code. It is criminal even if reserves to pay the liability were kept. (Charles Ponzi did pay his clients as promised until he was put out of business by the government.) Now the government assumes Ponzi's role and adjudicates that the very same activity when carried on by itself is legal and proper. [18] At the same time it makes it sure that every request for review by the Supreme Court is routinely turned down. Looking at this chicanery one question readily presents itself : what will hold citizens back from defrauding each other when the government sets the example of defrauding its own citizens by issuing and juggling irredeemable promises to pay?Our global monetary system in converting interest-bearing debt into inconvertible paper currency involves a form of currency manipulation which, as the various nations of the world have learned many times, is a method of defrauding the people. An inconvertible paper currency is a dishonest and immoral governmental and banking device, and no process of reasoning or sleight-of-hand device can change this fact. It is upon such fraudulent device that our global monetary system fundamentally rests.One argument of Fisher, also used by the protagonists of our global monetary system, is that the 100% plan eliminates the alleged fraud involved in 'fractional reserve banking'. However, fractional reserve banking, properly implemented, involves no fraud. [19] The commercial bank substitutes its credit, which is usable and generally acceptable, for the borrower's credit which is not in a readily usable or acceptable form, and charges a fee in the form of interest or discount for performing the service. Moreover, the law requires the bank to maintain a certain percentage of reserve against the credit which the bank extends so that cash can be paid out as needed. Thus Fisher and the protagonists of our global monetary system condemn fractional reserve banking traditionally performed by commercial banks, while offering as a substitute something far more dangerous. Besides, as we have seen, fractional reserve banking is neither dishonest nor immoral (See volume I) whereas Fisher's 100% money plan and our present global monetary system is thoroughly rotten as it squarely aims at defrauding helpless and innocent people.

Where Are We Now?

The Fed, the ECB and the Bank of Japan have together printed US$ 10 trillion [20] during the eleven years between 2006 and 2017. Global debt has grown exponentially and is now around US$ 250 trillion. The three main central banks' balance sheets have expanded at about the same rate in this period in their attempt to prevent the Banking system and the global monetary system from collapsing. Initially the Fed was in the lead, but since 2015 the ECB and the Bank of Japan have played catch-up. All three started from below $1 trillion at the beginning of the century and have added US$ 4.5 trillion each. It is expected that it is now the Fed's turn to play catch-up. Meanwhile the metric to measure the growth of global debt may have to be changed from US$ 1 trillion to US$ 10 trillion. But you cannot build prosperity on a lie, on the unlimited proliferation of inconvertible currency, by breaking laws that have stood the test of times. Governments' money scheme has lasted a century during which the value of all major currencies in the world declined between 97 and 99%. In the next few years we will see money-printing on a scale that will make all these currencies worthless by declining the final 1-3%. Most people cannot fathom the 100% destruction of currency values. Yet it has happened before. The central banks do not even try to conceal the fact that their aim is the destruction of the value of their own currencies. [21] By creating infinite amounts of inconvertible currencies central banks are not just putting off temporarily the demise of the global monetary system. They are also creating false prosperity by fuelling stock market and real estate price rises to unprecedented heights. [22] Stock market averages have duplicated the expansion of the balance sheets of the major central banks. Since March 2009 the combined balance sheet of the Fed, the ECB and the Bank of Japan is up 2.3 times while the Standard and Poor stock market average is up 3.5 times. This is where we are now. But for stock market averages to go further up, more money must be printed. At the same time, the marginal productivity of newly printed money is declining at an alarming rate. For the GDP to grow by US$ 1 credit must be expanded by several dollars! Worse still is the situation concerning the growth of global debt. The debt of the U.S. government at present is US$ 20 trillion and will at least double in the next 8 years as it has every 8 years since 1980. In addition, private and corporate debt is also increasing at similar rates. (U.S corporate debt is up US$ 8 trillion since 2010). The bad news is that that bad debt is also increasing apace. Eventually, all outstanding debt will become bad debt with no chance of ever being repaid.The belief that central banks keep the situation well in hand is false. It is true that the Fed, for example, can put more reserves at the disposal of member banks, but the latter may not want to use them (for being afraid to lend), or the latter could not use them (because businessmen may not want to borrow.) Fisher is not afraid of this. He says that 'if the tub is 100% full, then any additional water must overflow.' (p 110). This ignores the possibility that people may be prompted to use the additional currency created (because they feared its depreciation) to buy commodities (e.g., gold or silver). Fisher assumes that his inconvertible paper currency bubble would not make the paper dollar depreciate against gold. [23] People are being told that the millennium of fiat money is here to stay and the suspension of gold payments is no longer a temporary measure but an indefinite or permanent thing (in truth, no suspension has ever been permanent). At that point depreciation will necessarily set in. This means that gold would go abroad or into hiding as long as it can be obtained domestically, leaving the nation with nothing but its paper. If gold could no longer be obtained even at variable prices as now, then the value of inconvertible currency would decline sharply in terms of gold in anticipation of what all those wanting gold would realise must be the ultimate consequences of the increasing difficulty of obtaining physical gold. Using the technical language of the gold futures markets, the gold basis would go negative with no hope of ever turning back to positive. Permanent gold backwardation would set in. Physical gold could not be obtained at any price.[24] [I.e. exchanged against any amount of paper]It should be realised that there never has been a permanently well-managed inconvertible currency, just as there never has been a permanent suspension of specie payment. The suspension that we observe at present throughout the world should be viewed in the proper perspective. Who can guarantee that China, for example, will follow the lead of the Western powers and commit suicide in maintaining suspension of gold payments indefinitely? The advocates of our global monetary system seem to have lost their sense of proportion regarding these matters. They appear to have confused the efforts of countries to manage their currencies as best as they can with what they suppose would be the situation if these countries were openly to abandon the hope of ever resuming specie payments and were to embark officially upon a 'managed' inconvertible paper currency device as a matter of permanent monetary program. As a matter of fact, not one of the countries involved has officially announced its intention of doing so, nor has it passed a constitutional amendment ruling out a gold standard. No country has declared that it will never ever resume specie payments. No country has ever constitutionally mandated an inconvertible paper currency scheme (before Bretton-Woods). Not one dared to do it. Its policymakers have not got the intestinal fortitude. They lack the moral courage. The advocates of 'managed' inconvertible paper money seem to forget that people know the difference between a piece of paper convertible into gold at a fixed rate and one not convertible into gold at all, or convertible at varying rates.During a period of temporary suspension of specie payments people are unable to discriminate against paper currency because they do not know but that the government may resume the convertibility of its paper currency sooner or later. Should a government, however, put through a constitutional amendment that forbids the introduction of a gold standard of a fixed weight, the ordinary common sense of the people would undoubtedly lead them to discriminate against currencies which are inconvertible or have convertibility at a variable rate. Historically, the most poorly 'managed' currencies in the world have been precisely those severed from gold. All currencies that have not in time been re-anchored to gold or silver at a fixed rate have become unmanageable. When these inconvertible currencies get out of hand, the managed currency advocates disingenuously assert that the trouble lies in the fact that they are not properly managed. Thus the argument of the advocates of the managed inconvertible money simply boils down to this:

'A managed currency is managed when it is under control, but when it gets out of hand, it is not a managed currency!'

For the sake of emphasis let it be restated that in no country in which a managed inconvertible paper currency is functioning reasonably well has there been official pronouncement to the effect that this managed currency scheme is being turned into a permanent program, or that the country never intends to return to the gold standard. There is not one iota of evidence in monetary history to justify the unsupported and unsupportable assertion of the advocates of the 'managed' inconvertible paper currency that such a system can succeed or that we will never need to return to a gold standard.

Fisher says in his book 100% Money (p 218.): 'The French used to have an aphorism: 'after the printing press, the guillotine'
The word became flesh during the French revolution in 1793.

Endnotes to Chapter 36

[1] Many Europeans know very well their pensions look doubtful. However, who can afford to be the whistleblower?

[2] It did not escape J.M. Keynes, who had also read Conant on surplus capital.

[3] J.M. Keynes, Economic Consequences of the Peace, New York, 1920, pp 235.

[4] Please consult the Glossary to understand the three forms of socialism- communism. The Bolsheviks as such may have gone and ought not to be taken literally. However, ideology has nothing to do with it, except it is invented and spread among the gullible. Once it takes hold, the gullible are used and put to work. They are put to work by those who exploit government monopolies for their own benefit. Such practices are as old as the street, but for our purposes, a few cases will demonstrate the proof of concept, insofar it would still be necessary. See e.g. A.C. Sutton, Wall Street and the Bolshevik Revolution, Arlington House, 1974.

[5] Backwardation will be treated in volume IV as an advanced subject. For now backwardation is defined as the state of affairs where the spot price for gold or silver is above the future price. That state of affairs indicates a preference and premium for gold delivery now instead of promises.

[6] Irving Fisher, 100% Money, New York, 1935, Adelphi Publishers. It was republished one year later as '100% Money and the Public Debt', Economic Forum, Spring Number, April-June 1936, pp. 406-420. In this book or article he gives no other references than to his own publications and two others. There is however a long list of well-known fiat money experiments, stretching across the centuries. He mentions none.

[7] Although Fisher and his colleagues like Henri C. Simon appeared to attack free Banking in the United States, they misconstrued and misrepresented the U.S. Constitution; their lobbying in the political circles did encounter some resistance, but the public mood and opinion was on their side, due to the crisis. All experience with the civil war money was cast aside; John Law, the Mississippi Company and the French Assignat a distant memory. He even introduces his ideas by referring to the Bank of Amsterdam, which he misrepresents as a 100% reserve bank, instead of a commercial bank or bill discounter.

[8] All this 'knowledge' of what is good for us...All these people speaking in the name of others... Such attitudes can be traced back to the ancient gnostic dualist derailment of us, the enlightened, vs. the village idiots out there who do not know what is good for them...Combined with the animus dominandi, this quickly turns into an attitude of 'do as you are told or you will regret it'. This attitude will be found in law books and codes. See also note 25 and 32 part 6 page 107-109.

[9] The 'stock' of money returns to the concept of the Quantity Theory of Money, a religious superstition and very contagious amongst economists.

[10] The mortality rate of fiat money is 100%. See Ralph T. Foster, ISBN 978-0-

9643066-1-5, who makes this point abundantly clear.

[11] Alchemy is nothing but a strand of gnosticism, as old as history and pretending to produce solutions, in the form of potions, poisons, spells etc. to 'evil situations' mainly by prestidigitation, deception and if all else fails: lies.

[12] However, obfuscation remains a favourite technique. E. Voegelin: '... If anything is characteristic of ideologies, it is the destruction of language, sometimes on the level of intellectual jargon, on the high level of complication, sometimes on the vulgarian level. When we go beyond Marx, into the ideological *epigonai* of the late 19th and early 20th centuries, we are already far below the intellectual level that formed even the background of a Marx....' Autobiographical Reflections, Col. Works, vol. 34.

[13] In other words: it is the specialty field of the *pontifex maximus*, murmuring Latin spells to the wall with his back to the public– a complete scenario for an alchemist convention.

[14] Capital destruction under a fiat system consists of the marginalisation of plant and productive assets – not of cold capital itself, which is indestructible.

[15] Another infamous magician had promised to the French King exactly the same. His name may be familiar: John Law of Lauriston, the Scottish son of a banking family with rather narcissistic tendencies and a dandy lifestyle, that led to a duel and a manslaughter conviction, for which he left England to live in France. And Italy. And The Netherlands...

[16] 'On demand' means in the midst of a bank run crisis.

[17] Some strong alchemy involved here...

[18] Typical for gnostic dualists is the double standard: one for the masses and another standard for the 'enlightened ones'.

[19] See vol. II, Chapter 15 & 19 *The Chimera of Fractional Reserve Banking*, pp. 171.

[20] Do not take 'printed' literally. Printed here means brought into circulation and it could take the material form of notes or the dematerialised form of book credit.

[21] When finished, they think they can just start anew and announce the creation of a 'New Global Currency' like the Bancor or Amero or whatever...

[22] This happened exactly in those string of panics and market crashes ever since the early 19th century. E.g. The Panic of 1907, chronicled from a personal point of view in Reminiscences of A Stock Operator by Edwin Lefèvre, 1923.

[23] Against all odds. Instead of 100% money, irredeemable fiat currency is 100% mortal, or the denial of reality residing in the magician in his make-belief world.

[24] The permanency would entail that gold could only be obtained in exchange for real goods. Paper currencies would not trade at all - i.e. they suffer from a 100% discount or, what is the same, a 100% mortality rate.

Chapter 37

Burning Bridges and Halfway Houses

Liquidity Trap

The corner-stone of my deflation theory is the observation that there is a double-bias caused by the central bank's open market operations as it

(1) removes risks from bond (but not from commodity) speculation, and
(2) rewards bond bulls (while punishing the bears)

This double-bias distorts the economy in favour of deflation. It is palpable only when deflation is present in the economy in the first place, in which case it is made worse than it need be by prompting speculators to buy bonds in tandem with the central bank. Interest rates fall and through the mechanism of linkage prices fall, too, as the flow of money from commodities to bonds accelerates. In the worst-case scenario a vicious circle is activated and the economy plunges into depression.

The question arises why mainstream economists didn't discover the deflationary bias and alert central bankers to mend their ways. The answer is that they did. However, they had to proceed gingerly. The bridge of the gold standard leading back to monetary sanity and rectitude had already been burnt. They were looking at the incurable congenital disease of the regime of irredeemable currency. Mainstream economists could not talk openly about the dangers of snowballing bond speculation without exposing the fatal inner contradictions of their monetary regime. The diagnosis therefore had to be couched in the language of the liquidity trap. The term originated with Keynes himself who, in the second half of the 1930s, noted that his contra-cyclical prescription to inject new money in the economy through central-bank purchases of bonds in order to combat falling prices wasn't working. In fact, it produced just the opposite effect of what he had hoped. Deflation got worse, not better. As always, Keynes was ready with an explanation. The disease was so advanced that the patient didn't readily react to medication as it was supposed to. The first dose of money-injection administered by doctors from the central bank could not spread through the diseased organism but, instead, accumulated in a 'liquidity-trap'. Nevertheless, Keynes was for continuing the money-injection therapy. He was confident that, ultimately, prices would move higher, as they had to according to the Quantity Theory of Money. Of course, Keynes would not admit that the main cause of the malady was the surgical removal of the gold standard at his instigation earlier in the decade.

Pallas Athena Born In Full Armour

As the ownership of monetary gold was made illegal in 1933, the only competitor to government bonds was removed from the arena. Owners of monetary gold were forced by the strong arm of the government to invest in government bonds – not a very pretty sight in itself, even if the matter ended there. But the matter did not end there. As holders of gold were competing for the limited supply of government bonds, which rightly or wrongly they considered as the safest thing to have second only to gold, bond prices were driven to unprecedented heights and interest rates were plunged to unprecedented depths. The federal funds rate even went negative. Member banks were actually paid a premium for taking money overnight from the Federal Reserve banks.

At that point in time bond speculation was still unknown in the United States. But just as Pallas Athena was born in full armour when she sprang from the skull of Zeus after her father's bizarre pregnancy ended in a splitting headache, so did bond speculators, a whole army of them, spring from the skull of Keynes in a remarkable replay of the mythological story. The speculators did not need any training. They were ready. They did not need any capital either. It was made superfluous by the forcible removal of gold as a competitor of government bonds. Speculators (read: the banks) were literally paid by the Fed to take the money to buy the bonds. Thereafter their only worry was to keep writing up their assets month-after-month, quarter-after-quarter. Why should the banks risk their money by lending it to ailing business on their way to recovery, if they could invest it in steadily appreciating bonds, risk-free? The world had never seen anything like that before: banks betraying their mission to finance business and shepherding their resources into bond speculation. And why not? Not only did the continuous injection of irredeemable currency into the economy by the Fed make bond speculation risk-free, it actually guaranteed capital gains on their bond portfolio, on the top of the interest-income. The stock-market craze of the Roaring Twenties was nothing in comparison. The largest speculative orgy in history was on. It was in the 1930s, and it was in the bond market.

Of course, the theory of liquidity traps does not mention bond speculation. The s-word is taboo. It talks about liquidity being mysteriously siphoned off and trapped. As the central bank fighting recession drove interest rates close to zero, the fruits of any further monetary expansion would be stuck away in mattresses and cookie jars where they could do nothing for the economy. The process is described in detail in the first edition of Samuelson's textbook published in 1948 used in training Keynesian economists. Truth be told, the 'fruit' is not put in mattresses and cookie-jars. It is taken by the speculators to the bond market where the miraculous multiplication of money is taking place. But you are not supposed to utter the s-word as it would conjure up the fatal flaw of the regime of irredeemable currency.

The chapter on the liquidity trap did not stay in Samuelson's textbook for long. It was deleted from subsequent editions. Interest rates were edging up, and the author didn't think that there was a danger for them ever to come down again to the vicinity of zero. Surely inflation would see to that. The Fed convincingly demonstrated its power in ending recession after recession. There seemed no reason to doubt that it could always do so whenever needed. The regime of irredeemable currency was firmly implanted in the economy, and the central bank could control practically everything with the possible exception of the weather.

The Interest-Targeting Cabal

While out of the textbooks, the liquidity trap was not out of the ivory towers. It was still being discussed in the rarified atmosphere of academia. The world centre for liquidity-trap studies and for the inflation-targeting cabal is the *Woodrow Wilson School at Princeton University in New Jersey*. Under the leadership of department head Ben Bernanke a team consisting of Paul Krugman, Lars Svensson, and Mike Woodford has been busy investigating the liquidity trap and finding ways to unplug it through inflation-targeting should it get clogged again. The Princeton Plumbers worked out esoteric mathematical models to show that, indeed, the danger of liquidity traps was real. Here is the verbalisation of the mathematical hocus-pocus. (A less polite expression, the title of [1], could also be used. I stay with the more polite version. As the author points out, according to Goodwin's Law the party that blinks first and mentions bodily wastes loses the argument.) The cabal turns on the concept of 'potential output'. It is defined as maximum output consistent with a stable inflation-rate. (Please don't heckle the Plumbers with interjections that a stable inflation rate is an oxymoron.) If actual output exceeds potential, then the rate of inflation will rise; if below potential, then it will fall. In the latter the Princeton Plumbers sniff great danger. Suppose that, for whatever reasons, the economy is operating below potential output (there is an 'output-gap'). Then the situation is no longer stable. We are staring right into the liquidity trap. Disinflation makes inflationary expectations fade, leading to more disinflation, whereupon inflationary expectations fade more. The vicious circle is on and pushes the economy right into the liquidity trap. Once that happens, the central bank can pump money into the economy as much as it wants, it will all end up in the liquidity trap. The output-gap will worsen, leading to even lower inflation, and so on. The thing to worry about is the spiral of declining output relative to potential, and fading inflationary expectations . Krugman adds the punchline: 'zero is not a big number whether for growth, or whether for inflation'. In plain language, if you want growth, you had better target inflation, and target you must well above zero. The trouble with fading inflationary expectation is that it jerks the rug from underneath the interest-rate structure. Please note how the Princeton Plumbers studiously avoid any reference to bond speculation, a hard fact of the economy, and substitute for it 'fading inflationary expectations', a soft economic euphemism.

The Japanese Bubble Bursts

So when the Japanese bubble burst, the Princeton Plumbers were ready. The Fed quickly tapped Ben Bernanke, bringing him to Washington and making him the heir-apparent to Greenspan. Recent rumours have it that the threat of the Japanese sickness is so serious that Bernanke will have to be moved from Constitution Avenue to Pennsylvania Avenue, right into the White House, to head the council of the President's economic advisors. Well, we won't have to wait too long to learn where upstairs the head-plumber will be kicked. By 1996 Japan looked an awful lot like a country in a classic 'liquidity trap.' And that was scary. It meant that 'our grandfathers were not as stupid as we thought' in the words of Princeton Plumber Paul Krugman, who is moonlighting as staff writer for The New York Times. A 1930-style slump may not be that easy to fix, after all. A disease we had thought was under control reappeared in a form resistant to all the known antibiotics. Japan's trap was real.

But if Japan remains stuck in that trap, who cares? Well, you should. Not only is Japan the world's second largest economy; until recently it seemed to be the economy of the future. Worse still, if it could happen to Japan, why not to us? As the Princeton Plumbers must not utter the s-word in public, talking about the mechanism whereby depression can metastasise across the Pacific is taboo, just as well.

> This mechanism is the notorious yen-carry trade, or bond speculators doing arbitrage between the Japanese and the American bond markets. They sell the ultra-high-priced Japanese bonds and buy the relatively cheap American. The net effect is to push interest rates in the United States down to the unprecedented low levels prevailing in Japan.

Can One Prevent Deflation ?

This is the title of an article also written by Paul Krugman when he was still at MIT, from which the following quotations are taken. What gives it timeliness is that those six years have not solved any of the underlying problems but, in many ways, the economy has deteriorated in the wake of the continuing exponential growth of debt and its symbiotic parasite, bond speculation. The cover story from 'The Economist' makes it more or less official. Deflation, not inflation, is now the greatest concern for the world economy. Over the past year, producer prices have fallen throughout the advanced world; consumer prices have been falling for the last 6 months in France and Germany; in Japan wages have actually fallen 4 percent over the the past year...

> 'So far none of these price declines looks anything like the massive deflation that accompanied the Great Depression. But the appearance of deflation as a widespread problem is disturbing, not only because of its immediate economic implications, but because until recently most economists – myself included – regarded sustained deflation as a fundamentally implausible prospect, something that should not be a concern.

> 'The point is that deflation should – or so we thought – be easy to prevent: just print more money. And printing money is normally a pleasant experience for governments. In fact, the idea that governments have a hard time keeping their hands off the printing press has long been a staple of political economy; dozens of theoretical papers have argued that the temptation to engage

> in excessive money-creation causes an inherent inflationary bias in fiat-money economies. It is largely to combat that presumed bias that most of the world has accepted the notion that monetary policy should be conducted by an independent central bank, insulated from political influence – and has been written into the charters of those central banks that they should seek price stability as their main, often only, goal.
>
> 'Yet here we are, with deflation turning out to be a serious problem after all – and with policymakers finding that it is not as easy either to prevent or to reverse as we all thought.
>
> 'How can this be happening? What does it imply for policy? The purpose of this note is to argue that more or less conventional economic theory actually does suggest some answers to these questions – but that these answers fly in the face of conventional policy wisdom. And because the answers are so hard to accept, deflation is indeed a real risk.'

We may skip the hocus-pocus part of the article and go directly to its conclusions.

> 'The obvious answer to sustained deflationary pressures, then, is the now-notorious proposal for 'managed inflation'... But the idea sounds crazy, and that is a problem. How can we get finance ministers and central bankers, who have spent their whole careers preaching the evils of inflation and the virtues of price stability, to accept the idea that price stability may not be an available option?
>
> 'For if deflationary forces are as powerful as they are in Japan – and may soon be in the rest of the world, if The Economist is right – there is no middle ground... Attempts to find a halfway house – to aim merely for stable prices rather than sufficiently high inflation – will be doomed to failure.
>
> 'In short, if you really believe that deflation is now a global threat, you should also believe that only policies lying outside of the realm of what is conventionally regarded as responsible will contain that threat. And because unconventional thinking is not what one expects (or, in normal times, wants) from finance ministers and central bankers, there is now a real risk that deflation will indeed become a global scourge.'

Thus concludes the Princeton Plumber's article. It nicely explains what has happened in the intervening six years. The powers that be were scared by the deflationary threat much more than they ever admitted. Without any hesitation they took the advice of Krugman, abandoned policies 'conventionally regarded as responsible', unilaterally betrayed their mandate, burnt the halfway house of price stability, and hit the warpath of 'inflation', euphemistically calling it 'inflation-targeting'.

One Irresponsible Monetary Policy Deserves Another

What Krugman conveniently ignores is that inflation may not be 'manageable' like a pet dog. More like a hungry tiger smelling blood, it could get out of hand following reckless increases in the money supply. No less than burning bridges, burning halfway houses is not a very good idea. Mainstream economists burnt the bridge of the gold standard making it the whipping boy for the Great Depression. Through that bridge we could have retreated to monetary rectitude after the insane experiments with the fiat dollar. Now they burn the halfway house of price stability, too. Where will the Fed find shelter after the tornado of runaway inflation has struck?

The seriousness of the problem cannot be overstated. A steep rise in interest rates at this juncture would be the horror of horrors. Normally higher interest rates would strengthen the value of the currency as they attracted foreign investors. Not this time. Apart from the problem of pricking all the bubbles in the economy starting with the housing bubble, and ballooning the budget deficit into outer space, there is an even larger and more immediate problem. And that is the effect that steeply rising interest rates have on the value of bonds, widely held at home and abroad. The effect is inevitable and instantaneous.

Higher interest rates make bond values collapse.

You have to be very clear in your mind about this, so I spell it out. The dollar losing value on the foreign exchanges because of the trade gap is one thing. Dollar-bonds losing value due to higher interest rates is another thing. Nevertheless it is entirely possible, and right now appears highly probable, that the two losses will be inflicted **simultaneously**. Losses on bonds will compound the loss on the dollar. The compounded loss shall exceed the **critical mass** of bearable losses, and will trigger a chain reaction of further losses. The confidence in the dollar will be fatally and irreparably shaken, domestically as well as internationally.

How likely is that to happen? In my opinion not very likely. The

Fed must have a contingency plan to prevent a steep rise in interest rates. Krugman has convinced us that the money-managers at the Fed have got rid of their last scruples, if they ever had any. Paraphrasing him, if you really believe that runaway inflation is now a global threat, you should also believe that only policies lying outside of the realm what is conventionally regarded as responsible will contain that threat. One irresponsible monetary policy deserves another. **The contingency plan to prevent a steep rise in interest rates will have to involve a conspiracy between the Fed and the Bank of Japan to punish speculators short-selling the dollar and dollar bonds.** There is nothing else left in the Fed's bag of tricks but the check-kiting scheme with the Bank of Japan that could hold back the forces of monetary destruction waiting in the wings. Never mind that it is 'conventionally regarded' as irresponsible. Never mind that it is illegal. Never mind that it is criminal. Nothing else will defer the day of reckoning.

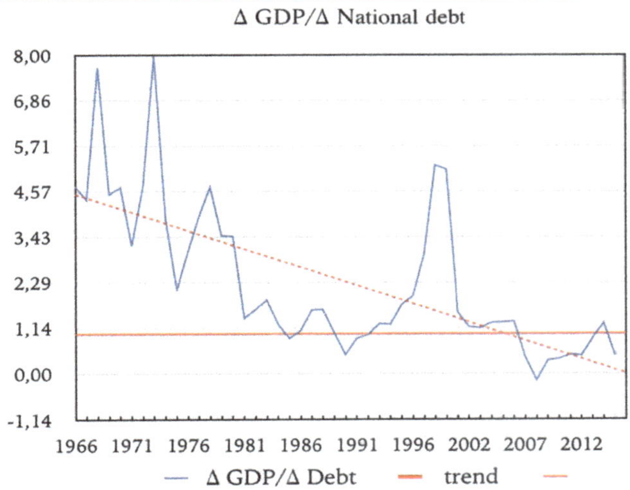

Fig. 7 50 years of 'scientific debt management'. No comments.

Bibliography

ENGLISH

Titles mentioned here are in English or refer to the English translation. Some of these titles may be difficult to obtain for the reader.

Anderson, B.A., *Economics and the Public Welfare, A Financial and Economic History of the United States, 1914-1946*, Princeton, D. Van Nostrand, 1949.

von Böhm-Bawerk, E., *Capital and Interest, A critical History of Economical Thought*, Transl. W. Smart), MacMillan, London, 1890.

__________ *Karl Marx and the Close of His System: A Criticism*, London, 1898.

__________ *Control or Economic Law*, LVMI, 2010, first appeared in 'Zeitschrift für Volkswirtschaft, Sozialpolitik und Verwaltung,' Volume XXIII (1914): 205–71; (tranlation. J.R. Mez)

Campagnolo, G., *Criticism of Classical Political Economy*, Menger, Austrian economics and the German Historical School, Routledge, New York, 2010.

De Roover, R., *The Rise and Decline of the Medici Bank, 1397-1494*, Cambridge, Mass. 1963.

__________ *Money, Banking and Credit in Mediaeval Bruges*, Cambridge, Mass. 1948.

Denniger, C., 'Bernanke Inserts Gun in Mouth', March 20, 2009 market-ticker.denniger.net

Einaudi,L., *Money and Politics : European Monetary Unification and the Gold Standard (1865-73)*, Oxford , 2001.

Eichengreen, B., and Temin, P., 'Fetters of Gold and Paper,' *Econometrics Laboratory*, Berkeley, California.

Fetter, F. A., *The Principles of Economics*, New York, 1905.

Fisher, D.H., *The Great Wave Price Revolutions and the Rhythm of History*, Oxford University Press, 1996

Fullarton, J., *On the Regulation of Currencies*, New York, A.M. Kelley, 1969.

Foster, R.T., *Fiat Paper Money - The History and Evolution of our Currency*, ISBN 978-0-964-3066-1-5

Friedman, M., *Optimum quantity of Money*, 1912.

Gillespie, A.M., *The Theological Origins of Modernity*, University of Chicago Press, Chicago and London, 2009.

Grice-Hutchinson, M., *The School of Salamanca, Readings in Spanish Monetary History 1544-1605*, Oxford, Clarendon, 1952.

Gonczy, A.M.L. *et al.*, 'Two Faces of Debt', *Federal Reserve Bank of Chicago*, 5th Rev. 1992.

Guttierrez, C., 'No Time For T-Bonds', March 28, 2009 forbes.com

Hayek, F.A., *Prices and Production and Other Works*, LVMI, 2008.

__________ *The Counter Revolution of Science, Studies on the Abuse of Reason*, MacMillan, London, 1955.

__________ *The Road To Serfdom*, Routledge, London, 1944

Hunt, I.L., (Col.) *American Military Government of Occupied Germany 1918-1920* - Report of the Officer in Charge of Civil Affairs, Third Army and American Forces in Germany, U.S. Government Printing Office, Washington, 1943.

Jastrow, M. Jr., *The War and the Bagdad Railway*, Philadelphia and London, J.B. Lippincott Company, 1918.

Keynes, J.M., *A Treatise on Money*, Vol I and II, MacMillan, 1914.

__________ *The General Theory of Employment, Interest and Money*, 1935.

Kisch, C.H., *The Portuguese Bank Note Case*, London, 1932.

Laughlin, L., *The History of Bimetallism in the United States*, Appleton, New York, 1896.

MacIntyre, A., *Whose Justice? Which Rationality?* Univ. Notre Dame, 1989.

Martin, J. S., *All Honorable Man - The Story of the Men on Both Sides of the Atlantic Who Successfully Thwarted Plans to Dismantle the Nazi Cartel System*, Little Brown, 1950. (ASIN B0000EEK-BR)

Menger, C., *Principles of Economics*, NYU Press, 1981, originally published in German in 1871 as *Grundsätze der Volkswirtschaftslehre.*

von Mises, L., *The Theory of Money and Credit*, Yale UP, New Haven,1953, translated by H.E. Batson.

__________ *The Anticapitalistic Mentality*, D. Van Nostrand Inc, 1956.

__________ *Human Action*, A Treatise on Economics, LVMI, 1998.

Nagel, Th., *Mind and Cosmos, Why the Materialist Neo-Darwinian Conception of Nature is Almost Certainly False*, Oxford University Press, 2012, 130 p.

Palyi, M., *The Twilight of Gold, 1914-1936*, Chicago, Henry Regnery, 1972.

Perkins, J., *Confessions of An Economic Hit Man*, Berrett Koehler, San Fransisco, 2004.

Pigou, A.C., *The Theory of Unemployment*, Macmillan, 1933.

Rist, Ch., *History of Money and Credit Theory from John Law to the Present Day, 1940.*

Röpke, W., *International Order and Economic Integration*, Reidel, Dordrecht,1959

Selgin, G., *Good Money: Birmingham Button Makers, the Royal Mint and the Beginnings of Modern Coinage (1775-1821)*, Institute of Economic Affairs, 2008.

Schumpeter, J.A., *History of Economic Analysis*, New York, 1954.

Shelldrake, R., *The Science Delusion*, Hodder & Stoughton, London, 2013

Smith, A., *An inquiry into the Nature and causes of the Wealth of Nations*, 1776.

Spahr, W. E., *Our Irredeemable Currency System, The Federal Reserve System and the Control of Credit*, Macmillan, 1931

__________ *A Proper Monetary and Banking System for the United States*, Ronald Press Co, NY, 1960.

Strachan, H., *The First World War*, Vol. I., To Arms, Oxford University Press, 2001, 1227 pages.

Sutton, A.C., *Wall Street and the Bolshevik Revolution*, Arlington House, New York, 1974.

__________ *Western Technology and Soviet Economic Development*, Hoover Institute, Stanford University, 1968.

Vieira, Edw. Jr., *Pieces of Eight: The Monetary Powers and Disabilities of the United States Constitution*, Sheridan Books, 2nd ed. , 2002.

Voegelin, E., *From Enlightenment to Revolution*, Duke Univ. Press, 1975.

__________ *Modernity Without Restraint*, Collected Works, Vol 5. University of Missouri Press, Columbia and London, 2000.

Warburton, P., *Debt and Delusion : Central Bank Follies That Threaten Economic Disaster*, World Meta View Press, 1999.

Wicksteed, P. H., *The Common Sense of Political Economy*, vol.I., London, Routledge & Keagan, 1933.

Willis, H.P., *A History of the Latin Monetary Union A study of International Monetary Action*, Chicago Press, 1901.

Withers, H., *The Meaning of Money*, London, 1910.

GERMAN

The titles mentioned here refer to German or Austrian works.

Moll, B., *Logik des Geldes,* F. Enke, Stuttgart, 1914.

__________ *Die modernen Geldtheorien und die Politik der Reichsbank,* F. Enke, Stuttgart, 1917.

Rittershausen, H., *Arbeitslosigkeit und Kapitalbildung zugleich ein bank-politischen Programm zur Bekämpfung der Wirtschaftkrise,* Jena, Verlag Gustav Fischer, 1930. (Translated by X, Unemployment as a Problem of Turnover Credits and the Supply of Means of Payments, Jena, 1930)

Alphabetical Index of Names

V

W

Alphabetical Index of Subjects

D

E

www.ingramcontent.com/pod-product-compliance
Lightning Source LLC
Chambersburg PA
CBHW041305210926
51851CB00006B/14/J
* 9 7 8 9 0 8 2 0 6 5 5 5 8 *